INTERNATIONAL STUDIES

of the
Committee on International Relations
University of Notre Dame

INTERNATIONAL STUDIES

Freedom and Reform in Latin America
Edited by FREDRICK B. PIKE
What America Stands For
Edited by STEPHEN D. KERTESZ AND M. A. FITZSIMONS
Diplomacy in a Changing World
Edited by STEPHEN D. KERTESZ AND M. A. FITZSIMONS
Soviet Policy Toward the Baltic States
ALBERT N. TARULIS
The Russian Revolution and Religion
BOLESLAW SZCZESNIAK
Catholicism, Nationalism and Democracy in Argentina
JOHN J. KENNEDY
The Representative Republic
FERDINAND A. HERMENS
Why Democracies Fail
NORMAN L. STAMPS
Christian Democracy in Western Europe, 1820–1953
M. P. FOGARTY
The Fate of East Central Europe:
Hopes and Failures of American Foreign Policy
Edited by STEPHEN D. KERTESZ
German Protestants Face the Social Question
WILLIAM O. SHANAHAN
Diplomacy in a Whirlpool: Hungary Between Nazi Germany and Soviet Russia
STEPHEN D. KERTESZ
Soviet Imperialism: Its Origins and Tactics
Edited by WALDEMAR GURIAN
Pan-Slavism: Its History and Ideology
HANS KOHN
The Foreign Policy of the British Labour Government, 1945–51
M. A. FITZSIMONS
Christian Democracy in Italy and France
MARIO EINAUDI AND FRANCOIS GOGUEL
Bolshevism: An Introduction to Soviet Communism
WALDEMAR GURIAN

(Out of Print)
The Soviet Union: Background, Ideology, Reality
Edited by WALDEMAR GURIAN
The Catholic Church in World Affairs
Edited by WALDEMAR GURIAN AND M. A. FITZSIMONS
Europe Between Democracy and Anarchy
FERDINAND A. HERMENS

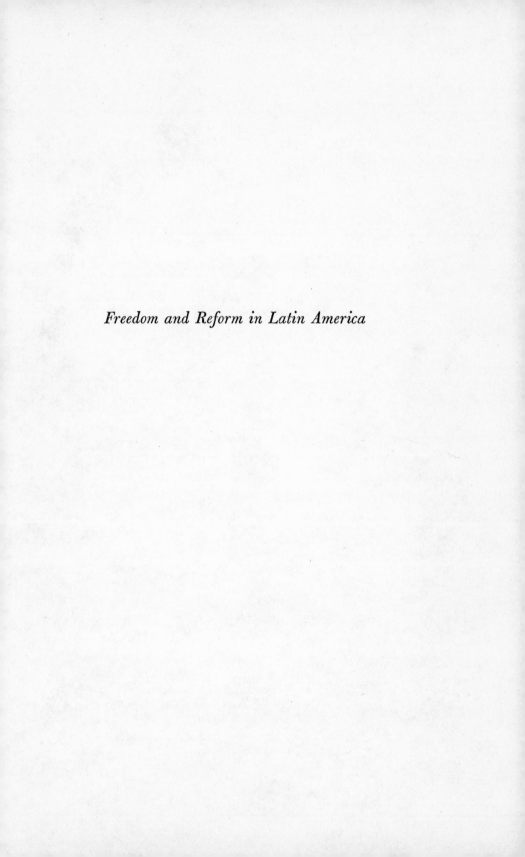

Freedom and Reform in Latin America

Freedom and Reform in Latin America

〰〰〰〰 EDITED BY 〰〰〰〰

FREDRICK B. PIKE

University of Notre Dame Press

1959

Library of Congress Catalog Card Number 59-10417

© *1959 University of Notre Dame Press*

Notre Dame, Indiana

Preface

Having produced numerous monographs and edited volumes dealing with areas of particular importance in the shaping of today's world, the Committee on International Relations of the University of Notre Dame began several years ago to contemplate a work concerned with Latin America. Particularly interested in this venture were Stephen D. Kertesz, the Committee's chairman, and John J. Kennedy, a specialist in Latin American studies of vast and distinguished experience. Owing to arrangements made by these two men there was held in May of 1957 on the Notre Dame campus a symposium pertaining to the problems of freedom and reform in Latin America.

After participating in this symposium, I was shortly given the opportunity of planning and editing the more extensive collection of essays which came to comprise the present volume. To the Committee on International Relations, then, I am initially indebted. In preparing my own essay on the revolutionary tradition I profited immensely from the suggestions of two Notre Dame professors, Rev. Thomas T. McAvoy, C.S.C., Head, Department of History, and Thomas J. Stritch, Head, Department of Communications Arts. And for his careful editorial reading of all the manuscripts and his many excellent suggestions, I owe a large debt of gratitude to Joseph M. Duffy, Jr., of the Notre Dame Department of English. Above all, in work of this nature, an editor becomes indebted to the specialists who generously agree to prepare contributions. The outstanding qualifications of the con-

vii

tributors to this volume have assured the readers of a valuable insight into the problems of freedom and reform in Latin America, and have rendered particularly rewarding and exciting the role of the editor.

Gratitude must also be expressed to two of my former mentors at the University of Texas. Lewis Hanke not only agreed to read the papers included in this volume but also extended wise suggestions as to contributors, and J. Lloyd Mecham offered invaluable suggestions in regard to the introduction.

To all of these men I, as well as those interested in the significant developments within modern Latin America who read this book, will be ever grateful.

FREDRICK B. PIKE

South Bend, Indiana
January 30, 1959

Contents

Contents

CHAPTER I

[FREDRICK B. PIKE *]

Introduction

A series of revolutions, mainly originating within the past fifty years, has transformed the modern world and the place of the United States within it. At the present time, Latin America is experiencing one of the most significant patterns of change evident in any portion of the world. These metamorphoses are of great import not only to the populations of the southern Americas, but to the United States, for they necessitate on the part of our statesmen and general public a basic revision of attitudes toward Latin America. Nor can the task of reappraisal be long delayed. The urgency of the need for hemisphere relations more secure and enduringly cordial than any heretofore developed becomes daily more abundantly lucid.

The drift away from the free trade that many international economists hoped for after World War II and the contrary tendency toward trade exclusivism, as exemplified by the Iron Curtain countries, the sterling bloc and now the European common market, may within a short time render us more than ever economically dependent upon Latin America. Senator Fulbright recently commented upon the irony of the fact that today, after

---

* Fredrick B. Pike received his B.A. from Loyola University of Los Angeles, 1949, and his M.A. and Ph.D. from the University of Texas, the latter degree in 1956. He joined the faculty of the University of Notre Dame in 1953, and now holds the rank of Assistant Professor of History. He has published articles and reviews in *The Americas, The Hispanic American Historical Review, The Review of Politics, Revista de las Indias* and *The Catholic Historical Review,* of which last he is now an advisory editor.

the United States has abandoned its isolationist proclivities, the rest of the world apparently seeks isolation from us. The departure from Paris and London as centers of the world approach to foreign relations, occasioned by the rapid rise of previously under-developed regions and lightly dismissed races, also dictates that we seek firm allies among the newly emergent areas of the world. Latin America, not because of territorial propinquity alone, deserves special consideration in our search for friends among the societies that have lately begun their evolution into more modern stages. While the "American Hemisphere Idea" of basic similarities and natural cohesion among the nations of the once New World has been largely based on superficial thinking in the past, it is conceivable that Latin America's present attempts to achieve both freedom and reform will serve to bring about for the first time a true solidarity among the American nations. Regard-less of significant deviations from United States paradigms which should never be underestimated, Latin America today manifests the classical Western origins of its civilization by recognizing the troublesome dichotomy between freedom and reform. The attempt to establish a *modus vivendi* between the claims of the two is a problem with which most oriental and African political structures appear to be only mildly concerned. In these ambients, it seems that reform as envisioned by a ruling clique is the only important consideration. This outlook is detectable even in the countries of so-called western Europe, especially when contemporary Russia is considered, as in many ways it must be, a part of the West. Latin America's preoccupation with the claims of freedom presents heartlifting evidence that the United States possesses an ally of nearly untapped potential in the world-wide struggle to preserve this fundamental human value while accomplishing reform. But allies can not be taken for granted. Our constant encouragement must be extended to Latin America, for the manner in which these republics resolve the dilemma posed by the often contrary demands of freedom and reform is likely to prove one of the most fascinating aspects of history as it is made in the twentieth century American states, and will ultimately evoke serious consequences upon the outcome of the titanic struggle in which the members of international society are now engaged.

To obtain the benefits that can flow from greater hemisphere unity necessitates an approach to Latin America different from any heretofore devised. One authority has remarked that the United States has previously paid adequate attention to its southern neighbors only during times of war, when it had severed relations with enemies and when affairs with allies were conducted by the military. At such times, the only sphere of operations remaining to keep State Department personnel in practice was Latin America. Although exaggerated, there is some element of truth in this appraisal, as a brief review of certain aspects of hemisphere relations may bring out.

The Latin American emancipation movement, and the fear of Holy Alliance intervention in the American hemisphere, produced among the statesmen and to some extent the general public of the United States the first signs of active interest in our southern neighbors. Since the time of this North American discovery of South and Central America, United States relations with Latin America have been characterized by long periods of forgetfulness, alternating with sudden, convulsive and ephemeral eras of concentrated heedfulness. The long periods of inattention, usually on the whole free from incidents of a sensational nature, have probably done more to damage hemisphere relations than the more notorious and publicized acts of indiscretion which have now and then produced giant headlines and drastically strained relations.

Thus far, by refocusing attention on the southern Americas, sometimes to an extreme extent, the United States has succeeded in undoing much of the damage wrought by preceding years of ignoring the area. When, for example, Mahan, Roosevelt, Lodge and their disciples, literally at the eleventh hour, rediscovered the strategic importance of the Caribbean, there still remained time for a rapidly moving United States to make of this sea its own lake. A few years later, and our renewed concern with a portion of Latin America might have come too late for the best interests of security. Joining with the naval globalists in the rediscovery of northern Latin America were United States oilmen, who began to profit from the generous concessions of Porfirio Díaz in Mexico, as well as banana and sugar producers and international bankers who found numerous opportunities in the Caribbean-Central American area. As side products of this development there occurred many unpleasant incidents, including troop landings. But these widely propagandized events may have done less to undermine hemisphere relations than the un-newsworthy fact that, aside from the Caribbean, Central America and Mexico, we continued by and large to ignore the Americas of the South. This indifference created the milieu necessary for southern Latin America to respond with unbridled bitterness and indignation to the security and financially motivated attentions which we accorded their often unreceptive northern brethren.

During the late 1920's, the Coolidge and Hoover administrations began to show signs of taking all Latin America more seriously. Certain faltering steps of this period, representing in part a hearkening back to the friendly inter-American relations eloquently championed by Elihu Root at the opening of the century, culminated in the Good Neighbor policy. This approach to hemisphere dealings, new at least in emphasis and degree, emerged barely in time to undo the bad impression made by the excesses of Caribbean intervention during the period of Isthmian-Dollar Diplomacy, and by the simultaneous neglect of the rest of Latin America, a neglect that was extended even to the Caribbean in the period immediately subsequent to World War I. In the case of one country, Argentina, the new policy did not come soon enough.

During its first two or three years, the Good Neighbor policy sought to correct previous mistakes by traditionally acceptable means, stopping short of extremes. At the 1933 Montevideo Conference, for example, the United States reserved the right to intervene under certain rather nebulous conditions in Latin American republics. Then, with the seriousness of the European crisis fully apparent, the Good Neighbor policy became a crash program desperately implemented for purposes of continental security. Concessions made at this juncture were of a type which could only impede restoration of a normal, give-and-take relationship once the emergency was over. Because the United States ignored certain customary necessities in the world of power politics and sought totally to substitute multilateral dealings with underdeveloped nations for the unilateral approach which any great power must occasionally pursue, it rendered friendly intercourse with the Americas to the South discouragingly difficult to achieve once the second World War ended. The principle of absolute non-intervention agreed to at Buenos Aires in 1936, and our somewhat weak stand in the face of Mexican and Bolivian oil expropriations demonstrated the inclination toward excesses inherent in the second stage of the Good Neighbor era.

The architects of the Good Neighbor approach can not be blamed for the ultimate consequences of the structure they fashioned. On the whole, their efforts were crowned with adequate, albeit temporary, success. But they might have won the same fruits without resorting to extremes, and thereby have paved the way for lasting amicable relations, if they had not had to clear away the debris and ruins occasioned by years of indifference.

If there is any validity to the foregoing appraisal, one is led to wonder what will be the price we will have to pay in the future upon once again becoming fully cognizant of the strategic importance of Latin America. The anti-United States feelings manifested in the Nixon incidents, the need for a brother of our President to mask in secrecy many details of his itinerary when touring Central America, the doctrine advanced by President Prado y Ugarteche of Peru that Latin Americans must once more look culturally and economically primarily to Europe, the increasing drift toward neutralism rather than an identification with the cause of the United States in the present world struggle, and the mounting tide of trade with Russia and Communist satellites, are all indications that the time for intensified attention is once more at hand, if not already almost past. Emerging from this picture is the conclusion that it would be advisable now gradually to enhance our concern for Latin America, to make certain guarded concessions, to encourage economic development even if to do so we must temporarily resort to expedients which do not in the immediate outlook appear to be economically justified. By adopting such policies now, we may be able to avoid what would truly constitute a give-away program at a later date.

None of the above implies necessary criticism of the United States Department of State. Some of the best informed recent appraisals of the Latin American situation have emanated from this molder of our international relations. Since the end of World War II, however, our foreign policy makers have understandably tended to ignore Latin America. The most acute problems confronting them and the free world they wish to defend stemmed from the spread of international Communism and were focused in other parts of the world. France, Italy, Greece, Turkey, China, the Middle and the Near East cried for more immediate attention, for here the challenge was of greater imminence than in Latin America. Consequently, the Truman Doctrine, the Marshall Plan, NATO, the Baghdad Pact and SEATO seemed more vital to security than the Organization of American States. In all of this there was no total forgetting of Latin America. Generous loans were made, and significant development and exchange of persons programs were inaugurated. Above all, our policy directors were convinced that in combating Communism's assault upon individual freedom they were making possible the preservation of a cherished way of life in the entire American hemisphere. They have found frustrating the Latin American inclination to dismiss the contribution to the Americas as a whole rendered by United States foreign policy in its over-all scope. Equally discouraging has been the fact that while calling for more aid, Latin Americans have been reluctant to overhaul their own capital formation structures, to combat corruption, favoritism and hyper-nationalism in government-business relations, and have continued to place increasing sums of money on deposit in United States banks. Perhaps a more underlying source of annoyance is the fact that the United States has now replaced Spain and England as the favorite Latin American scapegoat.

These extenuating circumstances do not alter the conclusion that apathy has been a general characteristic of United States relations with Latin America for most of the past decade. Today, the State Department is again coming to accord higher priority to the area, for its discontent and the subsequent opportunities for Communist agents have reached a level which dictates closer scrutiny and expanding cooperation. Congress, too, has manifested increasing awareness of the problem; before adjourning in 1958, it appropriated an additional two million dollars to support exchange of persons with our sister republics to the South. But the obstacles to sound hemisphere relations extend deeper than State Department and congressional attitudes. Our statesmen are confronted by insouciance, misinformation and oversimplification on the part of the general public which render their task disconcertingly laborious. There is still the common predisposition to take Latin Americans for granted, to consider them as so similar to us that they require no special attention. Geographic proximity and the fact that Spanish and to some degree Portuguese are considered easier languages and are more widely known here than Chinese and Russian, Arabic and Japanese, cause us to regard the Spanish and Portuguese Americans as basically non-esoteric and easily knowable. We do not devote to them the intellectual concentration necessary to gain understanding. The same approach is perhaps responsible for our frequent failure to try to comprehend attitudes of the United Kingdom. In both instances, superficial simplicity camouflages underlying complexity. There is also a tendency, arising from our custom to regard the United States as singularly and uniquely successful and virtuous in the American hemisphere, to disparage Latin American accomplishments while concentrating on incidents which reveal the area in an unflattering light. Other impediments to popular approbation and support for an enlightened Latin American policy are provided by the public's inertia in discarding fallacious and outmoded notions. Latin America has changed, and is changing with such velocity as to present a perplexing kaleidoscopic picture even to those who have dedicated their lives to understanding this part of the world. If calamity in hemisphere relations is to be avoided, it is now essential that a broader segment of the population than foreign policy experts in government and scholarly circles gain some basic awareness of the over-all trend of nascent patterns.

The widely admired former President of Ecuador, Galo Plaza Lasso, recently noted that Latin America is now undergoing social and economic transformations so profound as to threaten with obsolescence much of United States policy in dealing with the area. What is the nature of these changes, and in what fields lie the greatest possibilities of continuing change; in what ways are the changes such as to force us to modify our conceptions of and concrete policies toward Latin America?

It is hoped that the essays here collected will aid their readers in ferreting out answers to these questions. Of particular value in illuminating the contemporary period are the papers dealing with freedom and reform in urban and industrializing Latin America, in rural Latin America, with the role of democracy, and with changing patterns of constitutional and educational development. While the respective authors have not tried to blueprint doctrinaire solutions, they have emphasized the existence of problems within a basically new frame of reference and they suggest, at least by implication, the inadequacy of old approaches to the new challenges. Their papers reveal also the enormous difficulties encountered by Latin American reformers, such as the startling explosion of populations, today increasing at the most rapid rate of any area in the world, and the trials of essentially raw materials producing nations in matching the standard of living gains conspicuously scored by industrial regions. Sympathy with the magnitude of these problems should render the readers more tolerant when Latin America appears, by United States standards, to be advancing at a moderate pace.

Outstanding among the examples of change which must modify our dealings with the area is the already alluded to fact that Latin America now for the first time finds itself seriously confronting the quandary of establishing the appropriate balance between freedom and reform. This is in general an older dilemma for the United States, and currently puzzles us in a somewhat different manner than Latin Americans. For the past fifty years at least, our fundamental question has been, can we preserve freedom in the midst of the economic and social reforms to which we have increasingly grown accustomed? For Latin Americans, the query as it emerges today is, can we reform in the midst of the freedom we prize?

Reform has always imposed limitations upon what vested interests regarded as basic freedoms. It is not accidental that in the United States the liveliest concern over the disappearance of freedom has come in an age of reform. We have for some time shown an inclination to place reform above traditional freedoms. Poverty, for example, must be banished, we are told and many of us believe, even if this means that no one remains free to be rich. Finding the point of proper balance between freedom and reform constitutes one of the most insoluble riddles faced by all maturing civilizations. The quest for the solution has always served to underscore the fundamental duality of human existence, in which one set of desires is satisfied only at the expense of another. Each civilization must seek its own suitable equilibrium and Latin

America will work out a different sort of compromise than that being devised in the United States.

In the Latin America of the past, traditional ruling classes have been extremely sensitive to limitations of any kind. Juan Bautista Alberdi was one of the many writers to observe that life had been kind to these favored few, perhaps too kind. Values of land, upon which their fortunes were based, rose at dizzy rates even when no improvements were effected upon the estates. It was not necessary to work manually, for there were abundant sources of slave or semi-slave labor. In affairs of the spirit, works were not a pre-requisite of salvation, for this was assured by faith alone, not necessarily manifested by outer actions. Thinkers did not always find it necessary to perform the hard work of investigation and research in order to arrive at exalted conclusions, for within the Latin American temperament, reliance was placed on intuition in intellectual matters, rather than on the tedious spade work at which Germans and Anglo-Saxons, for example, have occasionally excelled. An upper class thus unaccustomed to discipline presented unfertile ground for the sowing of reform.

Today the picture is changing. Middle classes are coming more and more to control the destinies of Latin America. Although it has been noted that these newly dominant classes tend to fall into traditional upper class attitudes as quickly as circumstances permit, they have at least had some experience in taking orders from others and controlling their caprices. They are more apt to tolerate the fetters necessarily imposed by reform.

Perhaps alone of the Latin American republics, Uruguay exhibits similarity to the United States in that its struggle with the freedom-reform issue commenced at approximately the be-ginning of the twentieth century. Uruguay has been labeled the first New Deal country in the Americas, notwithstanding the lack of certain resources apparently essential to support a New Deal. Because of this tiny nation's longer experience with the central topic of this book, it appeared justifiable to depart from the usual procedure of treating changing patterns throughout as wide a selection of republics as possible, in order to concentrate in one complete essay on the trail-blazing country which has been re-garded by many as the model of the future for all Latin America.

For exactly opposite reasons, a separate paper was devoted to the most recent entry in the race toward freedom and reform, Bolivia. The virgin efforts of one of the world's most underdeveloped countries in undertaking to excavate itself from out of the past constitute not only an event of moment in the American hemisphere, but illustrate the rapidity with which long obscure and neglected areas in all portions of the globe are redirecting their attitudes, criteria and aspirations away from the past and toward the present and future. That this impoverished Andean republic has flirted menacingly with Communism as a potential aid in breaking forth from the cocoon of the past, but has now at least temporarily decided in favor of expedients judged acceptable under the circumstances by the United States, makes the study of this country all the more timely. A telling retort, moreover, to the oft-repeated charge that the United States exacts as its price for support to Latin America imposition of its own standards is the fact that we have extended unstinting aid to a country that has recently sought to alleviate its multifarious vexations through nationalization of mines and a land reform program that could be so applied as to threaten rights of private ownership, two measures surely at variance with our traditional system of values.

It may be noted that the papers in this volume dealing with Latin America in general often appear to apply primarily to the Hispanic American republics, according only passing attention, usually for purposes of comparison or contrast, to the product of Portuguese colonization in America. With its unique language among the Americas, its own distinct historical traditions, cultural backgrounds and mental attitudes, Brazil is striking proof that there is no Latin America; there are only different Latin American nations. The voices of freedom and reform have been raised amidst different circumstances in Brazil than in Hispanic America, and continue to this day to cry out in an ambient far different from that of the other Americas. For these reasons Brazil, too, required a separate study.

The very word reform, with which this volume is largely concerned, is profoundly ambiguous. There can be inner reform based on self discipline, and external reform of the physical environment and institutional structure. External reform produces dramatic and tangible effects although curbing freedom of action, while inner reform, the philosophers tell us, brings true freedom.

It is external reform with which the greater portions of the modern world, Western and Eastern, have been most concerned.

Latin America is no exception to the trend in contemporary world development. Attempts here to bring about external reform have generated the unavoidable concomitant of greater government control administered by apostolic bureaucrats. That the United States is now dealing with the external reformers has multiplied its difficulties in maintaining cordial relations. When it dealt with self-seeking aristocrats uninterested in the over-all progress of their countries, it encountered far fewer problems than when confronting nationalistic planners intent upon advancing their countries, not just their private fortunes. These new era statesmen are apt to be impatient when United States policy does not aid them to the extent deemed necessary for their ambitious programs. It is hoped that the essays in the present book, taken as a whole, will provide their readers with some insight into the aspirations of the new generations now shaping Latin America's domestic and foreign policies.

External and inward reform need not, of course, be mutually exclusive. As the realm of liberty of outer action is reduced by onrushing waves of external, nationalistic reform, men are thrown more back upon themselves in the endeavor to preserve a few patches and shreds of freedom. They must seek a type of liberty that can be practiced in private, and can not be subjected readily to outer checks. In the United States, the search for private freedom has resulted sometimes in a mere escape craze, leading to increasing reliance on the entertainment provided by the mass media, in an extensive audience for the syndicated columns of experts on peace of mind and soul, in do-it-yourself projects, and in recourse to tranquilizers. More noteworthy has been its effect in stimulating greater interest in the higher manifestations of culture. Our museums, libraries, book publishing firms, symphony orchestras and local opera companies, to cite a few examples, have progressed with giant strides, while United States scholarship has gained world-wide recognition. Even the art form represented by movies appears in recent years to have attained something of a pinnacle, demonstrating the concern of some portions of audiences with the deep and complex issues of human existence. There is evidence that we are shifting from an epic to a tragic or stoic approach to life, stressing inward strength rather than conquest of the outer environment alone. The search of Latin Americans for freedom in the midst of an intensely regulated and harrassed life may also result in notable achievements. The newly won privileges of the middle classes may provide them with opportunities to demonstrate the oft advanced claims concerning the cultural-spiritual superiority of Latin Americans, in brief, their greater qualities of inwardness. If they take advantage of these opportunities, Latin Americans could impart to Rodo's *Ariel y Caliban* the validity as a prediction that it always lacked as a description of actual circumstances.

Changing patterns of Latin American religious practices are largely ignored in this book. Religion is more associated with the inward reform to which Latin Americans may turn than with the external reform to which they have already directed themselves. Purely external reforms, however, could produce profound effects upon religion which might profitably be explored briefly in this introduction.

W. Rex Crawford points out in our first essay that Latin Americans in the past have equated freedom with absence of outer curbs. The excessive abhorrence of exteriorly applied restraints throughout the colonial period and the nineteenth century helps explain why a sense of citizenship did not develop, for citizenship requires the willingness to abide the demands of authority in the interest of national progress or the common good. In today's Latin America, the new classes, accustomed by an industrial revolution to mounting circumscription in their modes of living and earning a living, may be predisposed to suffer more graciously external restraint in matters of religion. The individualistic, anticlerical approach of Latin Americans to religion could be fundamentally altered. Moreover, as they are turned back upon themselves in the search for freedom, they may discover that religion affords a fruitful source of aid. In short, the coming of modern times to Latin America may, instead of debilitating religion, render it possible for the populace to discover for the first time a phase of their faith previously ignored, at least by most men: the value of inward discipline based upon formal dogma as interpreted by designated ministers.

The religion in which Latin Americans may discover a powerful

ally in the search for freedom based on inward discipline will not
be exclusively Roman Catholic. Already Protestantism has begun
to make notable gains in certain areas, such as Guatemala,
Uruguay and Chile, and can be expected to make continuing
progress; the advances of pentecostal, primitive religious sects in
Brazil have been startling. These facts, as well as the fear of Communism, have probably been in back of the fairly recent efforts of
the Vatican and Catholic prelates in Latin America to remold
their Church, as it operates in the southern Americas, into an
instrument more unequivocally dedicated to the quest for social
justice. In the past, the limited efforts of Protestant missionaries
seemed often more conducive to and more concerned with the
social and economic uplifting of the masses than those of the more
richly endowed Catholic Church. Clearly, the demand of the
lower classes for a share in the national wealth can no longer be
neglected, and the Catholic Church is now endeavoring to prove
that it can be as helpful as Protestants and Communists in fulfilling the "this worldly" aspirations of the people.

The new policies of the Catholic Church in trying to assume a
position of leadership rather than of feet-dragging in the social
and economic development of twentieth century Latin America
are highly commendable. At the same time, there is evidence that
at least some influential Catholics are adopting a pro-democratic
orientation, and shying away from authoritarianism in government. The *Per Un Mondo Migliore* organization in Rome, headed
by the Jesuit Father, Riccardo Lombardi, and the Institute of
Latin American Studies, functioning since 1957 as a part of the
International University of Social Studies *Pro Deo* of Rome, appear to be dedicated to democratic liberalism. This move may
produce a split within the Catholic Church in Latin America, for
William S. Stokes, in his article on democracy, freedom and reform,
points out the continuing conservatism of many leading Catholic
thinkers. Already in Argentina, the Christian Democrats have
divided into two parties, one pro-democratic, the other leaning
toward some measure of political authoritarianism.

Attention thus far has been directed to Latin America as it is
evolving at the present time. Included also in this volume are
papers which pertain almost as much to the past as to the present.
Especially is this true of those dealing with the revolutionary tradi-

tion and with cultural heterogeneity. Likewise concerned in large measure with the past is the analysis of Latin American concepts of freedom. These papers with a strong historical orientation are essential to an understanding of the area, helping to light the often obscure channels out of which contemporary Latin American civilization is emerging. Above all, they serve to stress how fundamentally different Latin America has in the past been from the United States, and strongly imply that differences will continue. They confute the widely held conviction in our country that once we become acquainted with people throughout the world, we will discover that they are all basically the same as we: reasonable people, that is, who, when we have explained our basic concepts and value systems to them will warmly embrace our way of life.

In dealing with Latin America, or with any part of the world, it is this sentimental one-worldism that has made basic understanding and cooperation so elusive. The writer feels that Latin Americans do not want to be treated as people who are the same as we; juridic equality they demand, but the notion of total equality, which sameness implies, they eschew. They desire us to respect their differences and, when possible, take these differences into account when dealing with them. We in the United States have been accused of being relativists, but perhaps we will never be relativistic enough until we cease equating sameness, equality and goodness on one hand, and differences, inferiority and evil on the other.

The egocentric belief that differences represent an evil, albeit one that can be remedied, has led to the wish for full and present equality, of sameness, and therefore goodness, among human beings and nations. Assuredly, this has not been exclusively a United States phenomenon. The belief-wish cycle has been an occasionally present factor in shaping domestic and foreign policies of Western republics since earliest historical times, but may have been lent new impetus by the eighteenth century philosophers. It has led, among other interpretive slants, to the deemphasis of heredity and historical tradition, and to the attempt to explain away all differences, which impede fulfillment of the wish for sameness, by controllable environment. Raynal was one of the first to apply this approach to Latin America. Refurbishing the Las Casas Black Legend, he blamed the Iberian colonial institutional structure, which he considered one aspect of environment, for the backwardness of the native races. If the institutions could be transformed so as to accord with the theories of the Enlightenment rationalists, Raynal was convinced that aboriginal backwardness would be eradicated. Many in the United States continue to believe in a new sort of Black Legend vis-a-vis Latin Americans: they are backward because of their arbitrarily chosen and readily discardable institutions; by substituting our institutions for theirs they could become our equals, the same as us, and therefore good. Little progress in hemisphere understanding can be anticipated until it is more widely realized that institutional variations reflect rather than cause diversity in national characteristics.

More fundamentally, the United States can not hope to maintain a position of world leadership unless it learns to recognize and respect the differences of the emerging areas of the Near, Middle and Far East and Africa. Here are cultures more radically different from our own than those of the Latin American republics, often seeming so mysterious as to defy comprehension. A reasonable attempt to understand Latin America and to appreciate its differences is essential to foster in us the ability to deal empathetically with the still more unfamiliar areas of the changing world. A sound outlook toward Latin America could become the bridge which will lead us out of our narrow preoccupation with classical, Caucasian, Greco-Roman, Judaic-Christian civilizations toward the startlingly new worlds which we now reluctantly perceive across a chasm.

The truth is that the world of which the Columbus discoveries made Europe aware has now become an Old World which can not deal effectively with the continents and peoples which have in the twentieth century attained to adolescent strength unless it learns more fully to understand its own depths and mysteries. The recent cult of Russian and non-Western studies, while in many ways fulfilling an essential function, can by overemphasis prove a shortcut to international maturity that is in reality a short circuit. The rise of the political and economic importance of Russia, Africa and the East should not diminish, but rather accentuate our scholarly and diplomatic interest in Latin America. To fail to achieve a rational comprehension of our own hemisphere will herald our hopeless inability to succeed in the world at large.

CHAPTER II

[W. REX CRAWFORD *]

The Concept of Freedom in
Latin America

The Love of Freedom in Latin America

Many currents of recent European thought have had a strong influence upon attentive Latin Americans. Among them, one can certainly point to the *obra* of José Ortega y Gasset, the Spanish lecturer, man of letters and philosopher, who died in 1955. The burden of his posthumous *Man and the People,* which appeared almost simultaneously in Spanish and English in 1957, is an insistence that a concept is a vital episode. In this approach one makes out the teaching of Ortega's master, Wilhelm Dilthey, and other Germans who have dealt with *Verstehen* and the *Geisteswissenschaften,* as well as a certain similarity to well-known existentialists. The *Erlebtes* is unavoidable.

Now if freedom is a thing lived for, fought for, if necessary died for, it is obvious that the concept has been for vast numbers

* W. Rex Crawford was an exchange professor at the University of Chile, under the Buenos Aires Convention, in 1941. From 1943 to 1945 he served as Cultural Attaché to the American Embassy in Brazil. He served once again as a lecturer in South America in the summer of 1952. His published works include: *A Century of Latin American Thought* (Cambridge, Massachusetts, 1944); *Cuatro Conferencias en la Universidad de Chile* (Santiago, Chile, 1942); *Panorama da Cultura Norte-americana* (São Paulo, 1945). He has also translated into English Fernando de Azevedo's, *Introduction to Brazilian Culture* (New York, 1950). He is at present Professor of Sociology and Director of the Institute of Humanistic Studies for Executives at the University of Pennsylvania.

16

of Latin Americans one of central importance. The inspiration for liberty came in part from ideas and books imported from the heady atmosphere of Europe. Readers boldly sent for and read the philosophers who "of course" were not supporters of the *ancien régime*. Professor Irving A. Leonard has amply documented this trend among colonial intellectuals.[1] Such literature, at once fiery and skeptical, was not approved by the Establishment of the time, either Church or state. It taught both independence and free thinking, and the latter in its religious context has always been more closely associated with liberalism in Latin America than the people of the United States would expect. The spirit of anticlericalism requires for its understanding by us a considerable exercise of academic empathy, but historical circumstances have made it a more natural phenomenon at times in Latin America.

The still rather lively corpus of ideas about the frontier and the freedom and individuality it fostered which we associate with the name of Frederick Jackson Turner,[2] has no very exact parallel in Latin America, although works as great as those of Sarmiento and da Cunha come to mind, and among more recent writings a notable essay by Vianna Moog which has not received the attention it deserves.[3]

The recurrent need for political independence and for throwing off dictatorial regimes has meant that large numbers of students, older intellectuals, officers and soldiers have cared sufficiently for freedom to risk all for it, to suffer imprisonment, torture, execution in its sacred name. What right have we, or anyone, to analyze and criticize with scientific detachment, when our own commitment has been less deeply felt, less tragically paid for?

And yet, the sacred is not always the well defined, and a willingness to rush into the streets behind the charismatic leader of revolt is not the same as a careful philosophical examination of the nature and limitations of liberty. Particularly is this true of cultures which have been criticized even by the French as being unduly given to the excitements of rhetoric. No ethnocentrism

[1] Irving A. Leonard, *Books of the Brave* (Cambridge, Massachusetts, 1949).

[2] For a judicious summary see Ray Allen Billington, *The American Frontier, with Bibliography*. The Service Center for Teachers of History (400 A. Street, S.E. Washington, D.C., 1958), pp. 32.

[3] Vianna Moog, *Bandeirantes e Pioneires; Palalelo entre duas Culturas* (Porte Alegre, 1954).

here, please, assuming a superior type of political philosophizing on the part of General Motors or the soap business, or a happy wedding between the deep thoughtfulness of German thought and the frequently lamented international action of German governments and general staffs. A sober, not-over-patriotic judgment might conclude that it would be most difficult to find in the whole corpus of Latin American writing anything that quite matches the doctor-of-philosophical balance and breadth of Dorothy Fosdick's *What is Liberty?*,[4] in spite of the fact that it bears the impress of its time and the then overwhelming concern with Fascism, Nazism, Liberty League, or that so incisively cuts through prevalent illusions in the discussion of freedom as does Reinhold Niebuhr in a recent article,[5] or that compares in depth of phenomenological insights with some of Max Scheler's notes.[6]

Freedom: The Absence of External Restraints or the Discipline of Self Mastery?

The preoccupation of our Latin American friends with the prolonged struggle for political independence has been at the same time a measure of their sincere devotion and a cause of a certain limitation in their ideas as to the nature of freedom. They turn back in their thinking to the period in which they achieved political separation from Spain (or somewhat less, Portugal), and their heroes are *Libertadores,* whereas ours are Founders and Fathers. A confusion between independence, which is only one aspect, and a beginning, and other possible meanings of freedom is one result. Occasionally in the chorus of huzzahs for freedom there is sounded a note that is, shall we say, more Anglo-Saxon, as when Juan Montalvo writes, "Any society in which freedom is the result of the laws, and the laws are sacred, is necessarily a free people," [7] and so seems to attach himself at least to the fringe of the school which equates "true" liberty with organization, duty, obedience, rather than with whim and impulse. Is this the very

---

[4] Dorothy Fosdick, *What is Liberty?* (New York, 1939).

[5] Reinhold Niebuhr, "Liberty and Equality," *Yale Review,* XLVII, No. 1 (Autumn, 1957), 1–14.

[6] Scheler, *Nachlass* (Bern, 1957).

[7] Montalvo, *Siete Tradados: Réplica a un Sofista Seudocatólica,* excerps quoted in José Gaos, *Antología del Pensamiento de Lengua Española en la Edad Contemporanea* (Mexico, D.F., 1950), pp. 499 ff.

voice of wisdom or presently a mere rationalization of the *status quo?*

Another characteristic of Latin American thought is that the sequel to freedom is the problem of organizing an orderly society, and so one flag bears the Comtian device *Ordem e Progresso,* one great book the subtitle *Barbarism or Civilization,* one slogan parts company with a glorious tradition to the extent of aiming to *matar al centauro.* José Victorino Lastarria, the Chilean firebrand, to be sure, linked independence with something more profound when he began the second part of his *América* with the proclamation:

the emancipation of men's minds, that is the real end of the Hispano-American revolution, which began as an independence movement, establishing the republics which flourish where once were the colonies through which Spain ruled the continent. Spanish civilization worshipped and still maintains in the Peninsula exactly the opposite principle. It is entirely based on the enslavement of the human mind.[8]

Looking back more than a century later, Francisco Romero hammers away at the same point when he maintains that "the American experience is first of all the experiencing of freedom." [9]

The politico-social orientation would imply, to those critics who think of the sociological as equivalent to the superficial, a certain blindness to the finer kinds of freedom. If freedom is absence of external coercion from other human beings, the temptation is to say it means doing what one wishes, and to leave it at that. At the other end of the scale, those who embark upon vaguer speculation as to freedom from impulse, passion and instinct, the Platonics, would tend to worry little about external restraints, and to emphasize the possible ties that in any social situation remain for the real or reasonable, the good or better personality. Between the extremes lies the area of control, of that which is done, that which is not done, usages, as Ortega y Gasset calls them, which are not exactly the will of anyone, but which float freely in the social atmosphere. Few insist on them, or could give good reasons for them, but nearly all are rendered uneasy by failure to keep them up.

Where does the Latin American, if one dares to use the haz-

---

[8] José Victorino Lastarria, *América,* excerps quoted in Gaos, *op. cit.,* p. 447.
[9] Francisco Romero, *Sobre la Filosofía en América* (Buenos Aires, 1952), p. 49.

ardous definite article, stand? If one surveys the *pensadores* of national and even American fame, there seem to be few exceptions to the statement that their basic inquietude is a political one, rather than the urge to get free from what is a part of man's own personality. Those who write of it repeat that we must "have faith in the excellence of freedom, without reservation, without fear, without change, and a firm, bold resolve to struggle for it."

The difficult questions which "the exercise of personality" or "the affirmation by an individual or group of his or its own essence" are likely to raise rather than to answer do not receive from Latin American thinkers, or perhaps from any of us, enough serious attention. Even the persistent problem of political life, how can we make the fundamental liberties ever more possible to realize, leaves the word fundamental to be explored. It may be doubted whether most of the ardent talk in recent years about the Free World has clarified the subject. Beyond lie the questions whether these fundamentals are things that society *qua* society can accomplish, and the practical historical question, to which this volume makes some answer, whether Latin America has found ways of its own of accomplishing them.

To return to the concept as vital episode, as a thing lived. Freedom belongs not only to a tradition of philosophical thought, but to Latin American life, to the Latin American psychology. The idea of freedom is always related both to the psyche that is claiming it and to the particular context in which it is sought. It grows from the typical personality and character. F. Oliver Brachfeld in discussing American philosophy analyses the personality as follows: "The Latin American of whose unbridled individualism we hear so much is not an individual separated from others, but on the contrary he needs sociability. Even if he should be solitary, his solitude is fundamentally different from German Einsamkeit. He is not an individual so much as he is always the *subject;* he conceives the world in the first person." [10] And Brachfeld adds the curious note that "he has very little feeling for the value of individual life, his own or another's." The cordial sociability of the Latin American and his goal as writer

[10] F. Oliver Brachfeld, *Discusión de la Filosofía Americana* (Primero Congreso Latinoamericano de Filosofía y Filosofía de la Educación. Quito, 1954), p. 197.

and teacher to assemble a group of disciples about him are indeed striking, but so is that *desconfianza* which perennially makes collaboration difficult, and which leads him often to regard academic cooperation in the United States with amazement. We can perhaps summarize our discussion thus far in Miss Fosdick's words: "Behind every demand for liberty is this desire to escape some unwelcome external restraint," [11] and add as a gloss that in Latin America, as surely among most men everywhere, external means external in the most obvious sense, rather than the subtler feeling that one's own passions and impulses can be the coercing enemy, and somehow external to the more essential self. Freedom is conceived in a political context more than in an ethical or aesthetic one, and that basic freedom from *tanha* or desire which Buddhism has taught for twenty-five-hundred years is a rare aspiration. Instead, "usually reference is made to the liberty of some group to do something in particular." [12]

To do something in particular is to do it at a given time, and so simple a query as, how do we so arrange our situation that we may continuously do as we wish, may lead us not only to constitutions and institutions, but to a deeper freedom which is independent of all written documents and institutional structures. The doubtful and cynical will interpret such "highfalutin" escape from circumstances as makeshift or hypocrisy, giving up when the path to what we wish to do is closed, and contenting ourselves *faute de vieux* with what it remains possible to do. Is the remnant of freedom thus preserved a poor thing or the truest and best kind of freedom?

Men of Action as Freedom Fighters

The fighters for freedom throughout Latin American history have included many varieties of men and it is impossible to do justice to them all. As university students they have typically exhibited anything but political apathy, have acquired an ideology with or before their textbooks, and have felt it their duty to rush into the streets or to strike, and have paid for these activities with imprisonment, blood and death, and often with the crippling of their careers. Many have gone on from student reform

[11] Fosdick, *op. cit.*, p. 3.
[12] *Ibid.*, p. 9.

and revolt to the dedication of their lives to political freedoms. While many of their teachers have been more stodgy and conservative, some of them, too, have been the source of libertarian ideas in the student body, and have sympathized with their impassioned action. We have only to remember the hundreds of Argentine professors who were dismissed or resigned under Perón to be convinced that freedom always involves risks, in Latin America at least. Corresponding cases are harder to find among ourselves. Have we so much freedom that we take it for granted, or does the American teacher hardly know what freedom is, which seems to be the conclusion that emerges from Howard K. Beale's study for the American Historical Association.[13] Deserving also of special mention as freedom-fighters, have been a long line of ardent *periodistas*. The Latin American newspaper-man has not restricted his protests to claims for his own freedom as a reporter; he has in many cases been frankly humanitarian and liberal in a political sense. The idea that his capacities and services as a writer have been hired has been repugnant to him. It must be remembered that the category of writers for the press includes many of the same persons who appear elsewhere as leaders, teachers and authors, for it seems much more natural to the Latin American press than to our highly specialized one to seek or welcome the "collaboration" of the intellectual. On all of this, our brilliant young contemporary, Roberto Esquenazi Mayo, has expressed himself warmly.[14]

The social novel, the novel of regions, occupations, exploitation, has repeatedly been studied. Perhaps it does not belong under the heading of "the concept of freedom," but it has made freedom and its lack burning issues, imprinted upon our consciousness in unforgettable images. The names of Azuela, Icaza, Gallegos, Rivera, Ciro Alegría, José Lins do Rego, Raquel Queiroz, Jorge Amado, are only part of a noble and talented company.

Philosophers as Champions of Freedom

It is at this point that we must turn from the fiery *discursos* and communiques of the action-geniuses like Bolívar and Martí to the closet of the philosopher.

[13] Howard K. Beale, *Are American Teachers Free?* (New York, 1936).
[14] Roberto Esquenazi Mayo, *Ensayos y Apuntes* (La Habana, 1952).

Francisco Romero writes of the admired master, to whom he returns again and again, that "Alejandro Korn was a philosopher of freedom. As an American philosopher, that is what he was bound to be, what every American philosopher must be." He could not stand for mere adjustment to the environment; man's task is to rise, to take a stand against tyranny, including that of any social environment. Less flamboyantly than Ortega y Gasset, another of Romero's contemporary gods, even Korn was at odds with all that is tribal, and phrases like "society demands" did not win his ready conformity. For the American philosopher there is the freedom of the new experience in a new environment; there is the struggle for freedom vis-a-vis oppression, whether it be political, religious or economic. Liberty is guaranteed (without an obeisance to Frederick Jackson Turner) by the limitless frontier. The very nations of the New World began not with slow, vegetative growth, but with a group decision to be free in relation to the mother country. Freedom, for Korn, and for his famous disciple, is not only something that pertains to the state, but also to the individual. It is the deeper, inner sense of freedom which is at the heart of Korn's thinking; he teaches the goal of autonomy. It is a state of mind, and it is a perpetual struggle. As consciousness and autonomy grow, man achieves even greater freedom, for that is his destiny; as he fights against nature, against his fellow-man, even against himself, his freedom becomes ever more real, more perfect, more complete.[15]

Historians may quarrel and quibble about the influence of these philosophers, even in countries with proud intellectual elites much given to conversations at midnight on philosophical themes. The widest influence may involve issuing forth from the closet to the market place. So we read of José Rafael Bustamante that "throughout his thought and his political life he devoted himself to defending and glorifying freedom." Even of Bustamante the highest praise is that in his *Philosophy of Liberty* he agreed with Alejandro Korn. So, even though there may be more question in Korn's case than in that of native South Americans whether he may fairly be taken as representative, we may be permitted to seek in this noble figure, who has been made as *The Philosopher of Freedom* the subject of a recent book by Francisco

[15] Romero, *op. cit.*, pp. 49–51.

Romero,[16] the best expression of thought on our subject in the sister republics to the south. One of his essays is entitled "Creative Liberty." [17] Alejandro O. Deustua [18] joins Korn in his zeal for creative freedom, and, thinking of creation in almost purely aesthetic terms, makes creation and freedom actual equivalents, two sides of a single coin.

Analyzing the work of the literary artist more profoundly, the wise Mexican, Alfonso Reyes,[19] joins T. S. Eliot in seeing that if the literary artist is in his playful and imaginative game freeing himself from the world of practical necessities, he also has a paradoxical need for obstacles, and where they do not exist outside will create them as the regulative canon of his own art, for there is no "freeing" where there is no confining.

Liberty Korn perceives as basically pertaining to the subject: affirming his freedom is the most genuine expression he can give to the heart of his being. In fact, personality and liberty are just two names for the same fact. We engage in the fight for our freedom, we are called upon to judge whether circumstances favor or stand in the way of this our aspiration and we consequently label external facts in the objective world useful or harmful to us. If we think straight we add to these pragmatic judgments others that must be called ethical; our judgment of the subjective factors that favor or hinder genuine freedom is conveyed by the terms good and bad. Korn further argues that while economic freedom is just as fundamental as ethical, there is real danger in confusing the two. The former term refers to the objective, the latter to the subjective. The useful, which belongs to outer circumstances, chiefly economic, is not always good, nor is the good always useful; the error of utilitarianism was just that of taking the useful for the good, and so of tending to deny autonomous personality. On the other hand, to insist only on the ethical concept is to close one's eyes to the fact that the full expression of personality is possible only in a world which has been already subjected to our will. If we lack both kinds of freedom we are

---

[16] Romero, *Korn, Filósofo de la Libertad* (Buenos Aires, 1956).

[17] Alejandro Korn, "La Libertad Creadora," in *Obras*, Vol. I (Buenos Aires, 1938).

[18] Alejandro O. Deustua, *Estética General*, parte segunda; *Cuestiones Estéticas*, Capítulo I; "El Valor Estético," excerpts quoted in Gaos, *op. cit.*, p. 1077.

[19] Alfonso Reyes, *El Deslinde: Prolegómena a la Teoría Literaria*, Vol. VI: *La Ficción Literaria*, excerpts quoted in Gaos, *op. cit.*, p. 1377.

subject to alien powers which annihilate our personality, and prevent our living a life of our own. There is an original note in Korn's remark that what the absence of ethical freedom delivers us over to is the domination of instincts and dogmas; the dogmas are usually forgotten, but play their pernicious part. With a fine realism that accepts the universe as the universe is, Korn mingles with his limitless aspiration for freedom, an implied admission of its impossibility: "If we could wholly achieve freedom, it would identify us with the Absolute." [20]

So for this Argentinian Socrates the prerequisite of human freedom is doing away with all subjection to economic limitations; but this is not the only prerequisite, for freedom and ethics are closely bound together. The heart of the immoral act is that it deprives of freedom, degrades the human condition which is, or ought to be, one of liberty. The good act, on the other hand, has its reward in itself, in the very consciousness that in acting freedom has been achieved. The word consciousness is vital here, for it furnishes as much definition as Korn will ever deign to give. Commenting on Cohen's epigramatic definition, freedom is the energy of the will, Korn replies with the cliché that freedom is the absence of coercion but only to reject it as tautological, getting us nowhere. His last word was, "If you don't know by introspection what freedom is, you and I have nothing to say to each other. You have not understood."

Abstract and Practical Freedom

Ringing words, and plausible. But there is something uncompromising and mystical, out-of-this-world, about them. Even a theologian from North America can be more realistic, more worldly. In a notable article, Niebuhr, a great thinker and truth seeker, goes so far as to speak of legitimate conservatism and legitimate liberalism, "which are nearer to each other than either is to a cynical conservatism or to an abstract liberalism." [21] Instead of merely "glorifying" or "defending," he is in effect asking how much freedom we can have, how we can decide when to sacrifice it to other goods that we value equally highly. One of these goods is equality. Presumably the first users of the sacred

[20] Korn, *Axiología*, excerpts quoted in Gaos, *op. cit.*, p. 1106.
[21] Niebuhr, *op. cit.*

trilogy, liberty, equality, fraternity, like the Marxists after them, had no inconvenient doubts as to the compatibility, almost the synonymity of the three goals. It is a question of fact how far this is true, as it is how far liberty is compatible with the unity and consensus of a society, how far equality can be indulged in the face of the necessity of some kind of hierarchy. Niebuhr concludes that "the unity and stability of the community makes liberty even today less than an absolute right," eliminating the ideal in its pure or abstract form as impossible. Further, the pursuit simultaneously of the two ideals lands us in a paradox: "it is possible to purchase the one only at the price of the other." The search for a realistic and viable form of liberalism necessitates awareness of the ineluctable nature of both unity and hierarchy, and willingness to struggle against the excesses of both. Fanatical and utopian liberalism is as much to be avoided as is unilateral, selfish liberalism. What we have attained, says Niebuhr, is not pure liberty, but as much liberty as one can in practice get, as a part of a larger thing, a just and stable society.

It is more than a little curious that a great Christian thinker should have neglected the third revolutionary ideal, which if it is neglected today, is nonetheless close to traditional religious values. It is to be hoped that he and other systematic thinkers will devote themselves some day to the relation between liberty and equality and fraternity. The first two are usually claims, but the latter is love, or close to it.

If both the thinkers and the fighters have seemed to give priority to the claims, we are in no position to assert that this is a phenomenon restricted to Latin America; the differences between them and ourselves are, if they exist, only a matter of degree. And when their claims are presented for all, for the other man as well as for the we-group, they are well on their way to adding brotherhood to the Anglo-Saxon ideal of the equal opportunity, of equality before the law and to the Latin American generous hope for freedom.

Ideas of reform can be understood best as related to the situations in which they arise, and to the enemy to which they are an attempted answer. Let us not forget that the image of capitalism that has been common in Latin America is not ours, but more resembles what comes to the European, or even the Asian mind, when capitalism is mentioned. There are overtones of colonialism. Extremes are natural under such circumstances, and a bitterness on the part of reform leaders toward foreign bosses, who as a matter of fact may be more generous in wages and welfare than domestic employers. Along with forces arrayed against each other, middle-of-the-road solutions have been found, too, and other parts of this volume may tell how Chile anticipated the United States in social security and preventive medicine, what real as well as dubious benefits Perón brought to the *descamisados,* and the like. And the reader can draw his own conclusions as to the number of citizens of our sister republics for whom the fine words in praise of freedom are little more than a sham.

CHAPTER III

[FREDRICK B. PIKE]

Sources of Revolution:

Their Impact on Freedom and

Reform in Latin America

Preliminary Considerations and Definition

So much a permanent and integral part of Latin American politics is the revolution that to many it appears to be the only important political institution developed in the southern Americas during nearly 150 years of independence, if indeed change can be institutionalized. (Mexicans, it may be noted, see nothing incongruous in such a possibility, having named their official party, the Party of Revolutionary Institutions.) Conservatives tend to decry this pattern of instability, believing it to evidence an immature flouting of authority that renders existence unproductive. Certain liberals, especially those of Latin America, argue the contrary, avowing revolutions to have been a vital bulwark of personal liberty and individualism, and a necessary means of achieving democracy. Adherents to both of these viewpoints claim too much. Despite revolutions, Latin America has made greater progress in the past century than have many of the more stable areas of the world, and has produced certain statesmen who by any standards must be considered mature. On the other hand, personal liberty has probably suffered from revolution as much as it has gained, with worthy administrations interested in human rights as often overthrown as despots, and with dictatorship tending to follow in the wake of genuinely disruptive social, economic or political change.

The Latin American revolutionary tradition involves the student at the very outset in grave difficulties, not only about effects, but more fundamentally about the nature of revolution itself. The word, for example, generally carries the connotation of radical and fundamental change. How are we to reconcile this with the fact that Venezuela is said by historians to have undergone fifty-two major revolutions in the first century of independence, and Bolivia well over sixty, while few if any truly basic changes could be detected in either republic within this time span? Obviously, this is a problem in semantics, and calls for a working definition of revolution.

By insisting on the Marxian concept that revolution represents an exchange of the classes which wield political and economic power, it can be argued that there are few evidences of revolution in Latin America since the 1820's. True, a middle class has gained significant power in certain areas, but often in a relatively peaceful and evolutionary manner which has left to the traditional landed aristocracy a significant veto power. If class uprising constitutes the essence of revolution, Venezuela, Bolivia and, for that matter, all Latin America have been singularly free from revolution. Nor is it possible to surmount all pitfalls by accepting less fundamental changes as sufficient for the making of a revolution, for the means by which change is effected are also important. Peaceful elections, for example, in the United States and other countries considered politically stable have often ushered in greater changes than political uprisings in allegedly revolutionary Latin America.

The obstacles to our quest can perhaps be overcome only by abandoning concern with universal applicability, which province we leave not too hopefully to the philosophers, and by insisting in advance that our definition's frame of reference be limited to Latin America. Additional complications can be avoided by confining this paper primarily to political rather than economic revolutions, although occasional attention will necessarily be directed to the interplay between politics and economics. With these limitations in mind, it is safe to conclude that a Latin

American revolution occurs when by means generally considered
extra-constitutional, a ruling group is forced to surrender sovereignty into the hands of others.

Colonial Tradition as a Source of Revolution

In many ways, the most decisive factor in producing the chaos
of nineteenth and even twentieth-century Latin America has
been the colonial heritage. It has now become trite to observe
that colonists of this area were rendered singularly ill prepared
for national existence by lack of opportunity for training in self
government. Revisionists, of course, have arisen to challenge this
appraisal, claiming that the *cabildo* or town council provided an
excellent source of experience in self government, comparable to
New England town meetings. By way of revising the revisionists'
theories, it is safe to affirm that training in local self administration provided by the *cabildo*, under the Hapsburgs at least,
represented a purposeful crown policy of permitting, even encouraging, local misgovernment as a means, cheap it was hoped,
of keeping creole elements content. When independence was
achieved, agencies of municipal government which had been instrumental in fomenting the movement apparently felt that they
had reacquired the right to irresponsibility which the Bourbon
monarchs had sought to curtail. Thus, in the new republics, attempts of central governments to establish sound rule were resisted as representing, in effect, a return to the Bourbon pattern
of reform. This was instrumental in provoking the centralism *v.*
federalism issue which nourished a bountiful crop of revolutions
in many Latin American countries.

Reference to Hapsburg and Bourbon monarchs raises the point
that there were two colonial traditions in Spanish America. That
of the Hapsburgs, after Philip II, often reduced itself in practical effects to a minimum of centralized government radiating
outwards from Madrid, and allowed much scope for individual
action as well as for gross inefficiency. To all of this, Bourbon
rule, at least until the death of Charles III, attempted to put an
end, by introducing the efficient and centralized administration
of competent bureaucrats. Within the new structure, in theory
that is, little room was left for the inefficiency of individualism
and the caprices of local institutions. Moreover, all colonial set-

tlers were goaded into producing for the common good, which meant the good of the mother country, rather than for their individual needs or those of the immediate locale. In many ways, the dichotomy between Hapsburg and Bourbon traditions has continued to the present time. Anglo-American colonies, it could be conjectured, might have enjoyed a less tranquil period of early independence if to their early customs of local self rule and relatively uninhibited pursuit of self and local interest had been added a century of exacting colonial administration and forced production for the advantage of a super government in which they had virtually no voice.

Lack of opportunity for developing responsible political skill, both in Hapsburg and Bourbon times, was closely paralleled in the economic field. The best and most lucrative business opportunities were largely reserved for *peninsulares* or contrabandists. When independence came, Latin Americans were as much novices in responsible business practices as in politics. The inevitable economic disasters, resulting both from malice and ignorance, were often productive of violent political disruption.

Another costly legacy of colonial rule, augmented by characteristics of Spanish and perhaps to a lesser degree Portuguese nature, has been personalism. Administration in colonial times was largely personal, rather than institutional. In Spanish America, the Bourbons tried to alter this condition, but their efforts were largely fruitless. The subdelegate, for example, soon became as much the agent of personalism as the *corregidor* had been. Nor did any assiduous Portuguese effort to replace the man with a system survive the fall of the Marquis of Pombal. Throughout colonial times, then, when laws were enforced, when an institution functioned smoothly, it was because of the popularity or strength of character of a particular administrator, not because of respect for laws or institutions in themselves. The Latin American has always been more impressed by the dramatic in life, by a good show, a strong and arresting personality, than by the dull and prosaic workings of efficient institutions. This has made for a political life noted for its color rather than its stability.

Personalism has manifested itself also in the notorious saying of colonial legal tradition, "Obedesco pero no cumplo." Viceroys and lesser officials thereby revealed that their own personal insights and their private opinions took precedence over any legal structure. In cavalier fashion, they disregarded laws on the grounds that the Council of the Indies did not truly understand the situation in the Indies. Even members of the Church hierarchy invoked scholastic philosophy to justify these practices. Martín Ignacio de Loyola, Bishop of La Plata, observed in 1616: "In interpreting a law, one must keep in mind the ultimate end of the king, and if strict execution of a law seems to militate against accomplishment of that ultimate end, one must respect the law with reverence, but need not execute it, for such is the teaching of true theology." [1]

Having rationalized their position in this or similar fashion, colonial administrators proceeded with unperturbed consciences to flaunt the law, at the same time professing obedience to it. Is it strange that this mentality of legal personalism has been exhibited by ambitious Latin American *políticos* to the present day? There issues from the central government of one of the republics a new directive or law. In the provinces, a man of some local importance chooses to ignore the legal prescript. He may not actually mouth the words, but clearly his actions are described by the classic sentence, "Obedesco pero no cumplo." And thus, another revolution has commenced, hallowed by the tradition of three centuries of colonial rule. Or, again, an administration finds it convenient to rule without annoying constitutional limitations, and invariably a stipulation in the fundamental charter, providing for the state of siege, makes this possible. In this, the administration is merely saying that it obeys the constitution but will not fulfill its provisions. Even in constitutional procedure, then, the principle of "obedesco pero no cumplo" has been perpetuated so as to render unconstitutional rule constitutional.

It is significant also that Latin America, veritably, was conceived in rebellion. Roldán rebelled against Columbus; Cortés against Velásquez; Olid against Cortés; Balboa against Enciso and Nicuesa; Córdoba against Pedrarias; Lugo the younger against his father; Orellana against Gonzalo Pizarro; Gonzalo

---

[1] Treatise of Don Fray Martín Ignacio de Loyola, Bishop of La Plata, to the *cabildo* of Buenos Aires, March 19, 1606. *Acuerdos del Extinguido Cabildo de Buenos Aires* (Buenos Aires, 1907–1925), I, pp. 193–198.

Pizarro and Carbajal against Viceroy Nuñez de Vela, and so on. In Brazil, conflicts between various *donatarios,* between civil settlers and Jesuits, between the *bandeirantes* and authorities in general, and between northerners and southerners, indicated a chronic willingness on the part of the colonists to ignore their officials and take the law into their own hands. Rebels against official power, when they managed to gain dramatic new wealth and prestige for the crown, generally went totally unpunished. Indeed, they were often rewarded with honor and office. A premium was attached to successful rebellion.

The tradition of revolution, never entirely dormant during colonial times, received new impetus in the eighteenth century, when a series of uprisings swept Spanish and Portuguese America from New Spain to La Plata. It is probable that only the semi-mystical allegiance to the crown prevented revolutionary tendencies from wholly submerging those of order and conservatism. Removal of the crown's authority in Spanish colonies during the early nineteenth century, and attempts to achieve this end in Brazil which ultimately succeeded in 1889, vastly strengthened centrifugal forces, and to this day Latin Americans have been unable to fashion a symbol of centripetal power comparable to that of monarchy.

Religion and the Revolutionary Tradition

The most unfortunate of all colonial traditions, in so far as it militated against stability in the first century of independence, may have been the intimate union of Church and state. Not only did this relationship make inevitable, once independence had been achieved, a bitter debate accompanied by frequent violence concerning exercise of patronage rights; it produced effects more fundamentally deleterious to both contestants. The scope of this paper limits us to considering only the manner in which the state was affected.

Involvement of religion in politics, the habit of confusing treason with heresy at which the Inquisition excelled, of justifying or censuring governments on the basis of theology, tended to introduce into politics a degree of fanatic, crusading zeal, destined to endure for generations after the colonial yoke had been discarded. A classic example of the mixing of religion and politics in the time-established pattern occurred in mid-nineteenth-century Mexico, when Archbishop Lázaro de la Garza and Bishop Munguía objected to those articles, among others, of the 1857 Constitution which established freedom of speech, press and assembly and proclaimed the principle of popular sovereignty. And the cry, *Religión y Fueros,* frequently in Mexico and elsewhere disturbed political peace by arousing the gullible faithful to defend religion when in reality only special temporal privileges of the Church were under attack.

Religious oneness may have produced a complementary effect in undermining stability. Owing at least in part to uniformity of religion, Latin Americans have tended without hesitation to think in terms of ultimates, to pursue all problems to their final theological implications. In present day Chile, for example, only three political parties, the Christian Democrats, Conservatives and Liberals, are approved by the Church for the votes of the faithful. The other parties, with programs that are judged to lean toward theologically unsound tenets, are frowned upon. By the same token, Argentine voters were advised by their prelates in 1946 not to vote for a party that advocated separation of Church and state. This admonition, which helped assure election of Perón, manifested once again the commonness of introducing what churchmen construe as theological concepts into politics.

Substantially different has been the situation in the United States, where variety of religions has made the consideration of ultimates socially and politically risky. Here, pragmatism came to prevail at an early time, with policies gaining acceptance because they worked, not because they were in accord with principles of faith.

Further complications have been introduced by the fact that Latin American Catholics seem to have exhibited at times certain leanings toward heresies which, in more fully developed form elsewhere in the world, have seriously challenged the teachings of Rome. Because of the typical male's lack of concern with outer actions manifesting religious convictions, it often appears that he is trusting in salvation by faith alone. There also appear traces of the inner light justification of the select few, as found in Calvinism and Jansenism. The Latin American is apt to be convinced that his particular views on questions sacred and mundane are rendered infallibly correct by inner light intuition, a facet of religion which may be denied prelates and even popes. Brazilian Catholics, for example, during the 1872–1875 controversy between Church and state chose to ignore papal and episcopal pronouncements on Freemasonry. And shortly before this, Father Vigil in Peru had furnished a classic example of Latin American Catholicism by writing the multi-volume *Defense of the Authority of Governments and Bishops against the Pretensions of the Court of Rome*. When his work was condemned by the Vatican, Fr. Vigil calmly wrote and published a reply, refuting the propositions of the papal condemnation. More recently, many sympathized with Laureano Gómez of Colombia, and with Juan Domingo Perón of Argentina, when these rulers professed their Catholicism but reserved the right to disagree even on spiritual matters with churchmen, including bishops and archbishops. Similarly, an Argentine writer shortly ago commented that although the majority of his countrymen were indifferent to religion, they did not fail at times to perform "acts which relinked them to the Church." [2] Of course, the individual determined what these acts would be, and when they would be performed, and was convinced that these self-determined acts would suffice for salvation, regardless of Church teachings on the matter.

Inner light and individual intuitive dogmatic certitude, combined with an eagerness to infuse theology into politics, have made of religion one of the most powerful historical forces in all Latin America working for violent political clashes and revolution. Numerous writers, among whom Francisco Bilbao has been one of the most outspoken, have criticized the Church because of its alleged authoritarian influence, inclining to equate it with conservatism and dictatorship. Yet, for every dictator that churchmen have backed in Latin America, it would probably be possible to find another ruler they have attempted to overthrow. The most recent additions to a long history are the Colombian revolution of May, 1957, and the Venezuelan insurrection of January, 1958. Although the role of the Church in these instances appears to have been laudatory, serving to solidify opposition to two

---

[2] Mario Amadeo, *Ayer y Mañana* (Buenos Aires, 1956), quoted by Fritz Hoffman, "Perón and After: A Review Article," *Hispanic American Historical Review*, XXXVII, No. 4 (November, 1956), 527.

despots who could hardly be termed enlightened, it is overly sanguine to believe that such excursions into politics are necessarily worthy undertakings. What does seem certain is that in the past, neither Church nor state has profited from the fact that whether attacking or defending governments, clergy and laity have often invoked the name of sacred faith and have seldom hesitated to make sweeping interpretations concerning the theological implications of politics.

It is, moreover, well nigh impossible to view the Church purely as a conserving and stabilizing institution when it has suffered so from internal dissension. The unseemly conflicts which occurred within the ranks of the Portuguese and Spanish American clergy are too well known to require at this time more than a passing reminder of their existence. It is well known, for example, that the role of some religious in favoring and others in opposing the independence movements resulted in a virtual civil war between the ministers of an institution which some writers would tell us has an official party-line solution for all problems, human as well as divine.

One of the most consequential splits in the ranks of the clergy occurred before the revolutionary wars, arising from the reception of the Enlightenment in the New World. Many churchmen, Jesuits and Franciscans prominent among them, helped spread in Latin America the ideas advanced in eighteenth century Europe by the new generation of philosophers and scientists. Others, notably the Dominicans, opposed many aspects of the new learning, and appear to have prevailed over their progressive opponents by the last decade of the eighteenth and the opening years of the following century. But permanent success these holders of the intellectual and spiritual dikes failed to achieve. Commencing their efforts too late, they succeeded only in palliating some of the symptoms of the Enlightenment, not in destroying the very germs. The Enlightenment had come to stay in Latin America, and to introduce a seemingly permanent new element into the Catholicism of the region, an element embodying the tendency to enhance the role of scientific knowledge, to exalt sensational over spiritual knowledge, and to undermine in general respect for tradition and authority.

Churchmen who broadcast the ideas of the Enlightenment in

Ibero-America have been unstintingly praised by liberal historians. In so far as they advanced the cause of true scientific knowledge and investigation, they have fully merited this praise. Yet, some of these churchmen, by their uncritical welcome of all aspects of the Enlightenment, were destroying the valuable conserving influences of the Catholic Church, thereby removing this institution as a bulwark against the ill-advised quest for change in itself, and as a barrier to the casual undertaking of revolutions.

That Catholicism of the southern Americas today is as much an offspring of the Enlightenment as of the Middle Ages which we are told continued in Latin America during much of the colonial period, has tended to produce a schizophrenic sort of religion. One pole of Church personality gravitates toward conservatism, authoritarianism and tradition, constantly shunning change, while the other seeks out the new and is violently repelled by the established and the traditional. There are ferment and restiveness within the Church, rather than unyielding dedication to the *status quo*.

Although the power and influence of the Church have declined drastically since independence, the pattern of dogmatic certitude regarding political issues that was a divisive element of the colonial tradition has continued. Even in their more secular modern society, many Latin Americans have apparently persisted in the belief that salvation, or at least self respect, lies in an interior faith, in adherence if not to the traditional orthodox creed, then to ideals and immutable standards of some sort. Thus, it is better for one to be associated with a government that conforms fully to his ideas, or to be plotting the overthrow of one that does not, rather than to risk compromising ideas merely in order to bring about political stability. This may help explain the paradox which has puzzled many as to how the freedom loving Latin Americans have often found dictatorship a more congenial form of government than democracy. To them, citizenship in the city of man depends on a belief in the ideals and guiding principles of that city, not necessarily manifested by outer acts consistent with those principles, just as citizenship in the city of God has ever depended on a belief not necessarily evidenced by deeds. This may help account for the fact that Mexicans feel freer in a political structure allowing only for victory of the official party, dedicated in the public mind to the revered principles of the 1910 Revolution, then they would in a truly democratic structure in which parties not properly oriented might gain power. Mexicans, as well as other Latin Americans, relish the sort of freedom provided by the undemocratic operation of a Rousseau-like General Will.

The Cult of Pure Reason and the Revolutionary Tradition

The real significance of colonial traditions, whether good or bad, is that they were the only patterns to which the newly emancipated republics of Latin America were accustomed. They had functioned with reasonable success for nearly twice as long as English counterparts in America. With modifications in detail, they might have continued to work. But Spanish Americans in 1824 were unwilling to change within the framework of tradition. The reason for this, essentially, was that between 1810 and 1824, Spain's colonists grew to hate the motherland, and all things Spanish, with a blind and uncompromising fervor. The love and affection between colonies and metropolis which had been fostered during three centuries came to an end in fourteen years of fanatical Spanish obstinacy and in an even longer period of refusal to recognize the *fait accompli* of independence. Contrast in this regard the events of the Anglo-American revolution, in which England yielded with a relatively graceful acknowledgement of the inevitable. The shock of independence was thereby minimized within the former colonies through the conscious preservation of links with the past. Moreover, England's colonists fought at least in part to preserve customs, practices and liberties which had evolved through the years. Although it may be said that the United States was conceived in revolution, it was also conceived in the principles of conservatism. To this day, we in this country tend to think in terms of conserving what we have rather than of experimenting with what is fundamentally new. Abraham Lincoln probably described this feature of our national life as succinctly as anyone when he observed: "A universal feeling, whether well or ill founded, cannot be safely disregarded." [3] John Dickinson had expressed the same conviction at the Consti-

[3] Quoted in Rachard Hofstadter, *The American Political Tradition* (New York, 1957), p. 111.

tutional Convention in Philadelphia: "Experience must be our only guide. Reason may mislead us."

In stark contrast to the Anglo-American pattern of conservatism in revolution, Spanish Americans, seeking to turn their backs on the seemingly discredited historical influences of the previous three centuries, committed the monumental blunder of bringing about the dominance of pure over practical reason. Refusing to consider the lessons of the past, zealously eschewing the practical, consistently ignoring the ineluctably acquired characteristics of colonial administration, they sought in the unchecked processes of abstract rationalism solutions to their problems. To a considerable extent, Brazilians were spared the orgies of idealism, as colonial traditions were preserved relatively intact by the monarchy which functioned until nearly the end of the nineteenth century.

There is a final irony to record. People can never escape totally from their traditions. In their desire to flee from the influence of Spain, Spanish Americans returned in part to the long enduring Spanish Middle Ages, to the ceaseless disputations of exhausted and decadent scholasticism. The difference was that in the secular age of freshly won independence in the New World, the disputants were politicians, not schoolmen, and disagreements led not to charges of heresy and use of the Inquisition, but to revolutions and civil wars.

Epic, Tragic and Revolutionary Traditions

The Anglo-Saxon sphere of civilization, especially in the United States, notes Patrick Romanell in *Making of the Mexican Mind,* is pervaded by the epic sense of life, and the Iberian world by the tragic. Romanell's observations can be expanded from an interpretation of individual characteristics to an explanation of the traits of political institutions and features of political life. In this broadened approach, life in the epic conscious United States is considered worth-while because of the opportunities it presents man *and* his institutions to conquer the environment and master physical nature.

The hero who embodies all of the virtues important to epic criteria for individual conduct is apt to be a rather simple, uncomplex individual. Consider the Horatio Alger brand of heroics.

The hero was born with certain endowments of industry, zeal and honesty, of a sort, which he did not have to develop through a long and tedious inner struggle with himself. The important thing was never what happened within him, but how he affected the world outside him, and eventually made a significant part of it his own. In the process of becoming successful no inner moral crisis developed. Success was simple, direct and complete, never marred by complications.

Like the human hero, revered political institutions, in the epic outlook, are expected to assume heroic proportions, propelling the country they govern ever upwards towards a life which is physically more comfortable for the vast majority. The thought of failure and collapse of institutions is avoided as assiduously as the thought of the failure and death of individuals: "Life is real, and life is earnest, and the grave is not its goal."

Latin Americans would ask, concerning the author of these lines, as Ernest Hemingway has asked in *Death in the Afternoon:* "And where did they bury him; and what became of the reality and the earnestness?" The Hemingway approach would strike a favorable response among Latin Americans because they have tended to possess the tragic sense of life. They can not believe that a man, a political regime or an institution can overcome all outer obstacles for an indefinite period. They think more of the inevitable failure and death of all things human. The highest goal of a person or a government is to overcome inner weakness, and thus be ready to die in honor. Men, governments and institutions pass away to make way for new endeavors. It would not be natural for them to impede this natural course of events. That the United States Constitution and its multiple institutions have survived in an epic sense, overcoming so many challenges for so long a time, might not engender admiration among Latin Americans so much as suspicion that the original principles of the founding fathers have been so undermined by compromise as to be unrecognizable. Better the death of a government or an institution, rather than a compromise with principle. But if political compromise and corruption should occur, and Latin Americans are usually realistic enough to know they must, the tainted regime and its institutions deserve no sympathy. The offenders, having discarded honor, must be turned out of office.

It would be an exaggeration to assert that the Latin American civilizations represent an undeviating adherence to the tragic sense of life, or even so consistent an adherence as that apparently maintained in parts of Spain. Portuguese America has had less of the tragic approach than Spanish America. One apparently trifling but actually profound indication of this is that in Portugal and Brazil the bull in the *corrida de toros* is not killed. There is no recognition, therefore, of the tragic drama represented by the bull fight. Even in Spanish America, shortly following the attainment of independence, the tragic sense of life appeared to be on the wane, and there was a conscious effort on the part of many thinkers to introduce more epic standards. It is possible today that the impact of industrialization is having the same effect. Spain's former colonies in America have thus been torn between two standards, and the result has been not only conflict and anxiety within the individual inhabitants of the region, but social and political disruption.

The split began long before independence, and was in part the result of the New World frontier. The abundance of land, mineral resources and cheap labor which the Ibero-American frontier afforded conquistadores must have begun at an early time to erode the bastions of stoicism and to inculcate certain epic values. This may indeed have been the most significant influence of the frontier in the southern Americas. If so, its influence was enhanced by the effects of the independence revolutions. In turning their backs on all things Spanish after winning their freedom, Latin Americans sought to dispense totally with the tragic sense of life. They actually came to believe they could translate their highest ideals and longings for perfection into concrete reality. In the pristine Spanish structure as it had developed on the peninsula, at least until the latter stages of the struggle with Islam, idealism had found nourishment in the high theoretical level of laws and in the dogmas of the Church. But men still acknowledged their own imperfection, and resigned themselves to their inability to put ideal laws or dogmas totally into practice. They recognized a dualism between the ideal and the real; while cherishing both, they were willing to keep them separate. This felicitous arrangement, allowing them to keep their highest ideals unsullied while living in a practical manner, had begun, it is true, to break down in the wake of religious fanaticism engendered by the successful Reconquest. Triumph over the Moors and the sudden opportunities for winning new converts to the faith afforded by the Columbus discoveries for a while led Spaniards to feel that they might succeed in bringing about the millennium by making Catholicism a truly universal religion. Their resounding failure led to a return to the tragic sense of life, and the earlier dualism.

Post-revolutionary Latin Americans had no time for this sort of dualism which had, as noted, been challenged even in the colonial period. They set out in search of governments which would do more than simply muddle through, which would be capable of transferring perfect laws into fact. They ceased to believe in a certain amount of necessary evil, and soon entered into a disastrous flirtation with positivism. The new seekers after epic success were often willing and anxious to capture control of political power through revolution so as to put their exalted notions into effect. When they failed to achieve the dramatic strides toward utopia that the faithful had been led to expect, the way was prepared for new revolutions. And always there lurked not far beneath the surface a certain boredom with utopian schemes, stemming from the temporarily dormant tragic sense of life. The struggle which has pitted preoccupation with a high standard of living against a way of life which includes the fatalistic resignation to adversity, an emphasis on the materially prosperous society against the priority of inner strength and fortitude has been reflected in the art and literature of the entire Western world. In Latin America, the struggle has more frequently than elsewhere been joined on a level beneath that of artistic expression. Emiliano Zapata fought in part because of the subconscious conviction that the rigors, the uncertainty and frustration of small scale rural land ownership would more nearly fulfill Mexican aspirations than generation of a modern, epic-conscious, efficient society. For partially the same reasons, Argentine gauchos resisted the advances of Sarmiento-style civilization, and the rude *sertanejos* of Canudos opposed the efforts of Republican Brazil to achieve national unity, material progress and efficiency.

Individualism and Revolutions

Probably the most obvious of all character traits contributing to revolutionary psychology is the extreme, even neurotic individualism of many Latin Americans, excepting of course the Indians. The excesses to which exaltation of the individual will can lead are well demonstrated by the remarks of a delegate to the 1950 Constitutional Assembly of El Salvador. In arguing against religious instruction in public schools, this deputy advised his auditors: "The light of liberty must first shine in the minds of children; only later, the light of truth." [4] This counsel provoked an outburst of enthusiastic approval, having described succinctly the very heart of the philosophy by which many a Latin American has lived, not only in youth, but in middle and old age. Once seduced by the liberty or license which promises all things, at least temporarily, one is apt to remain steadfastly obdurate before the less spectacular appeals of order, social regulation and wisdom.

A concomitant of individualism is the tendency to render judgment, to think in general, simply in terms of oneself, rather than to take into account broader and more objective considerations. This has led to great asperity in relations between Latin Americans. Criticism of a policy advocated by a particular politician is regarded by him as a personal affront, totally isolated from the broader frame of reference in which it might better be taken. Vengeance is demanded for the supposed insult, and thus is born another political war.

Individualism extends beyond the particular person and embraces his entire family, tending thereby to make the family unit always more important than society. The closeness of family ties has been much praised by many commentators on Latin America, but praised perhaps indiscriminately. An attitude which ignores the occasional need to temper family considerations in the light of society's demands does not make for political stability. It results instead in nepotism, both in politics and business, and leads to a vendetta complex which places private retribution for

---

[4] *Documentos Históricos de la Constitución Política Salvadoreña de 1950* (San Salvador, 1951), p. 269.

a purported affront to family honor above all requisites of a smoothly functioning body politic. It militates, in the final analysis, against a highly developed sense of responsibility to society.

This effect is demonstrated with particular clarity by the influence individualism has exercised upon many Latin Americans' concept of honor, leading them to regard this virtue primarily as a personal consideration. Honor is reduced to a set of rules governing conduct which one should abide by in order to gain the self-satisfaction of being a polished player of the game of protocol, and to win approval among a group that follows the same rules. It is similar to chivalry, whereby in a bygone age one gained an illustrious reputation by punctiliously performing the various rites and duties which established procedure demanded. But, the Latin American code of honor has taken no more heed than did chivalry of social implications in any broad sense. The praiseworthy acts required by honor have been intended to embrace, as were those of chivalry, only a small group at the top of society. Just treatment of the lower classes has remained the province of charity, not of honor. In the name of honor or chivalry men have performed feats of personal valor which have added immeasurably to their fame among a peer group, but which have unleashed the most disastrous and unjust effects upon other classes within the social structure. Latin Americans have taken to heart the sentiments expressed by Hamlet: "Rightly to be great is not to stir without great argument, but greatly to find quarrel in a straw when honor's at the stake."

The concept of honor is intimately connected with a sense of responsibility, a particular attribute which many critics have asserted to be practically non-extant in Latin Americans. Such blanket condemnation is not warranted. There is a sense of responsibility, but it is directed only toward the peer group. A politician who is not liked can conveniently be regarded by his detractors as outside the peer group and hence not deserving to be dealt with in responsible manner. In the United States, the notion of responsibility, although certainly honored as much in the breach as in observance, at least holds forth as an ideal a general or society-wide application. This has perhaps been one of the finest fruits of the spirit of equality.

The Influence of Economic Factors on the Revolutionary Tradition

Economic influences as well as the determinants of history, character and social usages have exercised puissant effects upon Latin American politics. The close interconnection between economics and one facet of politics, the revolutionary tradition, was demonstrated at the inception of the national period. By this time, the commercial, financial, manufacturing and agricultural advances of the colonial era had been largely dissipated by the bungling policies of Charles IV and the devastating wars of independence. There were scarcely to be found signs of a progressive, expanding, independent economy. Politics, in fact, was the most fruitful source of profit that one might discover, and was thereby transformed into a frenzied and unalloyed search for wealth in which public responsibility and general welfare were shamelessly ignored. Those who had no qualifications for public service other than a lust for money coveted high political office, and were willing to scheme and fight to attain it.

Another striking phenomenon of the Latin American area is so widespread in its ramifications that it is impossible to describe it simply as an economic, or a social, or a political condition. The concentration of land in the hands of a few produces effects in all phases of men's existence. Among its many influences has been the fact that the traditional forty families owning most of the land have generally controlled the government. There has seldom been widespread support for political administrations, and so there has been little room for negotiating, for playing one group against others. James Madison in Essay Number Ten of *The Federalist* described brilliantly the difficulties arising from factionalism in politics, and attempted to show how the proposed Federal Constitution would solve the problem. If the solution to factionalism envisioned by Madison is to be effective, there must be factions which represent more than one functional interest group. In Latin America, this condition has seldom been realized. When one of the forty families became discontent with an administration, its disaffection could not be offset by gaining support from other groups in society. Designs of one powerful family could thus upset entire political structures, with revolutions assuming the same insignificance which Metternich once disparagingly ascribed to constitutions: "What is called a constitution nowadays is nothing but get out so I can get in."

The class structure, arising from economic conditions of land and wealth distribution, may also contribute to the lawlessness which many observers have found to be at the root of instability in Latin America. It is likely that only when the private good of the upper classes can to some degree be made to coincide with the common good, will the lower classes feel any strong predisposition to obey laws passed by the ruling elite. Such coincidence has been extremely rare in Latin America. The rich have not depended on the majority of their country's inhabitants for their success, other than as a source of cheap labor. They have sold a great proportion of their goods, agricultural and mineral, abroad or to urban communities, and their market has not suffered from the fact that the rural masses comprising in the past by far the largest element of the population have been on the brink of economic annihilation. In the United States, where dependence is primarily upon the internal market, private interest of the producers and the common good have been more closely united, making possible a system which brings satisfaction to more people and results in greater stability.

Landed aristocrats have contributed indirectly to the frequency of revolutions not only by refusing themselves to play a responsible part in national administration and by abusing or ignoring the lower classes, but also by attempting to combat the interests of the small middle class which slowly emerged in the nineteenth century. To a considerable extent, the aristocrats continue to this day to cling to their attitude of contempt vis-a-vis the middle class. How this attitude has contributed to the revolutionary tradition can be understood through recalling one of the theories of Alexis de Tocqueville. In pondering over the basic conservatism of England, this remarkably perspicacious thinker noted:

The nobility . . . revealed in England a peculiar ability to merge and mix with other social groups, while in France it tended, on the contrary, to close its ranks and preserve its original purity of birth . . . some time in the middle ages. . . . The English nobility developed into an open aristocracy while the continental *noblesse* stubbornly remained within the rigid limits of a easte.[5]

The open aspects of the English nobility, contrasted with the closed features of the continental aristocracy, helped account, according to de Tocqueville, for England's having escaped the revolution which raged furiously across the channel at the close of the eighteenth century.

Applying this generalization to the present study leads to the discovery of similarities between the aristocracies of Latin America and continental Europe. In both instances, a burgeoning aristocracy of talent and wealth was denied access to the ranks of the aristocracy of birth. To gain recognition and political power, the frustrated aristocrats of talent and treasure felt constrained to resort to revolution.

To return to revolution inducing factors more purely economic in nature than latifundia and clashes of aristocracies, it may be noted that in many republics dependence for revenue upon export of one or even several raw materials has prevented attainment of long-term stability. It is a widely observed fact that a recession in the United States is likely to result in a full fledged depression in the southern Americas, one reason being the tendency for prices of raw materials to fall faster than those of manufactured goods during times of economic decline. A good example of a victim of this sort of economic squeeze play is present day Peru. Although unusually fortunate in enjoying a wide diversity of primary products which are sold abroad, this country finds itself now subject to a drastically adverse change in its terms of trade. Prices for such exports as copper, lead, zinc and cotton have declined, while the outlay for vitally needed finished goods, obtained largely from the United States, has remained the same or increased. The resultant economic crisis could have political repercussions, not only in Peru, but in other republics where similar conditions prevail.

Inflation is another force which throughout history has induced political turmoil. In mid-eighteenth-century England, for example, a price rise of thirty per cent from the middle fifties to the early nineties, followed by a precipitous jump of one hun-

[5] Ada Zemach, "Alexis de Tocqueville on England," *Review of Politics*, XIII, No. 3 (July, 1951), 336–337.

dred per cent the following quarter century, produced a situation in which wages failed to keep pace with rising prices. As a result of suffering among the industrial laborers, working class revolt was sporadic and violent. Inflation has produced like results in Latin America, lying behind much of the political restiveness at the end of the last century, and presently contributing to tensions in most of the republics. Its insidious influences constituted a telling factor in the recent Argentine revolution which toppled the Perón administration. Between 1943 and 1955, according to the *New York Times,* the working class cost of living index had increased 650 per cent. Nor is it permissible to blame these alarming statistics solely upon the economic bungling of Perón, for between 1948 and 1954 the cost of living increased 524 per cent in Bolivia, 1300 per cent in Paraguay, 307 per cent in Chile and an additional eighty-three per cent in 1955. Out of such conditions flow stresses and strains which bring on political convulsions.

Finally, the existence of a less obvious relationship between Latin American economy and the revolutionary tradition may be suggested by a point which Walter Prescott Webb has raised. In *The Great Frontier,* Professor Webb speculates that United States administrations were aided during the early and critical period of constitutional rule in winning the enthusiastic allegiance of the majority of citizens by the government's giving habits. People thought of their national administrators as wholesale distributors of land, as granters of subsidies and protection, as the providors of roads, harbors and other improvements. Quite to the contrary, in nineteenth-century Latin America, except at the rare times when a new confiscation of Church holdings or an Indian war made more land available, governments were very seldom cast in the role of givers. They simply were too poor. When lands or favors were dispensed, they were bestowed upon the few members of the elite, and no widespread support redounded to the political regime. The few members of the middle class, coming into tenuous existence through arduous individual effort, found an additional source of complaint in a tax structure that always favored agricultural interests. Gradually, as increasingly militant middle groups sought to induce governments to foment industry through imposition of tariffs, a new source of contention, warfare and revolution appeared. A great tariff debate, and all the implications therein involved, was, of course, a vital factor in the one momentous and violent revolution which has racked the United States since independence. The point to underscore is that by the time revolution occurred, the United States federal government had weathered an earlier period of crisis, and had won the loyal support of the greater number of its citizens, partially by what it had been able to give them.

The Role of Forces from Abroad in the Revolutionary Tradition

In addition to revolution making tendencies indigenous to Latin America which have thus far been considered, there are foreign influences which have contributed to the tumultuous estate of politics. Nicaragua and all Central America have suffered from the excursions of adventurers such as William Walker. Later, portions or all of the Caribbean area lay at the mercy of Minor Keith, Alfred Thayer Mahan, Theodore Roosevelt, William Howard Taft, Philander C. Knox, Woodrow Wilson, Calvin Coolidge and others of less renown. French intervention in Mexico precipitated a savage war and lent impetus to the revolutionary tradition. In more recent times, international Communism has been responsible for much unrest, and in 1935 launched an open revolution against the Vargas regime in Brazil. Nazi influence lay behind an attempt to unseat the same Brazilian strong man later in the 'thirties, as well as behind moves directed against Arturo Alessandri and Pedro Aguirre Cerda in Chile. It is doubtful, moreover, whether the June, 1943, Argentine revolution would have developed as it did had it not been for the example of Germany's national socialism. United States policy has also upon occasion facilitated the making of revolutions. The diplomacy of Sumner Welles helped lead, happily, to the ouster of Gerardo Machado from the Cuban presidency in 1933, and perhaps not so happily to the removal of Ramón Grau San Martín the following year. The 1945 speech of Adolf Berle, Jr., then United States Ambassador to Brazil, which criticized at least obliquely the penchant of Getulio Vargas for *continuismo* in office pushed the wily *caudilho* closer to his downfall. Nor can the Guatemalans be granted the totality of blame or praise for the 1954 revolution which toppled the Communist tinged Arbenz administration. One of the books dealing with this incident, written by Arbenz's Minister of Foreign Relations, develops in detail the charge, generally believed in Latin America, that the United States, urged on by the United Fruit Company, was directly responsible for this revolution. The same book contains an appendix listing thirty-five instances of United States armed intervention in Latin America since 1831.[6]

In far subtler, though in the long run no less effective manner, a different variety of foreign influences has shared in creating the state of chronic disorder in the southern Americas. Notwithstanding the efforts of a few brilliant men of letters, little in the way of an independent and indigenous culture was developed in Latin America during the first century following independence. As a result, the republics of this region depended for a great number of their attitudes, thoughts, customs and institutions on European and United States models. The area has been, therefore, frequently defenseless against foreign ideologies which have been incompatible with the local environment. Extreme federalism, radical democracy, *laissez-faire* business methods, positivism, Fascism and Hispanism represent some of the foreign pressures whose disruptive consequences Latin America might have been spared had she not been trying desperately to borrow a ready-made culture.

Revolutionary and Evolutionary Change

From the multiplicity of causes by now hinted at, there necessarily flowed numerous revolutions, or at least changes falling within the scope of the definition advanced at the beginning of this paper. In Mexico, for example, during the first fifty-three years of independence, there were over seventy administrations. Obviously, the revolutionists were enjoying a field day. Yet Mexican writers agree that within this period of over half a century only two revolutions were truly deserving of the name: the independence movement initiated by Hidalgo and Morelos but completed under the aegis of the conservatives in 1821, and the uprising beginning in 1854 which within three years had produced a liberal constitution, propelled Benito Juárez into prominence,

---

[6] Guillermo Toriello, *La Batalla de Guatemala* (Mexico, D.F., 1955). The appendix referred to was compiled by Professor Vicente Sáenz.

and touched off the War of *La Reforma*. In the present century there occurred one other capital R Revolution, that beginning in 1910 and lasting despite its passage through a number of convolutions at least until the end of the Cárdenas administration in 1940. Elsewhere in this book we are told that Bolivia, up to 1952, was ravaged by 179 revolutions. Yet it could be safely argued that only the pattern of events which elevated Víctor Paz Estenssoro to the presidency in 1952 deserves the name in capitalized form. Furthermore, in any attempt to determine the country boasting the highest number of revolutions since 1865, serious attention would have to be accorded the claims of Paraguay. But the land of the Guaraní and *mate* still awaits a political turnover amounting to much more than a change in the faces and names of those controlling the country. It is probable that in no Latin American country have there been more than three revolutions since independence which have produced permanently enduring changes of fundamental importance. In some countries, there has not been one.

While relatively few far reaching changes have resulted from revolution, many important shifts in Latin American life have been unaccompanied by violence, have been conducted within the constitutional framework, and have proceeded in slow or evolutionary manner. A large mass of evidence comes instantly to mind: Mexican industrialization, an increasingly friendly attitude toward foreign capital in the last seventeen years, and still more recently a gradual abatement of the Church-state problem and a religious revival; recent urbanization in Argentina and other countries; extension of the suffrage in early twentieth century Argentina, Chile and elsewhere; the recent enfranchisement of women in Mexico and other republics, accompanied by a general drift toward feminine emancipation; evidence of concern with the common good of society rather than individual liberty in all recent constitutions; the progress of Central American unification, at least on the economic level, which may serve as a pilot project for the rest of Latin America; increasing Church attentiveness to the social question; the rise of Christian Democratic movements; mounting success of Protestant sects in Guatemala, Chile, Brazil and elsewhere; increasing secularism; anti-Yankee sentiment since World War II of an intensity severe even for Latin America, and an increasing intellectual alignment with a so-called Third Position.

These and other occurrences make safe the conclusion that gradual, peaceful, non-revolutionary trends have accounted for many, if not most of the more consequential departures from the *status quo* in Latin America. Revolution is not nearly so essential a fuel to the machinery of politics as has been imagined. Instead, it has been a mere obbligato to the recent unfolding of events, seldom adding in an essential manner to the exposition and development of the theme that has been uppermost in the Western and even the Eastern world for the last century or two: the irresistibly mounting tide of material and emotional wants of once resigned groups that previously wielded no influence in shaping the course of human destiny.

Effects of Contemporary Developments on the Revolutionary Tradition

If so much of importance has been produced without any essential reliance upon revolution, will Latin Americans be willing henceforth to discard this method of political action? What follows is an attempt not to predict the future, but simply to analyze a few of the forces in present day Latin America which may logically be expected to have some bearing upon the whole revolutionary tradition.

Population trends produce effects on the revolutionary tradition which can be differently interpreted. Latin America's rapidly growing population, which may top 500,000,000 by the end of the century, results in short range dislocating effects. This is especially true when percentage increases in per capita gross national product are equalled or exceeded by percentage increases in population, thereby frustrating lower class desires for higher living standards. Ultimately, however, large populations, increasingly concentrated in cities, may create environments in which there will be greater willingness to accept closer governmental control in the interest of the common good and mutual security. It is quite possible that upward population spirals and urbanization explain basically the homage now accorded the nineteenth century Cuban philosopher Enrique José Varona, and the common agreement that Francisco Romero is the outstanding contemporary thinker resident in Latin America. Both have based morality upon the social nature of man and stressed the need for subordination of the individual to the organistic whole of society. And politicians now reflect the same attitude as the philosophers. "The new type office seeker," as John J. Johnson describes him, ". . . speaks in terms of larger loaves of bread and shoes . . . [and] goes to great pains to place society above the individual . . . he . . . emphasizes social equality rather than political equality. . . ." [7]

Urbanization has, in short, brought about government intervention in the lives of many people to a degree previously unexperienced, partially as a means of bringing protection through social legislation to the lower classes now that their old source of security springing from direct contact with rural land has been removed. In the wake of this process, people have become increasingly attached to the government and therefore apparently farther removed from revolutionary proclivities.

But the new stabilizing tendencies could be negated if the masses, now reliant upon the government, should feel that they are receiving inadequate attention from the bureaucrats. The issue is basically economic: if government income is not sufficient to maintain an acceptable standard of social security, particularly after peoples' hopes have been aroused, then the people may in bitter frustration arise and overthrow the government.

The effectiveness of the general strike has already demonstrated that urban living has equipped the Latin American proletariat with a new and highly efficient means of revolution. The success of the general strike in ending the rule of Chile's army supported Carlos Ibáñez in 1931 and that of El Salvador's Maximiliano Hernández Martínez in 1944; the role of city working classes in effecting the return of Paz Estenssoro to Bolivia in 1952 against the wishes of the military; the ability of civilian groups to force the hand of the army and accomplish the ouster of Colombia's Carlos Rojas Pinilla in 1957 and of Venezuela's Marcos Pérez Jiménez the following year, all reveal the power for waging revolution now possessed by discontent urban underlings.

Rapid increase in urban population does not, therefore, in

[7] John J. Johnson, "Middle Groups in National Politics in Latin America," *Hispanic American Historical Review*, XXXVII, No. 3 (August, 1957), 319.

itself necessarily constitute a revolution ending force. But accompanying urbanization in Latin America, and both a cause
and effect of it, has been industrialization. It is this development
which many confidently expect to generate the forces that will
banish instability from the land.

The assumption is commonly held that industrialization,
wherever it occurs, will produce the same stability and uniformiz-
ing trends that have been its side effects in the United States.
While it undoubtedly will exercise some persuasion along these
lines in Latin America, there may emerge significant differences.
Francisco Ayala has written of the Spaniard's refusal totally to
subordinate his individuality to the demands of industrialism.
By holding out against the criterion of efficiency and insisting
upon guiding actions by aesthetic considerations or individual
whim, the Spaniard creates situations in industry which bring
smiles of derision to the lips of Yankee production experts.[8] And
yet, the Spanish system may in final analysis be a greater guarantee of liberty, even though it results in less efficiency and perhaps
less basic stability. Along the same lines, when referring to the
South in today's United States, Ronald F. Howell has recently
written: "Industrialism must adapt itself to the South, not the
South to it. The function of integrating the spiritual and the material, the beautiful and the useful, is a peculiar task of southern
education today." [9] Similarly, it is possible that Latin America
may respond to industrialism by stressing human caprices rather
than machine-like efficiency. If so, industrialism will not provide
the inflexible stability often associated with it.

Latin America's attempt to industrialize has already demonstrated certain characteristics which may not be conducive to
stability. It is difficult to avoid concluding that in economic development, Latin America has often tried to do too much at the
same time. Today, for example, the republics are trying to build
industry as well as to encourage a sick agrarian economy, indulg-
ing a penchant for economic nationalism that often discourages
sorely needed foreign capital investments, pursuing programs of
government intervention in the economic order aimed in theory

[8] Francisco Ayala, "The Place of Spanish Culture," *Interrelations of Culture*
(Paris, 1953), p. 241.
[9] See Louis D. Rubin, Jr., and James Jackson Kilpatrick, editors, *The Lasting
South: Fourteen Southerners Look at Their Home* (Chicago, 1958).

at social justice but adding unduly at times to the burdens of entrepreneurs, and permitting if not encouraging the functions of left wing labor organizations whose leaders are perfectly willing to do what is in their power to discredit capitalism. Only the wildest optimism could lead to the conclusion that industrialization as pursued in Latin America will result in prompt stability.

Even if the above factors do tend to perpetuate rather than remove turbulence, it may be that long term trends inherent in any industrial revolution will ultimately strike a conclusive blow in favor of order and efficiency. Purchasing power in the hands of the many, a requisite accompaniment of industrialization, may lead to the fostering of an extensive middle class with a new found sense of social responsibility and interest in government. The disruptions and interruptions in the enjoyment of material comforts which serious revolution entails might thus become utterly intolerable to a vast majority of the citizenry, with political stability being considered as necessary to the good life as paved streets, sanitation facilities, work saving gadgets and canned food.

But there are no certain guarantees of stability. Not even the much vaunted middle class can be so categorized. Aristotle to the contrary notwithstanding, one could muster an imposing group of thinkers, headed by Plato, united in their suspicions of that class. In all probability, little in the way of conservatism can be expected from a middle class spawned by some new phenomenon, such as industrialization surely is in Latin America. Traditional restraints and value systems mean little to members of so recently created a class; they are likely to seek solutions to the physical problems still besetting them in expedients which have no relation to past experience. Benjamin Disraeli evidenced keen awareness of the middle class threat to stability and historical continuity when he sought new recruits to the principles of conservatism among the lower classes, convinced that they, rather than middle groups, could more naturally be expected to cherish the roots of the past.

Just as the lower classes or urban proletariat attached to government through security programs will remain loyal only so long as the security programs are maintained or expanded, so the middle class, thinking ever in terms of greater economic success, will remain content only so long as opportunities to achieve that greater success are multiplied. Can the Latin American economy develop rapidly enough to supply the main course of material comfort so ardently desired by middle groups who thus far have tasted only the appetizer?

Conflicting considerations also render doubtful what the future effects of foreign intervention and ideologies may be. In some ways, externally induced ferment appears to be declining as a cause of revolutions, and since the advent of the Organization of American States, Latin American nations have interfered less than heretofore in the affairs of their sister republics. Less encouraging are certain persisting signs of a colonial mentality, particularly the willingness to blame all unpopular developments upon a foreign country, generally the United States. If Latin America still inclines to look only abroad for the sources of its ills, it may be willing also to look abroad for solutions. Whether or not Communists derive sizeable gains from their stepped up attentiveness to the area may well depend not alone on the attitudes of Latin American leaders toward social reform, but upon United States willingness to extend during the next several years large scale assistance. This indicates that the question of stability or revolution remains to this day one that Latin America can not itself answer effectively. The answer, in large part, must be determined in Washington or Moscow.

Revolution, Freedom and Reform

While it is difficult to gauge what will be the effects of new developments upon the revolutionary tradition, it is far more baffling to determine what should ideally occur in order to bring about optimum well being in Latin America. It has been noted that violent political upheavals have directly accomplished relatively little. This does not mean that revolutionary activity has been without basic value. Some revolutions appear to have caused benefits both tangible and intangible. One of the intangible advantages has been the role of revolutions as a counterpart to the frontier in the United States, that is, as a psychological safety valve for the pressures of social, political and economic discontent. Owing to the concentration of most immediately usable land in the hands of a few great lords of estate, the frontier in republican Latin America never existed for the lower classes as a place of actual or imagined solace for the ills of an unfriendly society. Instead, escape and hope have been found in the revolutionary tradition. The dream of revolution as a means of improving one's destiny may simply have been the opium of the people, just as the dream of escape to the frontier was in the United States no more than a myth and delusion for poverty stricken urban dwellers. But myths and delusions are indispensable medications for emotional trauma. Revolution may pass in Latin America, just as the frontier passed in the United States. But is there any guarantee that the new tranquilizer to which Latin Americans may turn will prove in all ways better than the old?

On grounds more tangible, it is possible to find good words to speak for revolutions. Only those most stubbornly dedicated to the preservation of the old order in every detail now deny that the 1854 and 1910 Mexican Revolutions were salutary in many of their results. Latin American courage, daring and unwillingness permanently to abide the fetters of any political structure fundamentally repressive of human aspirations have contributed to the making of other notably beneficial revolutions. Had those sharing the opinions of Diego Portales in Chile been unwilling to fight for their convictions, the country might for an unmercifully lengthy period have continued under the chaotic and impractical rule of early nineteenth century liberals. The uprising, long urged by a brilliant school of writers and actually headed by Justo José de Urquiza which unseated Juan Manuel de Rosas stands as a permanent tribute to Argentine greatness. The more recent developments which brought about Perón's ouster may also be productive of important and worth-while effects, although it is much too soon to know. Nor should the many unfortunate consequences of the earlier revolutions which facilitated the rise of Perón blind one to the fact that from the ensuing decade of dictatorship there resulted the acquisition by the working classes of a greater sense of human dignity and a more enthusiastic interest in affairs of state. In Colombia, Rafael Núñez, although committing excesses, was able through his willingness to defend his beliefs with force of arms to deliver his countrymen from a mass of ill conceived legislation which doctrinaire liberals had forcefully imposed. Uruguay was also fortunate that its great President, José Batlle y Ordóñez, did not shirk from defending his revolutionarily new ideas by military means during his first term. In Brazil, the revolution which brought Getulio Vargas to the presidency, while ushering in many changes of dubious value, did succeed in curtailing exaggerated regionalism and helped check the dominance of São Paulo's coffee growers, thereby making possible the inception of a more balanced economic program. The Salvadorean revolution of 1944 which overthrew Maximiliano Hernández Martínez and the Guatemalan uprising of the same year ending the Jorge Ubico dictatorship appear also to have inaugurated long term developments of significance and merit. It is, in short, difficult to know which rivers to dam if one wishes to stem the revolutionary current.

Before looking forward with unconditional optimism to the day when revolution will be extirpated, it is necessary to ask what the alternatives may be. If the springs of human resources which have formerly welled up in revolutionary activity are allowed to run dry, Latin America may confront gradually intensifying absolutism, with the daring and personal endeavor of an imaginative though often irresponsible elite giving way to the passivity, conformity and security mania of the majority. A new revolutionless mass culture in Latin America, combined with long traditions of personalism, authoritarianism and dictatorship, could lead to the creation of political, social and economic institutions more totalitarian than any yet conceived in the American hemisphere.

The history of Ibero-America since independence offers striking demonstration of the awesome dilemma confronting man as he attempts to reconcile the spontaneous cravings of the individual with the considered responsibilities of society. Can we not, by paraphrasing the words Salvador de Madariaga uses in *Hernán Cortés* when making his final appraisal of the great conqueror of Mexico, summarize the entire history of Latin America in its gyrations between the poles of authority and revolution? Great in its achievements, it is greater still in that its existence has been a fit symbol of the tragedy of man on earth.

CHAPTER IV

[CHARLES C. CUMBERLAND *]

Political Implications of Cultural
Heterogeneity in Latin America

INTRODUCTION

Freedom and Reform in Theory and in Fact

The student of Latin American history is struck by the wide variety of reform movements in those countries since independence, and with the emotional intensity of public statements and documents dealing with the advantages of liberty and the necessity for reform. Whether well-conceived or no, the programs of Gómez Farías of Mexico, Balmaceda of Chile, Batlle of Uruguay, Haya de la Torre of Peru, Arévalo of Guatemala, Vargas of Brazil, and a host of others, widely separated in time and space, were designed to bring about fundamental change in the social and political structures. All were plans of great importance for

* The holder of an M.A. and Ph.D. from the University of Texas, Charles C. Cumberland served as Assistant Professor of History at Rutgers University from 1948 to 1955. Since the latter year he has been an Associate Professor of History at Michigan State University. He received a Social Science Research Council grant-in-aid, 1954–1955, and a Doherty Fellowship to Mexico the following academic year. In 1958 he traveled extensively in Mexico, Peru and Guatemala for the Institute for Research on Overseas Programs. He has published articles in *The Hispanic American Historical Review, The Southwestern Historical Quarterly, The Historian, Current History, The Americas, New Leader, The World Book Encyclopedia* and in A. C. Wilgus (editor), *The Caribbean: Its Political Problems* (Gainesville, Florida, 1956). He is the author of *Mexican Revolution: Genesis under Madero* (Austin, 1952).

the futures of their respective countries, all achieved great popular support, and in each case a serious attempt was made to inaugurate the proposals; these were not the empty mouthings of soapbox orators. Similarly, a large proportion of the Latin American leaders who have achieved fame or notoriety have done so as a result of advocating—frequently to the point of rebellion—freedom and liberty. That many of those who were the most vociferous in invoking the name of freedom were rank hypocrites is patent; since the beginning of the nineteenth century the dynamic personality has been able to obtain a large following by the simple expedient of speaking of liberty and freedom in glowing terms. But many of those who have fought in the name of freedom have done so at great personal risk and great personal sacrifice, seriously concerned over the importance of the concept. More importantly, the fact that leaders have been able to obtain popular support for freedom and liberty, regardless of the intentions and ambitions of the leaders themselves, attests to the strength of the idea of freedom; in all countries the concept has been popular and has stimulated waves of intense emotion.

On the other hand, the history of these nations demonstrates clearly that freedom and reform have been much more sought than found; a sense of frustration and disappointment, even despair, pervades the historical atmosphere. But this gloom is not historical only; a rapid run-down of the countries today turns up a discouragingly small proportion of countries in which fundamental change or reform has taken place, in which the citizen even approaches that condition of political and personal liberty to which the magnitude of the struggle would seem to entitle him. To be sure, the elements of reform and liberty have been incorporated into the constitutional and legal structures of all the countries, but most of the constitutions and much of the legislation of the first generation after independence were characterized by the same elements. The simple fact is, constitutions and legal codes to the contrary, that freedom (as expressed in terms of political, economic and sometimes personal freedom) and reform (as expressed in fundamental changes in the social structure and social action) have been and remain concepts and not conditions. Perhaps the most widely recognized—and the least understood—political phenomenon of contemporary Latin

America is this wide divergence between theory and practice, between constitutional provision and constitutional observance, between law as written and law as enforced. Throughout the national period this paradox has manifested itself in every country of Latin America, being only slightly less obvious today than it was fifty years ago. In spite of the growing tendency to draw theory and practice into closer relationship, it is now virtually impossible to determine the nature of political and legal actions merely through a reading of the constitutional and legal codes.[1]

Some cursory reading and a little reflection will serve to establish a degree of correlation between freedom and reform, political stability, and the relationship of theory to fact. Those countries in which there is a wide and obvious discrepancy between theory and practice are markedly unstable politically and have been unsuccessful in their attempts to institute reforms or freedom; on the other hand, where such deviations are either insignificant or infrequent there is greater political stability, and both freedom and reform are more in evidence. Apparent exceptions to this general rule may be found, but close analysis will indicate special circumstances. In the case of Venezuela in 1948, for example, the Gallegos government certainly attempted to correlate theory and practice, and both freedom and reform were much in evidence; but the government was obviously unstable. In fact, of course, the freedom was temporary and the coincidence of theory and practice fleeting; they were experimental and transient rather than a way of life.

Stemming from the above considerations a number of questions comes to mind. The most important of these is why, in spite of the great efforts expended and the long struggle involved— and the attraction of the ideas—so few of the countries of Latin America have been able to institute fundamental reforms and to introduce effective freedom. In the literature dealing with Latin American politics and history are to be found various explanations, none of which is satisfactory. The old canard that the "Latin temperament" makes the Latin American a poor subject

[1] In the absolute sense, this statement could be made about any country in the world today, and certainly there is a wide gap between British theory and British governmental practice. But no one in English politics expects or wants all theory to be put into practice, while in Latin America the constitutions are presumably working documents.

for free and progressive institutions scarcely needs serious consideration. Much of nineteenth-century chaos was explained in terms of ignorance and inexperience, but most of the countries have now had six generations of experience; in any equal span of years after the fifteenth century the English certainly made tremendous advances in both fields. Lack of education is another over-simplified explanation; poor educational facilities are symptomatic rather than causal, and there seems to be no clear correlation in Latin America between literacy rates and free institutions. Economic underdevelopment has received its share of attention as an explanation, but it, too, is often a symptom.

To what, then, may the limping pace of Latin American political development be ascribed? The present essay[2] is a presentation of a hypothesis which at the moment, in view of a dearth of data, cannot adequately be tested but which conforms with available information and which explains political instability and lack of freedom in terms of cultural heterogeneity.

The Concept of Cultural Heterogeneity

Some clarification of terms is needed before Latin American political development is discussed within this framework. In the first place, the hypothesis does not presume to clarify all questions of political instability; it suggests, rather, an examination of one aspect of the social structure and makes no attempt to dissect all parts of the functional and dysfunctional elements within the systems. Secondly, it must be made clear that cultural heterogeneity, homogeneity, integration and political instability are relative terms, impossible of succinct, meaningful definition and difficult of clear demonstration. All social systems include areas of tension and dysfunctional aspects; all systems are therefore potentially unstable. If the areas of tension are too great to be accommodated within the functional elements, and if the sublimation of these tensions depends upon an easily removable element—military force, for example—the system may be said to be unstable even though the government continues for a generation or more. In this sense neither the long Gómez regime in Venezuela nor the longer Díaz regime in Mexico was stable; in each case

---

[2] Haiti is excluded from the present discussion since its cultural heritage is distinct from that of the Iberian heirs.

apparent stability was maintained through the person of the dictator, and in each case the inherent instability of the system was clearly demonstrated with the disappearance of the power of that dictator. Furthermore, no modern state is culturally homogeneous in the strictest sense, and every existing culture has borrowed heavily from its past and from its contemporaries. Heterogeneity as here used describes a situation in which cultural elements of diverse origin are in conflict, inasmuch as they are expressive of fundamentally different bases; therefore there will be no attempt to examine cultural elements which are different but which at the moment are not in conflict.

It may be argued, with some justification, that the United States is the heir to widely divergent cultures, in spite of which it has demonstrated remarkable stability and growth. With respect to this point, however, two things are clear. In the first place, a major internal war was necessary to eradicate one area of culture conflict; the Civil War was the result of political instability stemming from essential cultural differences. In the second place, there were essential differences between the manner in which the United States and Latin America received their cultural heritages. The massive migration of the late nineteenth and early twentieth centuries brought to the United States a wide variety of southern and eastern European cultural elements, basically different from and often in conflict with the western European cultural values upon which the United States was constructed, and consequently the immigrant movement constituted an element of instability. Under existing circumstances, however, the immigrant was forced to conform to the pattern previously set; he was a member of a powerless minority, depending upon the largesse of the community into which he moved, pushed by circumstance into accepting and adopting the mores of the dominant group. Serious local trouble, indicating that accommodation was not complete, developed in areas where the immigrant minority was large enough to combat assimilation; witness the Oriental problem in California of the 1880's or the present uncomfortable situation with respect to the Spanish-speaking population of the Southwest. But in general the immigrant, coming from countries less advanced materially and in world power politics, and having little support from the nation of his birth, abided as best he could with the dominant pattern.

Cultural heterogeneity in Latin America, on the other hand, resulted from a different type of "immigration." In every case the conflicting cultural elements came from a source which was more advanced materially or militarily, but in no case was sufficiently strong to destroy existing culture patterns. Whereas the United States was able to modify areas of conflict and to accommodate areas of tension, the nature of the cultural impact in Latin America in many cases precluded either modification or accommodation.

Lofty Expressions and Grubby Realities

The nature and the extent of differences between theory and practice in Latin America are fundamental to the present discussion, since much of the conflict is reflected in and illustrated by these divergences. These differences fall into two general categories: deviations from the spirit of the constitution and laws, or overt actions by highly placed public officials against specific provisions of those instruments. The more common practice, a few examples of which will serve for illustration, has been a negation of the philosophy inherent in the codes. Juan Vicente Gómez retained a democratic constitution and insisted upon its validity even while he acted as a tyrannical dictator for over twenty-five years. Porfirio Díaz, although not as tyrannical, followed the same practice in Mexico for thirty-five years; Getulio Vargas ostensibly governed under a democratic constitution, but the constitution was not actually official and he changed it at will; the recently departed Perón made a mockery of the democratic constitution which he amended in part but never completely abrogated. One could compile for the twenty countries an almost endless catalog of situations in which the dictator-president maintained the fiction of constitutional government through the practice of amending by fiat certain restrictive clauses, and in so doing destroyed the basic philosophy upon which the constitution had presumably been based. In these cases the president's power was such that he apparently could have abrogated completely the constitution had he so desired, but he preferred to appear to be a constitutional president.

While negations of the spirit have been more frequent than total disregard for specific provisions, the records are certainly not barren of examples of highly unconstitutional or illegal acts by presidents and other important officials. The most common breach, of course, is the widespread corruption at all levels; but corruption in itself is not necessarily an indication of a general tendency to hold all laws in contempt even though its practice hardly gives support to law enforcement. Much more serious, insofar as the development of political institutions is concerned, have been practices which strike more nearly at the very roots of institutional growth. Gómez of Venezuela, for example, removed his political enemies by assassination or sequestration, denying to his victims the most elementary freedom or protection guaranteed by law and constitution. Elections in the majority of the countries have been "fixed" despite elaborate constitutional provisions designed to assure free expression of political choice. Vargas and Perón effectively muzzled the press in spite of guarantees for free expression in both Brazil and Argentina, and Perón made wide use of a twentieth century version of the *mazorca* [3] to keep opposition activity to a minimum. The constitution of the Dominican Republic guarantees freedom of expression, freedom of assembly, freedom from arbitrary arrest, and freedom from the demands of private monopolies—but this "bill of rights" has not prevented Trujillo from breaking up public demonstrations, censoring mail and newspapers, summarily committing his opponents to prison, or establishing numerous monopolies for the financial benefit of his family and friends. According to their respective constitutions, both the Mexican and Brazilian states are sovereign and free from intervention on the part of the Federal Government, but governors have been summarily removed from office, other governors have been designated by the presidents, and state laws have been abrogated by national officials. One may argue that many of these "interventions" were justified by corruption and inefficiency at the state level; this does not, however, remove the fact that these actions have been in contravention of constitutional provisions.[4] Other outstanding examples of presidents who have ignored practically all incon-

[3] A terror group used by Juan Manuel de Rosas to maintain his power in Argentina.
[4] Both constitutions provide means for intervening in states, under special circumstances; reference here is made to interventions which do not fall within this category.

venient legal and constitutional prohibitions are Leguía of Peru, Morínigo of Paraguay, Somoza of Nicaragua, Batista and Machado of Cuba, Pérez Jiménez of Venezuela and Huerta of Mexico.

Another aspect of this general category concerns the failure of the executive to fulfill mandates written into the constitution. The majority of these charters have long, detailed and all-inclusive provisions for social welfare and educational activity; in only a few of the countries is any serious effort made to put into effect the stated policy. Oftentimes the treasury is in no condition to support the schemes outlined, leaving the president with an impossible situation. In addition to the social welfare clauses, probably the most widely ignored mandates are those concerning compulsory voting by all qualified males; in spite of heavy penalties provided for by law, almost no attempt is made to force men to vote except in rare and special circumstances.

Without going more into detail concerning political action, it may be stated that we are faced with the indisputable fact that there is a wide divergence between the lofty expressions found in the constitutions [5] and in the laws on the one hand, and the rather grubby realities of day-to-day politics on the other. The written codes are expressive of the highest ideals of a democratic and representative government; from a theoretical standpoint the greatest criticism which can be made is that many of them spell out in too great detail the functions and responsibilities of government. Far from reflecting those ideals, daily operation is indicative of autocratic authoritarianism or some other attribute scarcely in consonance with the ideal.

Much more important than authoritarianism, which is a natural outgrowth of some culture patterns, is the political instability which has so characterized the region during at least the preceding 150 years and which, in spite of gradual change in this century, is still a common phenomenon. Since 1930 Latin America has seen nearly sixty forceful changes of government as well as roughly twice that number of unsuccessful rebellions; translated into mean averages, these data show that there were seven revolu-

[5] Generally speaking, Latin American constitution makers are interested in producing theoretically impressive documents rather than instruments of government completely applicable to existing conditions. They strive for the ideal, not the practicable, in the hope that ultimately the ideal can be achieved.

tions a year, two of which brought change in government. Applying the mean in another fashion, each country had nine revolutions during that span, three of which have been successful. This is (as is likely to be the case with any mean average) a distortion insofar as the individual country is concerned; Mexico, for example, has had only one minor and unsuccessful rebellion during that span of years.

CULTURAL HETEROGENEITY AND POLITICAL INSTABILITY

The Vain Longing for Stability

Instability in Latin America cannot be said to result from any inherent love for chaos or war; warlike virtues are not those most celebrated in the Latin's prose and poetry, nor do the military organizations rate high in the prestige scales according to the rather limited data now available. The products of their literary lions from Bello to Marín, and including such figures as Rodó, Ugarte, Azuela, Alegría, Vasconcelos, Darío, and Santos Chocano, exemplify the virtues of loyalty and suffering while exploring themes concerning the nature of man and his society. Judging from the literature, the reliability of which as a measuring device is admittedly open to question, the Latin Americans long for peaceful and orderly governments. Despite these desires, Latin American leadership has been unable to create stable political institutions. A clue to this failure may be found in the region's cultural heterogeneity.

It is axiomatic that governmental structure, in order to serve properly the needs of the society and to maintain stability, must be a reflection of the mores of the civilization which it pretends to serve. The institutions by which a people are governed must be in harmony with the culture; political practices which conflict with basic attitudes or patterns will lead inevitably to struggle. From this principle it would follow that a nation which is culturally heterogeneous will have difficulty in establishing political institutions which will be in harmony with different or conflicting social patterns; the greater the heterogeneity, or the greater the number of conflicting or contradictory elements, the more pronounced will be the difficulty. An examination of Latin American history will show heterogeneity of differing intensity among the countries.

Iberian Cultural Patterns

From Spain and Portugal the Latin Americans inherited a culture pattern which in itself had elements of heterogeneity, but which for the purposes of this paper (and without doing great violence to the hypothesis) will be considered as more nearly homogeneous than heterogeneous. For an elucidation of the hypothesis, one of the most important of these cultural elements was individualism or, perhaps more accurately, *personalismo* as defined by René de Visme Williamson. *Personalismo,* far from being the proclivity to follow one man blindly, is a mode of living, of thinking, of acting; it is the determination to rely on oneself and is intimately related to the vaunted Spanish pride and sensitivity. This fundamental self-reliance is manifested in myriad ways at both the personal and institutional level in contemporary Latin America. Peon or president expects, or even insists upon, treatment first as a person and then as a functionary in his particular niche; the excessive politeness which sometimes disturbs the North American visitor is a function of this expectation. Labor organizations, which to be effective must demand continuing loyalty to a cause, have been markedly unsuccessful until very recent times, except in rare instances and for short periods. Leaders of popular revolutions have never been able to maintain their positions through popularity alone, for as soon as the immediate objectives have been achieved *personalismo* becomes dominant and each individual reverts to reliance upon himself. The most striking evidence of *personalismo* is the fate of almost every political party in Latin America; the parties splinter, and then the splinters splinter in a never-ending cycle which effectively prevents the formation of truly national parties built around a solid core of political philosophy. In Chile this process was carried to an almost ludicrous extreme during the presidency of Juan Antonio Ríos, at which time there were three well-defined factions among the Socialists, two in the Conservative group, two among the Radicals, and a large variety of other groups clamoring for national recognition.

Of equal importance, and seemingly in basic contradiction to *personalismo,* are the related elements of authoritarianism and absolutism which were integral parts of the social and political structures of the Spanish and Portuguese empires in the new world. Colonial government was authoritarian, the Church was authoritarian, the family pattern of paternal authority was essentially the same, and economic enterprise was developed along authoritarian lines. The pattern carried over into the national period and still exists, accounting in part for the prevalence of dictatorship and absolute government; in general the same authoritarian Church presently holds sway, the same pattern of authoritarian family relationships is the norm even though it is tending to change, and paternalistic authoritarianism (the *patrón* system) is an important economic pattern in spite of organized labor's attempt to institutionalize on a different base the relationship between labor and management. During the long sweep of the colonial centuries, individual *personalismo* and institutional authoritarianism made their peace, each compromising with the other to the extent that the conflict was reconciled by allowing a general field in which each was to operate.

Strong in the contemporary pattern is an attitude toward holding public office, again a heritage from Iberian culture. The Spanish and Portuguese empires belonged to the respective crowns, not to the people, and as such those vast areas were private possessions. Public offices as now conceived did not exist, and public service was service to the crown. Accordingly, colonial administrators were awarded offices as a reward for duty performed for the crown, or they purchased the offices from the crown; in either event, the office was looked upon as personal property and a source of prestige or revenue, or both; it was rarely considered primarily as a responsibility assumed in order to render service to the community. Corruption (as we define it) became commonplace despite the elaborate system devised to prevent peculation; wealth obtained from public office was considered legitimate income from the judicious use of private property, not tainted sums coming from the misuse of public trust. Such a conception breeds a tendency to disregard legal codes when specific provisions circumscribe too closely the activities of the incumbent.

The final heritage of importance for the purpose of this paper is the conquistador tradition, closely related to *personalismo*. The conquistador was a man of action and the men accompanying him were his partners in the undertaking; nothing was impossible for intrepid men, to whom would come by conquest great wealth and prestige. On gaining the victory, whether over land or Indians, the conquistador was expected to divide the booty; the men who had, to some extent, sublimated themselves to his leadership were rewarded in proportion to the service rendered. During the colonial period the booty seized and divided consisted of land, cattle, mineral wealth or Indian labor; during the national period it has consisted of public office, sinecures, and monopolies.

Considering this rather sketchy outline of Iberian heritage, it is clear that such a heritage militates against democratic representative government—but nothing in the pattern precludes the establishment of a stable government reflecting the conventions of the society. That such a possibility exists is clearly demonstrated by the fact that such government did exist; for nearly two and a half centuries the region was almost completely free from rebellion [6] or instability in spite of trying economic conditions, the weakness of the home government, and the absence of large armed forces.

Indian Cultural Patterns

But pre-Columbian Indian concepts must be taken into consideration in any discussion of cultural heritage, and the difference between the institutions of the conquerors and those of the conquered was marked. Indian religions generally depended upon the adoration of visible objects, gods in themselves or representatives of gods, and the priesthood consisted of readers of auguries rather than interpreters of dogma. Even in those areas where a concept of a supreme god was well developed, the average individual depended upon the local and personal gods for his solace and his protection; the supreme god was impersonal, far away, and unconcerned with the fortunes of the unimportant individual. Furthermore, the majority of the Indians—those out-

---

[6] That is, among the *criollos* and *peninsulares;* reference is made below to Indian rebellions.

side the realm of the high civilizations—depended upon the "medicine man" priest who was an average member of the community on most occasions and priest only upon need or demand. In these areas there was no highly developed authoritarian priesthood, even though the religion itself might make great demands upon the people. Thus the attitude toward the function of religion, the nature and importance of the priesthood, and the efficacy of religious ceremony was distinctly different among the Indians than it was among the Spaniards who came to rule them.

Nonreligious institutions also differed materially from those introduced by the Spaniards. In most cases Indian government was gerontocratic rather than autocratic, even though some of the more highly organized groups were subject to an autocratic government. The nature of government controls was quite different, and in addition the function of civil authorities was based upon different assumptions regarding the position of the individual in the society. The Inca system, for example, assumed that every member of society had a responsibility to all other members of society as well as to the Inca himself.[7] Indian and Spanish concepts of property rights materially differed, particularly with regard to land, although the Spanish "common lands" practice approximated the basic New World attitude with regard to land. The role and prestige structures varied widely among the civilizations, but only infrequently coincided with those of the conquerors. In virtually every important respect, Indian and Spanish institutions were in essential conflict.

Iberian and Indian cultures were sufficiently diverse and contradictory to cause difficulties, but the nature of colonial government enabled the Iberians to seize and retain control, even though they were unable to eliminate conflicting cultural elements. Indian rebellions were, to be sure, frequent enough to demonstrate the situation's basic instability, but it was only with the introduction of additional exotic concepts that serious trouble developed. The new invasion, in the form of ideas rather than men, came from France and England; the ideas came both in their pure form and as they were strained through Spain and the

---

[7] No clear generalization which would be valid for all Indian groups can be made because of the great diversity of conventions; in every case, however, there were material differences from the Spanish.

United States. These additional ingredients of heterogeneity are particularly clearly defined in the field of political thought and governmental practices.

Patterns of Imported Thought and Techniques

Forced by censorship to read the foreign doctrines surreptitiously if at all, the colonial tended to accept the ideas slavishly without considering his own cultural, educational, and political environment. The result was imperfect understanding, incorrect application, and in some cases confusion between the doctrine and the political system presumably based upon the doctrine. The doctrines of Rousseau, Montesquieu, Harrington and Locke were attractive to political neophytes and to victims of discrimination, even though they did not agree among themselves as to the interpretation or application of the ideas. Each class selected that portion or interpretation best suited to its own needs; to the upper register creole, for instance, equality meant equality before the law within his social class, but to the mestizo equality meant social and economic equality for all. Similarly, liberty and sovereignty meant different things to different groups, depending upon experience and social position, but the general concepts were widely accepted. But in borrowing these concepts the Latin Americans were in reality superimposing foreign ideas upon their own civilization without due regard to the effects these ideas would have upon their culture pattern.

Furthermore, the newly-independent groups fell into even greater confusion when they adopted foreign techniques of government. Here the tendency to equate national progress with form of government led to wide acceptance of techniques as developed in the United States, for it was clear to the Latin American that the northern country had made amazing progress in the short span of two generations. As a result, most nations (including tiny Chile) accepted federalism although experience and tradition cried out for a centralistic form; [8] they introduced republicanism in spite of a heritage which almost demanded a permanent chief executive; they utilized the separation of pow-

[8] Certain elements of federalism were contained in the colonial system, but colonial federalism (e.g., the captaincy-general within the vice royalty) and national federalism were distinctly different in most areas.

ers doctrine regardless of a tradition of combined executive-legislative-judicial power; and they adopted frequent elections for a bicameral legislature in a region where none had either voted or legislated. These techniques of government so blithely adopted had sprung from a different culture, with different experiences, different value systems, different religions, different role structures, different family institutions. The techniques themselves were expressive of a cultural heritage, bearing no relationship to the realities of Latin American economic or political problems. They were foreign to the Latin Americans in every sense of the word, and as written into the constitutions they were adoptions rather than adaptations. They were in basic conflict with well-established patterns of culture.

But political ideas and techniques were not the only borrowings; immediately after independence most Latin American nations were introduced to English and American business and commercial practices which, on the demand by foreigners who controlled money and materials, the Latin attempted to emulate. British and American business methods were as foreign to Latin culture as were their political institutions, but in view of the solid economic achievement in both the United States and England these institutions seemed to hold out hope to Latin America.

The Confusing Mixture of Traditions

In spite of the diverse nature of the cultural elements, the Latin Americans accepted them as a part of their heritage and as a part of the tradition within which governmental activity must be carried on; within the context of these elements all decisions must be made. But accepting as a part of the culture such contradictory ideas as democracy and autocracy, equality and social stratification, community service and individualism, liberty and paternalism,[9] public responsibility and private use of official position, creates decision-making problems of a major order. Furthermore, any theoretical concept would of necessity eliminate areas of contradiction, but such elimination would be done on paper only and would bear no relationship to reality. In any

---

[9] Leopold Zea has traced the development, in Mexico, of the struggle involved in making a compromise between abstract, absolute liberty on the one hand and governmental needs on the other.

state in which it is easy to label the concepts and practices as rather pure representations of one or another heritage, the problem of government becomes highly complicated. Presidential change in Peru may be used as an illustration of the confusion caused by lack of cultural integration, since Peru is a prime example of cultural heterogeneity, and an examination of the various traditions which may be applied will be enlightening.

Classical Spanish tradition suggests the selection of the new executive through the application of authoritarian and plutocratic principles, and social stratification supports this solution; but borrowed traditions encourage democratic election. The borrowed American system demands election through a federal system, while French ideas suggest election through a popular majority. Indian tradition calls for a gerontocratic method of selection, but North American ideas demand essentially universal participation. These are conflicting traditions, but they are all common to the Peruvian, open to him as a framework within which to make decisions, and they lead to confusion and unpredictability. But within all this structure there is no *Peruvian* tradition. Since there is no positive, common and unique set of traditions, the politician makes his decision within that framework which seems at the moment to give the greatest opportunity for the problem's successful solution. Since every problem is unique, and inasmuch as every situation has a possible solution within more than one traditional complex, the ultimate framework within which a problem is solved is impossible to predict. This condition makes consistency a virtual impossibility; since constitutional and legal provisions cannot reflect traditional values and needs, the legal structure reflects an esoteric ideal largely unrelated to the decision-making process. This in turn makes wide discrepancy between structure and practice not only logical but mandatory.

Patterns of Stability and Instability

If we examine the various Latin American countries with this in mind, the dim outline of a definite pattern emerges. Those countries which are made up largely of one ethnic group have shown a greater degree of stability during the past fifty years than have their neighbors; Costa Rica and Uruguay are the best examples. Conversely, those nations containing large elements of distinct ethnic groups have tended toward instability during the same time. Further examination of the laws and customs of each country reveals a startlingly high coincidence between instability, discrepancy between theory and practice, and the absence of a distinctive tradition.

Further evidence in support of the general hypothesis here presented may be found through a comparison between Peru and Mexico, which had roughly parallel experiences during the colonial and part of the national periods. Both were colonial centers of mining wealth, both had great Indian populations well advanced in the intellectual and material arts when the Spaniards arrived, and both were turbulent and unstable during the nineteenth century. In the early part of the twentieth century the similarity between the two countries began to disappear rapidly. Peru continued as it had in the past, but Mexico immersed itself in a political, social and economic experiment designed to create a new Mexico with a distinctly Mexican culture.[10] The experiment has met with surprising success. Contemporary Mexican plastic arts are distinctly Mexican; the legal structure and the legal attitudes are unique to Mexico even though many administrative techniques earlier borrowed have been retained; the methods used to attack economic or social problems were devised in Mexico for use in Mexico; and the various other aspects of life which determine a culture pattern differ not only from nineteenth century Mexico but from other countries as well. These changes were accomplished at enormous costs in blood, gold, and social disorganization, and certainly have not completely erased cultural differences; but as the "Mexicanization" process has solidified, the discrepancy between theory and practice has decreased and political stability has increased. Since 1930 only one minor revolutionary movement has occurred, and at the present moment there are few evidences of political instability in spite of considerable dissatisfaction. In contrast, Peru has contended with seven revolutions or other violent attempts to change government. Three of these attempts have been successful, and the government has oscillated between constitutionality and dictator-

[10] An examination of the factors which brought revolution in Mexico and those which prevented such a program in Peru is beyond the purview of this essay.

ship. Furthermore, most students familiar with the Peruvian situation (and many Peruvians) expect rebellion or revolution at any time, while those familiar with Mexico expect continued stability in that country; the 1958 presidential campaign and election in Mexico seems to justify that expectation.

The same general comparison, with somewhat the same conclusions, may be drawn between Chile, Costa Rica, Uruguay, Colombia and Brazil [11] on the one hand, and Guatemala, Paraguay, Venezuela and Bolivia on the other. Nicaragua, the Dominican Republic, El Salvador, Panama, Cuba and Honduras fall into a third class and, at the moment, present difficulties for analysis. In these countries there have been few violent changes of government during the past generation and one could argue, particularly in the cases of the Dominican Republic and of Nicaragua, that the governments are more stable than those of Colombia, Costa Rica or Brazil. But the same argument could have been presented—and indeed was—respecting Mexico during the late Díaz regime and Venezuela during the latter days of the Gómez period, and yet conditions following the disappearance of those dictators—conditions arising from the situation within the countries themselves and not brought on through outside intervention—demonstrated quite clearly that quiescence, not stability, prevailed. On the basis of internal conditions and developments in the relatively recent past, it would be safe to predict that each of these countries will see violence in the near future.[12]

Argentina is in a separate class, offering evidence that cultural integration is not sufficient to guarantee stability. With a considerable degree of cultural integration, Argentina, in the late nineteenth and early twentieth centuries, made steady progress in the direction of stability and further integration until a combination of historical accidents—Irigoyen's disastrous second

[11] In view of the long civil disturbances in Colombia and of the tenuous situation in Brazil, it may be wondered why these two countries are included in this list of "stable" countries. The line between stability and instability is thin indeed, and the author has been able to devise no adequate yardstick for making an absolute division. A like difficulty is involved in defining "integration." But both countries have demonstrated greater stability and integration over the past fifty years than have any of the countries in the subsequent lists, save Argentina.

[12] The apparent ease with which "Tacho" Somoza's sons continued his power in Nicaragua may cast some doubt on this assertion.

term, the world-wide depression, Roberto Ortiz' blindness—brought the movement to an end and paved the way for the new governmental experiment under Perón.[13] Whether the interjection of Perón's *justicialismo*, with its heavy dependence upon twentieth century European totalitarian doctrines, has introduced another element of cultural heterogeneity remains to be seen. If it has, Argentina will not only have made no progress since Irigoyen, but she will have retrograded.

Charismatic, Traditional and Legal-Rational Political Organization

One additional test, using data now available, may be applied to the hypothesis: the applicability of Weberian bureaucratic principles with the progression of charismatic, traditional, and legal-rational systems as expressive of the steps to sophisticated and efficient government. Although Weber did not conceive of his discussion of bureaucracy as constituting a theory of evolution from charismatic to legal-rational as characteristic of the development of government, implicit in his principles is the concept that the charismatic is the most primitive and the legal-rational the most sophisticated form of bureaucratic development. But form is not the only important element; substance is even more telling, and in Latin America are many examples of a legal-rational form used for the purpose of maintaining a charismatic or traditional substance. The discussion here with reference to these bureaucratic developments is concerned with the substance of government rather than form. Even though we do not have sufficient data to determine the coefficients of correlation between the various elements, general observations and a study of governmental practices indicate a close correlation between the level of bureaucratic development and cultural integration. Mexico, Costa Rica, Uruguay, and to some extent Brazil and Colombia, have a well-developed bureaucracy of the legal-rational type; Guatemala, Peru, Bolivia, Paraguay, Venezuela, El Salvador, Honduras, Cuba, Nicaragua, and the Dominican Republic have moved back and forth between the charismatic and traditional types, with some of them moving in the direction of the legal-rational. Available evidence seems to indicate, for example, that

[13] This is, of course, a vast oversimplification of a complicated situation.

Bolivia has recently gone far in that direction, but this may be temporary. Since those nations which have the legal-rational form are precisely those in which distinctive and unique national characteristics are observable, and those nations which have the charismatic or traditional form are those in which the various strains of cultural tradition are easily discernible, it follows that one is probably dependent upon the other. The degeneration of a legal-rational type into either the charismatic or the traditional type does not deny the validity of the general principle; it demonstrates merely that within the terms of the culture pattern the legal-rational is unrealistic and perforce must give way. The common characteristics of stable government (cultural integration, unity of theory and practice, and a highly developed bureaucratic form) in some countries, along with other countries in which prevail characteristics of instability (lack of cultural integration, discrepancy between theory and practice, and the more primitive bureaucratic practice) would logically lead one to inquire whether this is the result of coincidence or of correlation.

One step more may be added to the analysis. Implicit in legal-rational bureaucratic government is freedom of much greater magnitude than in either the traditional or the charismatic, and this freedom of selection in turn depends upon the acceptance of democratic processes. This, then, adds a fourth characteristic to the pattern, and those countries which have demonstrated the greatest cultural integration have ultimately made the greatest progress in the direction of democratic government. Theoretically, cultural integration does not necessarily lead to democratic or representative government; a rigidly authoritarian government may be—and historically often has been—perfectly representative of the cultural elements of the society over which it presides. Nor does cultural integration necessarily lead to a legal-rational bureaucratic form. But inasmuch as one of the major adopted cultural components has been a complex of political doctrines generally supporting democratic growth, the integration has had to include this element within the structure. The adoption or adaptation of new and non-democratic concepts in the past generation has added an element of confusion, and has been a strong influence in the rise and fall of Arbenz, Perón, and Pérez Jiménez.

CONCLUSIONS

It may be argued, using both Latin American and non-Latin American examples, that cultural integration is not a prerequisite for stable government; India, for example, represents a wide variety of distinct cultures, including languages. Close analysis, however, will show that some form of ultimate power is accepted as the supreme arbiter. This power, whether laic or clerical, is in itself a demonstration of a kind of cultural integration in which a type of compromise is reached with respect to conflicting elements of sub-cultures; the disappearance of that power for any reason immediately brings forth the situation's inherent instability.

Restated in positive form, the hypothesis consists of three parts, only a portion of which can be substantiated by available data but all of which seem to be supported by the information at hand. The first of these parts is that all the Latin American nations have been the heirs of a variety of cultural traditions, some more widely divergent than others, and that either through the passage of time or through experimentation some of the countries have managed to weld the component parts into a cohesive whole. The majority have been unable to do so. Historical evidence seems to be quite clear on the nature of the ideas and practices introduced into each country, but considerably less conclusive on the customs and beliefs of the Indians. The extent to which integration has occurred is open to question in view of the dearth of fundamental research in the field.

Secondly, the hypothesis includes the proposition that the extent of cultural integration determines the number of traditional methods applicable to the solution of a particular problem, which in turn determines the degree of discrepancy between theory and practice; and a concomitant proposition is that instability is a function of this discrepancy. Available evidence here is certainly more limited and less conclusive than the evidence supporting the first part of the hypothesis, but the apparent correlation indicates a fruitful field for further research.

And finally, cultural integration in itself is no guarantee of stable government or of democratic institutions, but without such integration any hope for either stability or democracy is unrealistic. Historical evidence demonstrates that many states with apparently unique cultures have been the victims of civil wars and other factors of instability when new ideas or new conditions, not yet traditionalized, have interceded. On the other hand, demonstration of the first two parts would lead logically to the conclusion that stability is dependent on cultural integration.

CHAPTER V

[FERDINAND A. HERMENS *]

Constitutionalism, Freedom and

Reform in Latin America

INTRODUCTION

The Ideals of Constitutional Government

The Latin American nations will continue as the valued allies of and source of strength to the United States, not only in the United Nations but in many other fields of importance in the struggle to preserve the free world, if ideals of constitutional government continue to guide their political destinies. Democratic governments may not always be as easy to deal with as are certain dictatorships. Democracies would, however, be unfaithful to the processes of freedom upon which they themselves are based if they did not attempt to extend those peaceful processes to the international sphere.

Totalitarian dictatorship, however, so alien to the Latin tradi-

* Ferdinand A. Hermens received his Ph.D. from the University of Bonn in 1930, and subsequently undertook post-doctoral research at the Faculté de Droit, Paris, and the London School of Economics and Political Science. From 1935 to 1938 he served as Assistant Professor of Economics at the Catholic University of America. Since 1938 he has been a member of the Notre Dame faculty, coming to that University as an Associate Professor and rising to the rank of Professor in 1945. He has been a visiting professor at the Universities of Muenster and Bonn, 1948, and the University of Munich, 1953. His publications in English include: *Democracy or Anarchy? A Study of Proportional Representation* (Notre Dame, 1941); *The Tyrants' War and the Peoples' Peace* (Chicago, 1944); *Europe Between Democracy and Anarchy* (Notre Dame, 1951); *The Representative Republic* (Notre Dame, 1958).

tion, has raised its head south of the Rio Grande. Neither in its rightist version, represented by Perón in Argentina, nor in its leftist variety, represented by Arbenz in Guatemala, has it been able to "go all the way"; in both countries there remained islands of freedom which had much to do with the eventual overthrow of dictatorship. What happened in these cases could, however, happen again and might, in the future, assume a more radical form. If so, there would be consequences in the field of international relations. Just as the democracies will tend to carry the process of peaceful persuasion upon which they are based into the field of foreign relations, a totalitarian dictatorship will find it natural to resort, in its foreign policy, to the processes of coercion on which its domestic political structure rests.

Much depends, then, on the possibility of establishing the principles of democratic constitutionalism firmly in Latin America. In this regard, the difficulties appear, at first sight, forbidding, and there is, understandably, an undertone of pessimism in most of the writings on the subject. Closer examination may, however, reveal that some, at least, of the tendencies characteristic of present-day Latin American society make the prospects of constitutional government a little brighter than they have been in the past, even if rigorous realism must guide the evaluation of these tendencies.

The Society and the State

Realism requires, in particular, that we act in full awareness of the nature of constitutional government. Latin writers have clarified this concept by contrasting the *personalismo* characteristic of one-man rule to *institucionalismo*. The latter prevails if, in a given framework, persons, parties and policies can change without affecting the stability of the framework itself. In this sense, the governments of the northern part of the Western Hemisphere, the United States and Canada, are institutional; both have, for generations, experienced far-reaching political changes within the same set of institutions.

If we ask why it is that what is taken for granted in these countries is so difficult to attain in the rest of the hemisphere, we must refer to the general task which the institutions of constitutional government have to perform. It is to bridge the difference between society and the state.[1] Society is, of necessity, characterized by what John Locke called "the variety of opinions and the contrariety of interests which unavoidably happen in all collections of men."[2] To this array of differences, be they based on religion, on the social structure, on political beliefs, or on other factors, the state must, if it is to serve its vital functions, oppose unity—certainly unity of action, and to some extent, also unity of thought.

This transition from the diversity of society to the unity of the state is never spontaneous. A group of specific factors must intervene, and add an element of unity which society as such lacks. We call these factors "political form," in the sense that it is their task to "form" these social forces in such a way that a state can emerge.[3]

The "matter" of all political life is constituted by society, as it exists at a particular time. There is never a lack of elements making for difference and discord within any society, and if political form is to solve the task of making *one* will prevail, it will have to be strong enough to grapple with recalcitrant forces. This means, at the same time, that while political form must, to some extent stand *above* society, it must also be deeply rooted *within* society; it must succeed in bringing stronger forces to its side than are opposing it.

Montesquieu made a substantial contribution to the analysis of these problems when he emphasized that every form of government needs certain "intermediate powers"; these are the social foundations upon which government rests. In the case of monarchy, the nobility constituted the intermediate powers: "no nobility, no monarchy; no monarchy, no nobility." Inevitably, the combined rule of monarchy and nobility began to fail as soon as the industrial revolution brought social forces of a different kind to the fore.[4] The time was to come when these forces per-

---

[1] For details, see Ferdinand A. Hermens, *The Representative Republic* (Notre Dame, 1958), in particular Chapters I and VII.

[2] John Locke, *Of Civil Government* (New York, 1924), p. 166 (Book II, Chapter VIII).

[3] For details, see Hermens, *op. cit.*, pp. 5 ff.

[4] *Ibid.*, pp. 91 ff.

mitted a truly stable equilibrium between society and government only in the forms of democracy.

Anglo-Saxon and Latin Constitutional Development

At this juncture suffice it to compare briefly the Anglo-Saxon type of constitutional development to the Latin, particularly the French. Much of the tragedy of Latin American government is due to the fact that it was to follow the latter rather than the former. The experience of Britain is, perhaps, more significant than that of the United States, where no real feudalism developed, and where the problems resulting from the transition to modern society, and to a government corresponding to it, did not arise.

The first characteristic of British constitutional history is the recognized "inevitability of gradualness." Old political forms were not toppled at once. The new forces entered the existing political structures by degrees, and replaced the powers of the old only to the extent that they themselves were ready to assume responsibility. Only after the second and third electoral reforms (1867 and 1885) did Britain become a modern "mass democracy" with a plebiscitary basis, the voters themselves determining which party was to form the government.

In the Latin countries there was no such gradual and peaceful transition. France, Spain and Portugal, and their colonial dependencies, passed through a period of absolutism, which terminated the experiment with constitutionalism made during the Middle Ages and the beginning of modern times. The institutions of absolutism could not be penetrated gradually and peacefully; their very nature excluded compromise. The representatives of the new society, in fact, found themselves excluded from political power, and from the training in political responsibility which such power entails. Their opposition became all the more violent for this fact. When the transition came, it came all at once, the new social forces assuming political power in its entirety although they were ready to exercise at best only a part of it.

Doctrinairism and negativism were an inevitable part of such developments. Edmund Burke characterized these qualities as soon as they appeared on the scene in revolutionary France. He said of the French revolutionary leaders that "the best were only

men of theory;"[5] he reproached them for both lacking and de-
spising experience. In fine, he held, these men were "speculatists,"
characterized by "a clumsy subtilty of their political meta-
physics."[6] These charges were exaggerated, and they were unfair insofar as the faults of these men were not primarily due
to their personal characteristics. The old political order had
not given them the opportunity to share in the exercise of political authority, and to learn of its requirements. Still, the doctrinaire element is, to this day, strong in France and it exists in
all other Latin nations, in particular in Latin America.

Negativism became a part of doctrinairism. Many Latin writers
have conceived the freedom for which they struggle in the terms
of what Max Weber has called "freedom *from* the state," as opposed to "freedom *within* the state." Where the absolutism of
colonial rule was to be opposed, it was understandable that there
should develop a doctrine that separated freedom from authority,
to which, in reality, it is complementary; there is no freedom
without authority just as there is no true authority without freedom.[7] The tendency to conceive freedom in these negative terms
is not only a legacy from the past. It also follows from the need
of reconquering freedom again and again from dictatorship. The
latter implies such a concentration of physical power (if not moral
authority) that authority itself becomes suspect. The pendulum is
made to swing from this extreme to the other, and it is overlooked
that, for this very reason, it will tend to move back to the other
side again.

Power, Freedom and Human Rights

Where a constitutional government is stable, it is based upon
three interrelated factors. In the first place, in the words of Alexander Hamilton, "Power must be granted, or civil society cannot

---

[5] Edmund Burke, *Reflections on the Revolution in France* (New York, 1955),
p. 46.
[6] *Ibid.*, p. 66.
[7] Yves R. Simon, *The Nature and Functions of Authority* (Milwaukee, 1940), and
The Philosophy of Democratic Government (Chicago, 1951). President López
Mateos of Mexico expressed the basic relationship clearly when he said: "Liberty
is fruitful only when it is accompanied by order. Liberty without order is anarchy,
and order without liberty is dictatorship." "Mexico Installs a New President,"
The New York Times, December 2, 1958.

exist." [8] This implies that before power can be limited, there must *be* power, for, as Clinton Rossiter has said: "Power is the price of freedom." [9]

In the second place, power must be channeled in such a way that its very structure makes freedom *possible* as well as *necessary*. Where, for example, free and competitive elections are the source of all political power, there is—if majority rule applies— reason to assume that the dependence upon an electorate which consists of a variety of groups, none of which it is safe to antagonize, constitutes, in the long run, the best guarantee for the rights of all.[10] Precisely as elements of a potential majority, these minorities have a political leverage which no constitutional provision attempting to guarantee their status can give them.

The protection of human rights is, of course, not in all respects an automatic result of even the best functioning constitutional government. There is, therefore, every reason to include specific guarantees in a written constitution. Where there is a government with adequate power, and where this power is based upon political processes in which the free decision of the electorate plays a vital part, concrete provisions may spell out the limits within which individuals and groups are to be free from the encroachments of governmental power. A strong society must, indeed, ultimately be based on strong individuals. It must be repeated, however, that written guarantees of individual rights will prove ineffective unless there is a government which is strong enough to make them respected by others and which, by its very nature, will be inclined to respect them itself. Many authors of written constitutions—not *only* in Latin America, but *in particular* in Latin America—have neglected this basic dependence of freedom on free government. By ignoring the needs of the latter they have failed to lay the ground upon which the former could have grown. Besides, in many cases extensive listings of human rights in constitutional documents have served merely declamatory purposes.

[8] Speech of Alexander Hamilton in the New York Assembly, January 19, 1787, here quoted from Lynton K. Caldwell, *The Administrative Theories of Hamilton and Jefferson* (Chicago, 1944), p. 19.

[9] Clinton Rossiter, *The American Presidency* (New York, 1956), p. 153.

[10] For details, see Hermens, *The Representative Republic*, pp. 150 ff. For the charge that government by majority threatens to become "a tyranny of the majority," consult pp. 182 ff.

Roman and Anglo-Saxon Law

The discussion of political life in terms of a one-sided ideal is not, however, the only way in which reality can be ignored. Latin America has been deeply influenced by the type of written law which owes its origin to Roman law. Whereas the Anglo-Saxon common law was always, and of necessity, close to practice, the kind of written law characteristic of the Roman tradition came to be based on legal fictions as well as on fact. Juridical fictions can, of course, have a positive function, but so far as constitutional law is concerned, this function turned out to be one of concealment. Thus, the Roman emperors never formally abolished the republic, and their laws were promulgated, as before, as the will of "The Senate and the People of Rome." The Roman jurists knew that any attempt to point out the difference between the letter of the law and its actual meaning would have brought them into conflict with "the powers that be;" it was easier to write in terms of a fictional identity between the two. The thinking of Latin American jurists has been deeply steeped in these traditions; they, too, accustomed themselves to treat the written law as if its provisions corresponded to actual political processes.[11] Juridical positivism strengthened this tendency, as it had done in other parts of the world.

We must not, however, assume that what went wrong in Latin America was in the main the result of erroneous intellectual attitudes. These attitudes exist, and they constitute a factor of their own. Yet, they arose largely because general conditions were favorable to them. Latin America finds itself in the "twilight zone of government" through which nations in other parts of the world have passed and are passing now. The foundations of the old order are gone, and those of a new order have not yet reached the degree of solidity which is the prime prerequisite of political stability.

Social Stratification and the Political Structure

Latin American society has, in the first place, never possessed the degree of basic equality characteristic of North American

---

[11] There have always been exceptions to that rule. Thus, Ramón Infiesta, in his *Derecho Constitucional* (second edition, Havana, 1954), deals as vigorously with constitutional practice as with constitutional theory.

society from the start. There have always been rigid social differences within the Latin American nations and, as a result, there was no properly functioning "circulation of the elites." There applies even now to most of them what a Cuban daily recently wrote when summarizing a book on Cuban politics:

This work, as few others, underlines the scarcity of leadership which in Cuba has always, since the very beginning of the movements for independence, characterized the struggle for power. And, above all, one can see better how the top positions in political life have been in a small group of families for more than two hundred years. The recurrence of the same names in such different situations causes the versatility of the members of these familes to stand out . . . even if their conduct was inconsistent and contradictory to the family tradition.[12]

Social rigidity need not be an element of instability. It can, during a period of transition, provide a fairly stable, if oligarchic, constitutional rule. James Bryce ascribed much of the relative political stability of Chile at the turn of the century to an oligarchy consisting primarily of large land owners.[13] The same could be said for certain periods in the constitutional history of Brazil and Argentina. Bryce felt that the *de facto* rule of the leading families was preferable to an attempt to take democratic institutions seriously at a time when the people were not ready for them. His hope, however, that "in the fullness of time" such oligarchies might pass naturally and peacefully into "a more popular form of government" was not to materialize.[14]

There might have been an exception in the case of Brazil, the one country in Latin America in which monarchy came to grow roots in the native soil. Many observers have felt that under the type of conditions which existed in nineteenth-century Latin America monarchy would have been the solution, and in Brazil matters seemed to work out well in that direction. The Braganza dynasty, driven from Portugal by Napoleon, had established its court in Brazil in 1808, and the country was proclaimed a kingdom in 1815, to become independent in 1822.

The Brazilian monarchy worked well for two generations. At

[12] Review of León Primelles, *Crónica Cubana*, two volumes, 1955 and 1958 (Havana) in *El Diario de la Marina*, April 6, 1958.
[13] James Bryce, *Modern Democracies*, Vol. I (New York, 1931), p. 206.
[14] *Ibid.*

first, the crown held substantial powers; it was the *Poder Moderador* which was to decide conflicts between government and parliament.[15] This was the theory of monarchy during the reign of Louis Philippe in France and it seemed well adapted to the needs of a period of transition.[16] In the long run, however, the monarch could fulfill the important symbolic functions which required him to stand above parties only if he did not have to take part in day-to-day political decisions. In Brazil matters seemed to proceed in the right direction when in 1847, the office of prime minister (President of the Ministry) was established; and it appeared that a democratic monarchy might eventually become a reality. The monarch continued, however, to be a power of his own,[17] and to be held responsible for important decisions. When, in 1888, Pedro's daughter, Isabella, who was regent during her father's absence in Europe, signed the decree abolishing slavery, which was followed by economic dislocations, republican sentiment (fostered also by other factors) burst forth, and the Republic was proclaimed in 1889.

Still the Brazilian monarchy might have continued to render great service to the country for the reasons which Walter Bagehot expressed in these words: "Constitutional royalty . . . acts as a *disguise*. It enables rulers to change without heedless people knowing it. The masses of Englishmen are not fit for an elective government; if they knew how near they were to it, they would be surprised, and almost tremble." [18]

English fitness for "elective government" proved greater than Bagehot expected, but Brazilians might, indeed, have "trembled" when considering the transition to open elective government. They took the plunge, however, and perhaps, monarchy was after all not in the long run suited to the requirements of Latin American society. This conclusion suggests itself even more strongly on the basis of other monarchical experiments, such as those undertaken by Iturbide and Maximilian in Mexico and the two empires in Haiti, which ended amidst ridicule.

[15] For a brief abstract of Brazil's constitutional history, see Karl Loewenstein, *Brazil Under Vargas* (New York, 1942), pp. 4 ff.

[16] When General de Gaulle tried to revive this concept with his Constitution of 1958, critics characterized this immediately as an anachronism.

[17] A. Machado Pauperio, *Presidencialismo, Parlamentarismo e Govêrno Colegial* (Rio de Janeiro, 1956), pp. 80–82.

[18] Walter Bagehot, *The English Constitution* (London, 1933), p. 48.

The Quest for Democracy in Latin America

Latin America, then, had no real choice but to plunge into attempts to make democratic government a reality. In this regard, all concepts are, of course, relative,[19] and we shall do well not to demand perfection, bearing in mind that in this country, too, the democratic process does not always work as it should —witness the existence of "boss" and "machine" rule in certain cities. Still, there is a difference between the older democracies and Latin America.

The political leadership of the Anglo-Saxon countries is not only mobile; it also has its roots everywhere. This has been the case since mass parties developed in the United States during the time of Andrew Jackson, and in England after the second and third electoral reforms. Such parties extend their organization into every city block and into every hamlet. Thus there exists a comprehensive network of leadership, beginning at the "grass root" level and extending, through stages, to the highest levels of government. These leaders, and the organizations which they run all over the country, constitute the "intermediate powers" of democracy. They represent true social and political forces, as they have absorbed into themselves most of the elements capable of active leadership. The opposition to democracy, which is never entirely absent, finds itself deprived of the type of leader without which it cannot succeed.[20]

The recognized political leadership of a country in which democracy is firmly established includes the leaders of the opposition as well as those of the majority. The "outs" do not have an official share in power, but the "ins" are always aware that it may sooner or later be their turn to be the "outs." They also know that they will hasten the advent of that calamity if they disregard any popular argument advanced by their opponents.

---

[19] "The efficiency of any process is a relative matter, and all structures are marked by imperfection. Nevertheless, in a political system where both structure and process are sufficiently effective to make government by the people a reasonable and attainable possibility, a claim may be made for the existence of democracy." John J. Kennedy, *Catholicism, Nationalism, and Democracy in Argentina* (Notre Dame, 1958), p. 110.

[20] Opposition to democracy is, in the countries in question, much stronger in the ideological field than in that of practical politics, which might be taken to prove that political ideology is largely irrelevant.

Therefore, while the latter do not have a real share in political power, they do exercise influence on the holders of power. As the existence of this relationship is recognized there develops an attitude of "live and let live" between majority and minority. The charges that there might arise a "tyranny of the majority" are contrary to the very nature of the process in which majorities are formed, which is one of peaceful persuasion, and implies that those who are members of the minority today might be members of the majority tomorrow.[21]

To list these ingredients of democratic government as they have developed in the Anglo-Saxon countries is to underline the great difference between them and the Latin American nations. It also, however, indicates, even if only in the most general way, the direction in which our neighbors to the South will have to go, and the means which they will have to apply, if they are to establish a stable constitutional government. For the forms which such government has to assume are not, in any essentials, tied to any cultural environment. There are a few basic choices to be made, and they are the same the world over, even if, for the time being, certain solutions will not work everywhere, and even if modifications are always required according to time and place. On the active side of the ledger there are, in addition, clear indications that the general condition of society in Latin America tends to evolve away from the past and to move, even if haltingly, in the same general direction as the society of the older democratic countries has moved since the industrial revolution; this movement means that political choices will become more similar.

This applies, in the first place, to illiteracy, the most characteristic symptom of politically underdeveloped countries. Illiteracy is part and parcel of a general pattern of society in which a government based upon the active consent of the governed is difficult. The illiterate, or partly literate, constitute what Italian writers have termed "the absentee masses." In Latin America some of them are separated from the rest of the nation by language barriers; in a few cases, Indians still live under their own form of tribal organization with little awareness of the government of the country within the borders of which they reside. To all of

[21] See the chapter on "The Tyranny of the Majority," in Hermens, *The Representative Republic*, pp. 182 ff.

these people there applies what Lord Bryce said: "They are citizens in name only, knowing nothing and caring nothing, except in a few cities, of what passes in the sphere of government." [22] What makes illiteracy so onerous in the countries which find themselves in the "twilight zone of government" is, of course, the fact that it is no longer easy to limit the active rights of citizenship. In the past, all major democratic countries extended the franchise slowly and gradually; if a particular extension ran ahead of the increase in literacy, conditions were such that the latter followed in short order. In recent decades, however, the demand for universal suffrage, regardless of qualifications, has been so strong that in some cases it has swept aside even the most legitimate objections.

Dictatorship in Latin America

Illiteracy, indifference of the masses, graft and corruption are a few of the abundant elements in Latin American society which make for weakness so far as suitability for constitutional government is concerned. Wherever these deficiencies came to exceed the breaking point, dictators rushed in to fill the vacuum.

In the evaluation of these dictatorships it is necessary to distinguish between the "authoritarian" dictatorship characteristic of Latin America and its totalitarian counterpart as it has developed in Russia, Italy and Germany, and, more recently, in China and the satellite countries. The authoritarian dictatorship is established by someone high in the government—at times the president himself—or in the army, rather than by a mass party rising from below. When the leader of such a mass party wins control of a country he disposes of "intermediate powers" much more ubiquitous, much more ruthless, and much more imaginative than the regular army and police upon which the typical "authoritarian" dictator must rely. The totalitarian party and its subsidiary organizations reach into every nook and cranny of the country's social life. Its members will never hesitate to act immediately, without waiting for orders, when they encounter opposition, and the organs of the regular government will, in all essentials, be at their disposal. In spite of all attempts in this direction made by Perón and Arbenz, Latin American dictators have never disposed of "intermediate powers" of this kind; large

[22] Bryce, *Modern Democracies*, p. 189.

areas of their countries' societies have always been beyond their grasp.

Nor has Latin America ever seen a successful attempt to pervert public opinion as is done in totalitarian dictatorships. By and large, the authoritarian dictator will be satisfied when the expression of views differing from his own has been made impossible; if he does not try to fill the gap with an ideology of his own the result will remain superficial. Under a truly totalitarian government, on the other hand, it is not enough that people keep critical opinions to themselves; they must be made to profess, and if possible to believe, what their leaders tell them to profess and to believe. Hitler told us that terror could, indeed, be used as a method to mold opinion; Lenin, Stalin and their successors have acted on this assumption all along. The opinion which develops under such conditions is a hothouse plant which will wilt away as soon as normal temperatures return—witness what happened after the Hungarian revolt of 1956—but it looks impressive in the meantime. Latin America has never known anything of the kind.

The comparative mildness of the authoritarian dictatorship does not mean that it fails to lead to a violation of human rights; this fate no true dictatorship can escape. Also, if the relative freedom which an "authoritarian" dictator, such as Batista in Cuba, permitted leads to armed opposition, there may be an interplay of terrorism by both the revolutionaries and the government which can hold its own with the worst in the annals of atrocities. It is, however, vital to remember that this is a situation where neither moralizing nor crusading will help. As it was expressed in an anguished article written by a Cuban journalist during the early stages of the Fidel Castro uprising: "America has had, and will have, dictatorships. Why? Because dictators are not the results of personal caprice, but a consequence of an entire situation or level of political culture in each nation." [23]

In some cases it is also well to bear in mind what Harry Stark expresses in these words:

It is my belief that the oft-observed transition of Latin American presidents into dictators comes about not from premeditated evil design, but rather from a desire not to frustrate the hopes placed in

[23] Gastón Baquero, "De Dictadores en América," *El Diario de la Marina,* February 9, 1958.

them by their peoples. The metamorphosis takes place gradually as, little by little, they grasp the futility of getting done anything constructive if it must travel through the tangled maze of bureaucratic processes, stymied at every turn by red tape and by the personal ambition and greed of politicians who, to pursue selfish ends, are sometimes not above playing upon the ignorance of the masses.[24]

Personal ambition may still have played its part in these decisions and, at times, may have been decisive. Yet, basically, the abovementioned Cuban commentator was right when he said that the old error was "to combat dictators, but not to combat the bases, the foundations and the moving forces of dictatorship." [25]

If we are to eliminate the foundations of dictatorship the accent must, indeed, lie on the positive. As Danton, the French revolutionary leader, put it: "On ne détruit que ce qu'on remplace." In this case, we want to replace dictatorship with constitutional government and the question arises whether there is anything discernible on the Latin American horizon which provides reasons for hope. Our quest will have to go in two directions. We shall first have to ask whether there is a prospect of an economic development which may lead to a more democratic society. We shall then have to ask whether the devices adopted to strengthen constitutional government have been adequate to the task.

THE BASES FOR CONSTITUTIONALISM AND DEMOCRACY IN MODERN LATIN AMERICA

Economic Development and Democracy

So far as the prospects of economic development in Latin America are concerned, there are two schools of thought. There is first an impressive number of pessimists, led by Gunnar Myrdal,[26] whose views have been endorsed by so many others that they have been referred as "the new orthodoxy" of international development.[27] They are opposed by a group whose optimism is only

[24] Harry Stark, *Modern Latin America* (Coral Gables, Florida, 1957), p. 58.
[25] Baquero "De Dictadores en America," *op. cit.*
[26] Gunnar Myrdal, *An International Economy* (New York, 1956), and *Rich Lands and Poor* (New York, 1957).
[27] P. T. Bauer and B. S. Yamey, *The Economics of Underdeveloped Countries* (London and Chicago, 1957), and two papers presented by Dr. Bauer at the conference of the Mont Pèlerin Society at Princeton University in September,

relative;[28] they hold that while the objective conditions for economic development are better than is frequently assumed, their utilization depends on mental attitudes and government policies which may be absent. They agree with the old saying that the Latin Americans are "Beggars on Golden Stools;"[29] the subcontinent as a whole—if not every country by itself—contains, in their view, enough natural resources to make a prospering economy possible.[30]

We need not discuss the theoretical arguments involved in detail. Suffice it to say that at least some Latin American countries have broken the supposed vicious circle of poverty, and that their example seems to exert a measure of influence upon others. First, of course, there is the case of Mexico, where economic development has, for some time now, managed to keep well ahead of the annual population increase of three per cent. The economic change which has occurred in that country since 1950 has been rapid, and it has come about with a minimum of foreign aid. Oscar Lewis has called it "a model for underdeveloped countries."[31] These changes have been accompanied by a new mental attitude: "It is the American concept of substituting for increasing class and civil warfare over a small economic pie, a larger ever-growing pie that makes Mexico different from most Latin American republics."[32] This philosophy permeates as yet only a part of Mexican economic policy, but the areas of the Mexican economy where action was based on these premises have been the most dynamic.

Fairly rapid economic development has also taken place in Puerto Rico, where the affiliation with the United States has

---

1958: "The New Orthodoxy of Economic Development," and "Regulated Wages in Underdeveloped Countries," mimeo.

[28] In addition to the publications by P. T. Bauer there are those of an increasing number of Latin American economists and businessmen who emphasize that wherever free enterprise is given a reasonable chance it is likely to prove itself. The most active group is centered around the "Instituto de Investigaciones Sociales y Económicas" in Mexico, which circulates leaflets and books all over Latin America.

[29] A book under this title was published by Peter Schmid (New York, 1955).

[30] For a vigorous expression of this point of view by a Latin American, see Leopoldo Aragón Escalana, Letter to the Editor of *The New York Times*, April 4, 1957.

[31] See *The New York Times*, Nov. 8, 1957, and Daniel James, "Is Mexico Going Capitalist?" *The New Leader* (July 21–8, 1958).

[32] Irving Pflaum, "Mexico 1958," *The Chicago Sun-Times*, April 20, 1958.

created an unusual situation, but where two other factors have also been present: the old fatalism has been shaken off, and Governor Muñoz Marín, whose early thought had gone in a socialistic direction, has turned to the encouragement of free enterprise.[33] In this case there is no doubt that not only has over-all production increased greatly, but that living standards have risen, and continue to rise, substantially.[34]

The case of Venezuela may be less significant because the rise of the over-all national income has, so far, affected the rural area but little. Yet, the increase of production has not been limited to the extraction of oil; there have been sizable gains in cattle breeding and sugar production, and much has been done to remove urban slums. Between 1945 and 1955 the average annual increase in industrial production has been fifteen per cent.[35] A good part of these gains was possible only because Venezuela presented better conditions for foreign capital than did other Latin American countries with comparable natural resources. The Pérez Jiménez dictatorship claimed much of the credit for this policy.[36] Its basis had, however, been laid by the administration of the then provisional President Rómulo Betancourt (1945–1948), which pioneered the historic 50:50 oil contracts. The overthrow of the dictatorship in 1958 reopened many issues of economic policy, but some observers, at least, seemed to feel that the generally favorable climate for free enterprise, both domestic and foreign, would be maintained. No harm would be done, of course, if in government spending public works of a spectacular type would have to yield to overdue improvements in the field of education and in agricultural development. Naturally, it remains to be seen whether newly-elected President Betancourt will

[33] See "Puerto Rico: Fact vs. Fiction." A Report by the Inter-American Association for Democracy and Freedom, Supplement to *The New Leader* (January 24, 1955); "Puerto Rico, The Bard of the Bootstrap," *Time* (June 23, 1958).

[34] Puerto Rico admittedly enjoys the advantage, as one economist put it to the author, of being able to "export its unemployed to the United States."

[35] Chase National Bank, *Latin American Highlights* (September, 1956), p. 6. For general economic conditions in Latin America, see the various Economic Surveys of Latin America published by the United Nations; the latest one, dealing with conditions in 1956, was published in 1957.

[36] The general claims of the Pérez Jiménez regime have been set forth in an advertisement published in *The New York Times*, July 11, 1957, under the title, "The Case for Venezuela," by the Venezuelan Consulate General in New York. For a more detailed discussion of recent Venezuelan economic history, see Tad Szulc, "Venezuela Lags in Social Effort," *The New York Times*, August 8, 1957.

be able to adhere to the moderate views which he professed before the December, 1958, elections, and whether he will be able to maintain political stability.

Whatever Venezuela will do, it seems obvious that official attitudes favorable to primary reliance on the market as the regulator of economic activities are developing in more than one country. Presidents Mario Echandi Jiménez of Costa Rica, Miguel Ydígoras Fuentes in Guatemala, and Jorge Alessandri in Chile are well known advocates of a "liberal" economic policy. The Guatemalan Minister of Foregn Affairs declared, in a speech delivered before the General Assembly of the United Nations on September 26, 1958: ". . . in 1958 we can place ourselves among the countries showing satisfactory monetary balance, where a definite tendency of economic activity towards progress exists and where there prevails a state of consolidation, each time greater, of mutual respect and understanding between the forces of labor and enterprise." [37] While such declarations may express as much an aspiration as a reality, they do indicate a new trend in official policy. Even President Arturo Frondizi of Argentina has been trying to feel his way toward a more liberal economic policy, and the victory of the National Party (*Blancos*) in the December, 1958, elections in Uruguay points to a shift in the same direction.

These economic policies will favor the trend to a society more favorable to constitutional government in the first place simply because to the extent that they succeed in providing for a gradual improvement of living standards they eliminate a part of the social friction which tends to express itself in political unrest. We must not forget that most of the recent dictatorships in Latin America owe their success either to the world economic crisis, or to post-war economic dislocations. The danger of such dislocations has not passed. There remains substantial unemployment and underemployment, but in this regard there has also been progress. New enterprises, native as well as foreign, have provided for employment with wages several times higher than used to be paid in the agricultural regions from which many of these workers came. "Full employment" remains, of course, a very distant goal for most of Latin America.

Lastly, where economic improvement has been noticeable it

[37] Mimeographed press release, p. 6.

has been accompanied not only by a general increase in literacy but by the development of the type of literacy which matters because it becomes an essential element of the people's daily living. Reliable statistics are difficult to obtain so far as the general advance of literacy is concerned, but figures for high school enrollment are more readily available and perhaps also more significant. Roy R. Rubottom, Assistant Secretary of State for Inter-American Affairs, recently reported:

In Chile, matriculations in the secondary school level increased 104% between 1940 and 1953, while the population increase registered 22%. In the ten-year period of 1940 to 1950, Brazil had a 135% increase in secondary school matriculations, and a 26% increase in population. Panama, between 1948 and 1953, recorded a 53% increase in secondary school attendance, against a population increase of 14%. Mexico, between 1940 and 1954, increased secondary school matriculations by 266%, while its population total went up 46%.[38]

What these figures mean is that in the countries in question the supply of leadership is increasing rapidly, and the "intermediate powers" needed for a functioning democracy are being strengthened.

The Catholic Church and Democracy

There has been a considerable change also so far as another potent force for civic betterment is concerned. The Catholic Church has, during the past decade, become increasingly aware of the fact that the apparent or real alliance with what may be called the "unthinking Right," and, at times also with dictatorship, was unnatural. There have been individual members of both the clergy and the laity who were prominent in the struggle for independence and in the fight for internal freedom, but they have more often than not had to fight in isolation, and have lacked official encouragement. In more recent years they have become better organized. The gain in strength which the Christian Democratic parties have made in several countries has provided a focus for the Catholics working for democratic govern-

---

[38] Speech of Roy R. Rubottom delivered before the Pan American Society of the United States, November 14, 1957. State Department press release, Number 626, issued November 13, p. 9.

ment, and improved the position of those who preferred to work within the framework of other parties. By now many active Catholics, including not a few members of the hierarchy, have become aware that dictatorship involves never-ending conflict with the moral law. Where jailings and tortures become an everyday experience the guardians of morality cannot be indifferent. Direct conflicts with dictatorships have arisen from attempts, usually made by younger priests and by members of the laity, to organize Catholic social action as demanded in the papal encyclicals. The encyclical, *Quadragesimo Anno,* so often misunderstood, insisted that "Men have complete freedom to choose a form [of occupational endeavor] which they prefer provided that they satisfy the demands for justice and for the common good." When the encyclical appeared the Italian Fascists took it as a challenge to their claim for a totalitarian monopoly of organization. The result was the conflict which arose in 1931 and led to an even more explicit rejection of totalitarian pretensions in the encyclical *Non Abbiamo Bisogno.*

The implications of this conflict were not fully recognized by Latin American Catholics until recently. Events brought their significance home, however, when, in 1954 and 1955, attempts made by both the Argentine clergy and laity to activate work on behalf of social justice led to open conflicts with Perón,[39] in the course of which one of the spokesmen for the dictatorship called the Church "a factor of political anarchy." [40] Subsequently, the hierarchy took a stand against dictatorship in Colombia and Venezuela. While the attempt made by the Cuban Bishops in 1958 to arrange for a peaceful transition to a constitutional government was not successful—largely because Fidel Castro rejected any compromise—the fact that it was made is significant in a country where the Church had previously been regarded as so weak that it was not expected to raise its voice at all.

[39] What had priority? According to my information friction started with the organizing efforts of young priests and the laity along the lines mentioned. Subsequently, Perón moved against the Church by way of retaliation. "The Church" is, of course, not always the same thing. It was privilege minded in the past and most of the members of the hierarchy may remain so, but the younger priests are something else again. For material relating to this topic see A. P. Whitaker, *Argentine Upheaval* (New York, 1956); Fritz L. Hoffman, "Perón and After," *Hispanic American Historical Review* (November, 1956), pp. 510–528.

[40] "La Iglesia: Factor de Anarquía Política," *Ideas y Hechos* (June–July, 1955).

Prospects for Constitutional Government

There is, then, something to be said for the assumption that
there may, after all, now be something new under the Latin
American sun as far as the prospects of democracy are concerned.
As a matter of fact, the electoral process seems to have worked
better recently than it has done for some time. The year 1958
witnessed elections in Costa Rica, Guatemala, Argentina, Chile
and Uruguay in which the opposition won, and the government
allowed it to take over peacefully. Colombia, with its pact providing for bipartisan government for sixteen years is a case of its
own; it is not easy to visualize such an arrangement working for
so long. Yet, the pact did provide a chance to bridge the partisan
differences which are said to have led to the killing of more than
100,000 people during the past ten years. In Puerto Rico honest
elections have come to be taken as much for granted as honest and
efficient administration. The achievements of Governor Muñoz
Marín in the political field may be based as much on exceptional
conditions as those in the economic field. Still, what has been
done in both respects by Latins and for Latins has not failed to
attract the attention—and at times the envy—of others.

Parliamentary and Presidential Systems

Constitutional government can, however, suffer shipwreck not
only because the social conditions are lacking which it presupposes but also because, in the words of Alexander Hamilton,
"improper channels of government" are chosen.[41] As we have
seen, the transition from the multiplicity of society to the unity
of action needed by the state is not automatic; specific factors have
to intervene in order to bring it about. If the wrong choice is
made, if, in other words, the goal of establishing unity of action
is sought with the help of institutions which are not suited to this
purpose, democracy may perish even in a country where all other
conditions for its success are granted.

So far as constitutional details are concerned, all Latin American nations, with the exception of Uruguay, now have a presidential system. Thus, as in the United States, the offices of head

[41] Letter of Alexander Hamilton to Gouverneur Morris, 1777, here quoted from
Lynton K. Caldwell, *The Administrative Theories of Hamilton and Jefferson*, p. 20.

of the state and of the head of the government are united in one person. The president is elected by popular vote and the members of his cabinet are appointed and dismissed by him. This arrangement has not infrequently led to what has often been called "democratic caesarism," and some presidents have been "exercising supreme power in glorious irresponsibility." [42]

Many Latin observers are aware of this situation, and have looked to parliamentary government as it works so successfully in England and, on this side of the Atlantic, in Canada, as a hope for a less personal type of rule. Under the parliamentary system the existence of a separate head of state—the Queen in England, and the Governor General as her representative in Canada—has the result that not all attention can be concentrated on the · president. Furthermore, a British or Canadian prime minister has to share his executive functions with a cabinet consisting of leading members of his party, each of whom is a political power on his own. The cabinet has to resign if a vote of censure is adopted or if parliament fails to approve an essential part of the government's policies.

Where a parliamentary system works, it does, indeed, provide a less personal type of government than the presidential system. Where it does not work it may, however, become the "hair-trigger government" as described by Charles A. Beard,[43] with legislatures forever overthrowing the cabinet, as happened in the France of the Third and Fourth Republics. Such results can be avoided only if there exists a coherent party system with a firm popular foundation, and if the government has the right of dissolution. The first of these conditions is, for the time being, unattainable in Latin America. There have been, of course, cases in which the parliamentary system did give reasonable satisfaction, as during part of the Imperial period of Brazil and in the Chile of the turn of the century. But then it was based on the rule of an oligarchy, which developed forms of cohesion of its own, just as the British aristocracy had done during the time when it controlled parliamentary government. In our day there is no longer an

[42] William S. Stokes, *The Politics of Latin America*, Chapter XIX (to be published in 1959), here quoted from the manuscript made available to the author by Professor Stokes. A. Machado Pauperio, *Presidencialismo, Parlamentarismo e Govẽrno Colegial*, p. 33 ff. expresses himself with similar force.
[43] Charles Beard, *The Republic* (New York, 1943), p. 248.

oligarchy stable enough to rule a country, and both Brazil and Chile have abandoned parliamentary government. Significantly, Chile did so on account of the serious drawbacks to which this system led and which caused President Arturo Alessandri to have it abolished in 1925.

We must conclude that under Latin American conditions a presidential system, with the president in all countries save Uruguay being elected by popular vote, is, for the time being, the only solution.[44] The elements of disintegration, so prevalent in the countries of the subcontinent ever since they won their independence, persist to this day. Apparently, the "strong man" in the president's chair is needed to pull the many divergent forces together. To state the problem in these terms implies, of course, that Latin America still needs a certain degree of *personalismo;* it also implies that, although constitutions usually give the president ample powers he may, when confronted with a recalcitrant legislature, try to impose his will by means not easily compatible with the spirit, and sometimes the letter, of the constitution. This is one of the reasons why Latin America would, while rejecting the parliamentary system for the present, do well to hold the doors open for its future development. Where the parliamentary system works, it does eliminate the friction between the legislature and the executive which may either cause harmful deadlocks, or lead one part of the government—usually the executive—to ride rough-shod over the other.

If the presidential system appears, for the time being, as the only one capable of easing Latin America into the paths of true constitutionalism it follows that no purpose is served by limiting the president's legal powers unduly. A "strong" president will do illegally what he cannot do legally, and a weak one may permit the country to slide into that condition of near-paralysis which has so often been the prelude to dictatorship. The frequent abuse of executive power has none the less made some Latin American leaders incline to look for constitutional safeguards by narrowly

---

[44] The exception, Uruguay, is dealt with in Professor Fitzgibbons' contribution to this volume. For details on the Latin American executive as a whole, see Joseph Francis Menez, *A Constitutional and Political Comparison of the Executive Office in Latin America and the United States*, unpublished Ph.D. thesis (Notre Dame, 1953); Leo Benjamin Lott, *Venezuelan Federalism: A Case Study in Frustration*, unpublished Ph.D. thesis (University of Wisconsin, 1954), and Leo B. Lott, "Executive Power in Venezuela," *The American Political Science Review* (June, 1956).

circumscribing the powers of the president. Thus the plans of provisional President Aramburu for a reform of the Argentine Constitution were described as follows: "He has declared that the reformed charter will be 'the tomb of tyrants' inasmuch as it will be designed to prevent any future president from assuming dictatorial powers." [45]

The accent of the proposed reforms lay, therefore, on the negative: since executive power was to be feared, it had to be surrounded by so many fetters that it could not possibly go too far. It was overlooked that it is equally dangerous when the executive can hardly move at all, and when, in particular, it cannot move effectively against the opponents of constitutional rule.[46]

Proportional Representation and Constitutional Government

Actually, General Aramburu's reform plan came to naught because he anticipated what he considered one of its essential ingredients: he decreed that the elections to the Constituent Assembly be held under proportional representation (P.R.), the *pièce de résistance* of those who conceive democracy in negative terms. The results of the elections, held on July 28, 1957, were that there were no less than sixteen parties represented in an Assembly of 205 members.[47] Theoretically, a clear majority of 118 favored the reform of the Constitution. The Assembly had barely met, however, before it became clear that there was no agreement as to the type of reform to be adopted. The Peoples' Radicals, the strongest of the pro-reform groups, attempted to follow the time-honored Latin American custom of writing their party platform into the new Constitution, demanding, for example, a government monopoly of education, agrarian reform, and state monopolies in the field of public utilities—matters which, what-

[45] Edward R. Morrow, "Argentines Vote on Charter Today," *The New York Times*, July 28, 1957.

[46] The general philosophy behind the reform plans of the provisional government have been stated well by Carlos Luzzetti in his article: "La Dictadura Presidencial y la Reforma Constitucional," *Civis*, Vol. II, No. 5 (March, 1956). On the other hand, Argentina has never lacked men who realized that a feeble executive was no guarantee of democratic stability. See, for example, Ricardo Arribillaga, "El Poder Ejecutivo y sus Ministros," *Colegio de Abogados de Rosario, Curso de Divulgación de la Constitución Nacional* (Rosario, 1942), pp. 250 ff.

[47] Edward R. Morrow, "Argentine Vote Led by Radicals," *The New York Times*, July 31, 1957.

ever their merits, belonged to the field of ordinary legislation. The Centrist deputies disagreed strongly with these demands, and left the Assembly, as other groups had done before. The existence of a complete deadlock was, in fact, clear after the first two sessions of the Assembly. President Aramburu then remarked that the country was in a state of "paralysis." [48] The word "paralysis" recurs, of course, again and again in the record of parliaments elected by P.R.; one of the most remarkable illustrations of this fact occurred in pre-Fascist Italy.[49]

As in post-war Italy there were serious problems in post-Perón Argentina; the dictatorship had left a legacy of hate and disruption in its wake. To master the tasks resulting from this fact was bound to be difficult under any type of constitution and under any kind of electoral system. Yet, an assembly elected with majority voting had at least a chance to do its job, whereas the one which came to be elected under P.R. fell apart almost as soon as it met.

Since the Constituent Assembly had failed to pass a new election law, the presidential as well as congressional elections of February 23, 1958, were held under the old system, embodied in the Sáenz-Peña law of 1912.[50] It provided for the "incomplete list" system for both the election of the presidential electors and of the deputies in each of the twenty-two provinces and the city of Buenos Aires. In general, the voter was allowed to ballot for two-thirds of the seats to be filled, although the proportion differed somewhat from province to province. (Thus, where only two seats were to be filled the voters could vote for two; where seven were to be elected he would vote for five, etc.)

Under this system the 1958 presidential elections became practically a choice between Dr. Arturo Frondizi, the candidate of the Intransigent Radicals, and his former running mate Dr. Ricardo Balbín, the leader of the People's Radicals. Frondizi secured a margin of well above a million and a half votes over Balbín. This was due to Peronist support, a fact which was to plague the new

---

[48] "Argentine Leader Spurs the Assembly," *The New York Times*, September 2, 1957.

[49] F. A. Hermens, *Democracy or Anarchy?* (Notre Dame, 1941), pp. 159 ff.

[50] Law No. 8871 of February 13, 1912, modified by laws No. 9147 and 10269. For text see *Recapitulación de leyes usuales de la república de Argentina* (Buenos Aires, 1922).

President after he assumed office. Still, at least, these elections did produce a result.

The same happened in the parliamentary elections: the Intransigent Radicals won a plurality in every province, followed, in each case, by the People's Radicals. This meant—with the exception of two seats going to the Liberal Party of the province of Corrientes—that only two parties obtained seats in the Chamber of Deputies. In the Senate, which was elected indirectly, the supporters of Frondizi took all the seats.

This result was open to serious criticism. A majority system in single member constituencies would have offered a reasonable chance for a coherent majority, and it would have resulted in more seats for the opposition. As it was, with the strongest party holding two thirds of the seats in the Chamber and all of the seats in the Senate, the opposition party inevitably felt disheartened; so bulky a majority, moreover, is apt to result in dissension within the ranks of the victors.

One of the reasons why the Sáenz-Peña law had been adopted was the wish to encourage something as close to a two-party system as conditions in Argentina would permit. The question is whether the means adopted are not a little radical. Elections in single-member districts have led to clear-cut two party systems in England and in the United States,[51] not to mention Canada and other commonwealth countries. In Argentina, it was assumed there would be too many variations from constituency to constituency to make this possible. Also, Latin individualism was believed to be so strong that in single member districts, local issues and personalities would overshadow national issues.

It is, however, always a question whether artificial means should be adopted to create a two party system. To the extent that the popular party organization makes progress in Latin countries it will, even in single-member districts, provide for more coordination on the national level and, therefore, enhance the prospects of either a two party system, or of an approximation to it: a situation in which two major coalitions of parties emerge and one of

[51] The term "two-party system" does, of course, not mean that only two parties are in the field. There may be a number of them, and minor parties may even secure seats in Parliament or Congress. What matters is that, ordinarily, one party secures an over-all majority, with the result that governments are "one party majority governments." See Hermens, *Democracy or Anarchy?*, pp. 99 ff.

them secures an over-all majority. There is all the difference in the world between coalitions of this type and those formed under P.R. Under majority voting parties must form their coalitions before the voting takes place; their alliance will, therefore, be confirmed and strengthened by the voters themselves. Futhermore, partners to such an alliance must agree on men as well as measures, as in each constituency all of them can support only one candidate even if, where there is a second ballot, they may combat one another in the first. Lastly, under such elections truly extremist parties which are unable to conclude alliances with others will be under a severe handicap.

As of now, P.R. is, in one form or another, used in most Latin American countries. Its results are always mitigated by a number of factors, in particular the presidential elections which have, of necessity, to be held under the majority system. Frequently several parties combine to present a common presidential candidate, and this process carries some of the integrating effects of majority voting over into the parliamentary elections. Besides, the strong position which the president usually holds enables him to offset some of the divisions existing in his country's parliamentary bodies, even if a badly split legislature increases the temptation for the president to assert himself by unconstitutional means.

There have, however, been cases in which the president was not able to offset the effects of P.R. in the legislature. Chile provides the best illustration. Article 25 of its 1925 Constitution prescribes P.R. both for the elections of the Chamber and of the Senate. The technicalities of these elections make for a number of disconcerting and confusing possibilities,[52] which cannot be discussed here. Suffice it to refer to the over-all results. In the congressional elections of March 3, 1957, seventeen recognized parties and three illegal ones competed for all of the 147 seats in the Chamber of Deputies and for twenty out of a total of forty-five Senate seats. According to the *Political Handbook of the World,* the composition of the two bodies after election was:

[52] For the details see K. H. Silvert, "Elections, Parties and the Law," *American Universities Field Staff Letter* (Santiago de Chile, March 10, 1947). Some of the technical aspects of the law as dealt with by Silvert have since been changed: Law No. 24079 (*Diario Oficial,* June 26, 1949) has been corrected by law No. 24085 (*Diario Oficial,* July 3, 1958).

UPPER CHAMBER		LOWER CHAMBER	
Parties	*Seats*	*Parties*	*Seats*
Liberal	9	Radical	36
Radical	9	Liberal	29
Socialist	8	United Conservative	22
Agrarian Laborites		Christian Democratic	14
(dissidents)	4	Socialist	11
United Conservative	6	Agrarian Laborite	10
National	4	National	6
Christian Democratic	1	Democratic	5
Independents	2	Agrarian Laborite	
Democratic	1	(dissidents)	3
		Others	9
Republican Movement	1	Vacancies	2
Total	45		147

[The Communists were legally banned in 1957 but elected certain candidates on other tickets. The ban on them was lifted in 1958 and, in the future, they are expected to elect senators as well as deputies.]

It was quite a problem to govern with the help of a parliamentary majority under such conditions. Chile had a presidential system, but President Ibáñez experienced great difficulty in securing the passage of those measures which needed parliamentary approval; they included, of course, all laws and the budget. During this time, Chile suffered from rampant inflation. This has happened in other Latin American countries, and there would have been an inflationary tendency even with clear-cut congressional majorities. Still, the type of dispersion made possible by P.R. did make a difference.

In the case of Chile as well as that of other Latin American countries the question arises whether a multiple party system does not make the adoption of P.R. "natural," much as the latter tends to aggravate the former. It is, of course, easier to get P.R. adopted when a country's political structure is already divided, but then, this outcome is not necessary. In these cases ideology, such as the presumed "justice" of P.R. and its anticipated—but not often realized—results, plays its part.[53] By the time the true effects of this system come to be realized it may be impossible to abolish

[53] For a criticism of these claims see Hermens, *Democracy or Anarchy?*, pp. 78-85.

it by regular constitutional processes; the vested interests in the respective parliamentary bodies may then be strong enough to prevent such action.

A country's political divisions do not, therefore, predetermine the choice of the electoral system. The extent of disunion makes a difference in regard to what parties will do, in particular if they act on what they assume to be their own interests, and neglect the over-riding interests of the country as a whole. The latter may turn out to be identical with the interests of at least the moderate parties, as long as these are viewed "in the long run" rather than "in the short run." Therefore, when decisions in favor of P.R. were made, a misinterpretation of its effects has often played a vital part.

While political splintering never went as far in Brazil as in Chile, the type of multiple party system which rose under P.R. has added to the burdens of government. Thus President Juscelino Kubitschek (elected, incidentally, in 1955 with thirty-four per cent of the popular vote) lacked neither ability nor courage. Yet when, in the fall of 1958, he submitted to the Congress legislation needed to put a plan of economic stabilization into effect which Minister of Finance Lucas Lopes had prepared, *The New York Times* reported as follows on the prospects of these measures:

Although most political and public opinion seems to favor the Lopes plan in principle, different political groups have started maneuvering to extract concessions from the Administration in exchange for their votes on the stabilization measures.
Thus the Oppositionist National Democratic Union has made it clear that it will oppose the stabilization plan unless Dr. Kubitschek agrees —which he will not—to abandon or delay the idea of moving Brazil's capital to the new city of Brazilia.[54]

This type of political horse-trading is typical of that system of parties not related to one another by campaign alliances which, as a rule, is a result of P.R.[55] Opposition to that system has not been

[54] "Economic Policies Stir Rio Opposition," *The New York Times*, November 2, 1958.

[55] Horse trading occurred in spite of the fact that at that time the two parties which had supported the candidacies of President Kubitschek and Vice-President Goulart (Social Democrats and Labor) held a majority in both the Senate and the Chamber of Deputies. The majority was lost in the congressional elections of 1958, a fact which greatly contributed to the woes of the President.

lacking. Thus, in 1954 Herbert Levy, a Deputy belonging to the National Democratic Union, declared: "If we keep the electoral law as it stands, we will compromise the whole regime." [56]

Like all other devices of constitutional government, systems of voting will become more significant in Latin America as the democratic process takes root. Where elections become more honest, majorities can no longer be fabricated, and a president will not be able to prevail over a balky legislature with the—comparative! —ease with which this has been done in the past. Nor must it be overlooked that the "matter" of Latin American society is particularly vulnerable to the effects of P.R. The passionate character of the people, and the tendencies to doctrinaire politics on the part of the "elite," make for disintegration, and P.R. gives more scope to both.

Christian Democratic parties raise one of the most serious questions concerning P.R. Their rise is one of the reasons for relative optimism in regard to the future of Latin American democracy. In the words of Professor John J. Johnson:

The Church and Catholic lay organizations in league with the middle sector political leadership might inject into politics a moral force for the most part lacking at present. They might also be highly effective in discouraging workers from deserting to the extreme Left Wing organizations, especially to the Communists, for many workers have a deep and abiding loyalty to the Roman Catholic Church.[57]

These effects of Christian Democratic parties can, however, be nullified if they insist on the use of P.R., as practically all of them are doing in Latin America. They feel that, as a minority, they cannot secure an adequate number of seats under majority voting. Furthermore, they are reluctant to form campaign alliances with parties differing from them in matters which they consider fundamental. Yet they can hardly accomplish much by securing a minority—and at times a small minority—of the seats in a legislature. The compromising with others which has been rejected in the campaign will then have to take place in parliament, and it will be rendered difficult not only by political splintering but also by

---

[56] Sam Pope Brewer, "Electoral Reform Urged in Brazil as Vote Returns Continue to Lag," *The New York Times,* October 18, 1954.

[57] John Johnson, *Political Change in Latin America: The Emergence of the Middle Sectors* (Palo Alto, California, 1958), p. 192.

the fact that radical anti-religious parties including the Communists will secure seats as a result of P.R.[58]

The advantages enjoyed by Communist groups within the Latin American political structure are summarized in a remarkable article written recently by Michael Scully. The evils of which he complains are only in part attributable to P.R., but it requires little effort to see that this part is real. In Mr. Scully's words:

Some of them [the Latin American countries] have 10–15 parties and sub-parties. This leads to minority presidents who must win the support of other parties by favors that include the gross overloading of the public payrolls with henchmen. In Congress it means incessant debate, delay, amendment and weak compromise legislation. This often leads to tolerance of a legal or thinly disguised Communist party whose small vote and aggressive tactics can give a non-Communist coalition the margin it needs for victory. A major objective of Communism at the present is to promote such fragmentary parties and finally paralyze the democratic process.[59]

The effects of a multi-party system are serious. If there is ever to be a constructive attempt in the countries concerned to secure a broader political alignment there has to be the type of incentive that majority voting provides. This means that agreement with others is the price of electoral success; that price will be paid by many who turn a deaf ear to any appeal to patriotism.

[58] Communists will, of course, try to succeed under any electoral system; they will infiltrate other parties if they cannot build up their own sufficiently. Yet, it is interesting to note that P.R. is being advocated by every Communist party in the world. Palmiro Togliatti, the Italian Communist leader, provided the most cogent justification for this stand in an article entitled "On the Possibility of Using the Parliamentary Path for the Transition to Socialism," published in the Moscow *Pravda* of March 7, 1956. He stated that under a majority system the Communist "representatives splinter into small groups in parliament and sometimes disappear altogether."

The French elections of November, 1958, seemed to confirm this prediction. The Communists, who (together with the "Progressists") had won 150 seats under P.R. in 1956, lost votes as well as seats in 1958, electing only ten deputies at a time when P.R. would have still given them eighty-eight. This result was followed by vigorous denunciations of majority voting on the part of Russia's leading papers as well as the official news agency, Tass, and the Moscow radio. For details see Michel Tatu, "Moscou: Le recul des communistes français est compensé par les succès obtenus dans d'autres pays," *Le Monde*, December 3, 1958. According to this report, the Communists expect to make up for their French losses by gains in underdeveloped areas, including Latin America.

[59] Michael Scully, "What's Behind Our Troubles with Latin America?" *The Reader's Digest* (August, 1958), pp. 65–66.

Presidential Elections

A few words might also be said about the rules governing presidential elections in Latin America. Given the multiplication of parties it happens not infrequently that a candidate who secures the largest number of votes fails to obtain an absolute majority. If this occurs in the United States the democratic process will not be affected. Thus in 1912 the Republicans split, causing Woodrow Wilson to win with about forty per cent of the votes. The Republicans accepted their defeat as "part of the game." On the other hand, Wilson was aware of the fact that he had to do his best to win Republican voters to his side; failing to do so he had little chance of being reelected in 1916. The fact that in 1916 he did outscore a reunited Republican Party goes to show that his administration, the record of which this vote approved, had been based on majority support all along.

In Latin America the situation is different. Where, as in Colombia, something resembling a two party system exists, a candidate who owes his success to a split among his opponents will find his authority severely limited. Thus, when in 1946 a split in the ranks of the Liberals brought about the election of a Conservative (for the first time in twenty years), Colombian politics, which had been restive for some time, entered into that period of turbulence which was to culminate in an undeclared civil war between the major parties, and the establishment of the Laureano Gómez and Rojas Pinilla dictatorships.

In countries with a multiple party system, elections by mere pluralities are a more frequent occurrence. In 1958 they took place in Costa Rica, Chile and Guatemala. The anticipation of such results has caused the adoption of provisions intended to limit the chances of electing a president whose popular support rests on too small a basis; the final decision is made by the Congress. Costa Rica has, however, the sensible rule that if a candidate secures at least forty per cent of the votes he is automatically elected. This simple provision reduces the range of uncertainty and of political maneuvering. Thus in 1958 Mario Echandi polled 103,000 votes as against 97,000 for Francisco Orlich, the candidate of outgoing President José Figueres, and 23,000 for Jorge Rossi, a member of Figueres' party who had split with his chief. Echandi's plurality was small, but he had secured more than forty per cent and there was little doubt that the result was genuine since, at the request of President Figueres, foreign observers selected with the assistance of the United Nations had supervised the vote—the first case of international supervision of elections in Latin America. Figueres could not but accept the result. He promised to act as the leader of a "loyal opposition," [60] a role made easier for him by the fact that he expected to control the majority of the new legislature.[61]

In the case of Chile matters also proceeded relatively smoothly. In 1958 Jorge Alessandri obtained 386,192 votes, the left-wing candidate Salvador Allende 354,300, the Christian Democrat Eduardo Frei 254,323 votes, and two other candidates 189,182 and 41,224 each.[62] Alessandri's victory over Allende was won by a small margin. Had the latter, who was supported by the extreme Left, been the winner, serious consequences might have resulted. In this case decision by a mere plurality—the Chilean Congress customarily declares the candidate with the highest vote elected—would not have been accepted easily.

More serious difficulties were bound to arise in Guatemala where the electoral process was subjected to certain strains, both during the Communist infiltrated administrations of Presidents Arévalo and Arbenz, and during the period following the revolt of Colonel Castillo Armas in 1954.

The election of Colonel Castillo Armas in 1954 was held under conditions which do not make it possible to speak of a free vote, although it seems likely that, at that time, Castillo would have won even in free elections. When Castillo was assassinated in 1957 his supporters split; General Miguel Ydígoras Fuentes entered the field and claimed to have defeated the government's candidate, who had been credited with the most votes. There followed street demonstrations during which Ydígoras accepted left-wing support, and the Congress invalidated the election. New balloting took place on January 19, 1958, and the committee examining it

[60] Paul Kennedy, "Figueres Pledges Loyal Opposition," *The New York Times*, February 6, 1958.

[61] For details see, "Resultados Definitivos en la Elección de Diputados," *Diario de Costa Rica*, April 3, 1958.

[62] "Cuadro General Entregado por el Ministerio del Interior," *El Mercurio*, September 5, 1958.

claimed that in its course "the popular will could manifest itself under the most propitious conditions which our civil annals register." [63] General Ydígoras was credited with 190,972 out of a total of 492,272 votes. He was followed by José Luis Cruz Salazar, the candidate of the Castillo Armas group. Theoretically the legislature could have declared Cruz Salazar elected; a majority of its members would have liked to have done so. Actually there was no alternative to handing the presidency over to Ydígoras; anything else would have meant a revolution. The strain which a presidential election by a mere plurality had imposed upon the country was real, however, and its results were bound to affect the nation's political life for some time to come.

What happened in Colombia in 1946 and in Costa Rica, Chile and Guatemala in 1958—to mention only a few examples—does raise the question whether in Latin America presidential elections by a mere plurality promote political stability. Several parties can, of course, sponsor a common candidate and elect him with a popular majority, but with the type of multiple party system promoted by the use of P.R. in legislative elections this will not always be the case.

The best long-run solution would be the development of something as close as possible to a two party system. If the majority system—preferably the plurality system—were used for *both* legislative and presidential elections there would at least be a *tendency* in this direction. As long as present conditions exist a check on the election of minority candidates appears to be needed. Still, a legislature can, apparently, no longer provide it; if it fails to endorse the candidate with the largest number of votes, its choice is unlikely to be accepted by the people.

Under the circumstances one wonders whether a second ballot might not be the solution. It would provide another chance for parties to form a coalition and to provide true majority support for the new president. Furthermore, it would entail a measure of agreement on measures as well as on the man. True, a second ballot may encourage additional candidacies in the first ballot, but then in Latin America so many parties present presidential

---

[63] Comisión Extraordinaria de Escrutinio, presided over by José Francisco Gómez Carranza, p. 3. The report, submitted on February 9, 1958, is quoted from a typewritten copy.

candidates anyway that additions would be immaterial. This, of course, is a stop-gap solution. In the long-run Latin America would benefit more from plurality elections for both the presidency and the legislature than from any other arrangement.

CONCLUSIONS

The proponents of constitutional government have a hard row to hoe in Latin America; the terrain could hardly be more difficult than it is. The development of stable democratic government presupposes the development of a democratic society, in which the authority at the top can rise from the active consent expressed by the people from below, through the medium of a popular party system.

The changes needed in this direction will, in the main, have to come through economic progress. In this field Latin America can, as mentioned above, do much for itself. Assistance from the outside must, however, play the essential part of helping to eliminate certain bottle-necks; after this has been done, and after a country has developed the momentum characteristic of the Mexico and the Puerto Rico of the last decade it can largely shift for itself. The fact that much foreign assistance is channeled through such agencies as the International Bank makes it easier to secure acceptance for the advice which it may be desirable to give in regard to the proper utilization of the resources placed at a country's disposal.

There remains the political side of Latin America's progress toward constitutionalism. Let us again quote Michael Scully: "But all the gold in Fort Knox will not remedy the root-evil of political instability that drains the economies of most southern countries and gives Communism its chance. The solution for that half of the inter-American problem must be—and can be—found by the Latin American nations." [64] Even in this field, North Americans need not altogether stand by idly. So much erroneous advice on these matters has crossed the Rio Grande from the North that a little counteraction could not do any harm. Thus, the Latin Americans have been told that either the class structure, or their cultural environment, predetermined their political life; the im-

[64] Scully, "What's Behind our Troubles with Latin America?" *op. cit.*, p. 66.

plication was that nothing could be done about it. We might recall that our own "Representative Republic" was founded on the assumption that something *could* be done to offset divisions arising in a country from economic and other cleavages. The proper type of political institutions can, as Madison told us in essay number ten of *The Federalist,* do much to "break and control the violence of factions." These institutions may not as yet work as well in Latin America as they do in this country, but there is no reason not to give them a chance.

An awareness of what a country can do for itself with the proper kind of institutions will also help to overcome the despair, as well as the cynicism, which one now encounters so frequently in Latin America. A prominent Latin journalist told this writer: "Constitutionalism is an ideology in the Marxist sense of the term: it is a device with the help of which the rulers and the ruled mutually deceive one another." The country in which this was said was, at the time, in the throes of a political turmoil which more consistent attempts to establish constitutional government might have helped prevent. Latin American pessimists should be aware that, in the repeatedly mentioned words of Alexander Hamilton, constitutional government is bound to suffer if it is "made to operate within an improper channel." [65] Where deficiencies in the condition of society are compounded by mistakes in the constitutional field, bad effects may be imputed to democracy which actually result from attempts to make it work with devices not suited to this purpose.

Last but not least, it should be borne in mind that while constitutional government has frequently failed, dictatorship will, in the end, always fail. After a breakdown of democratic institutions, followed, sooner or later by a breakdown of dictatorship, there is nothing to be done except to start all over again. Latin American leaders have expressed this need repeatedly. Thus, when Rafael Caldera returned to Venezuela from the exile imposed upon him by the Pérez Jiménez dictatorship he made a speech which was later published under the title "Lucha Constante Por La Libertad." [66] Former Costa Rican President, José Figueres, expressed

[65] Letter of Hamilton to Gouverneur Morris, 1777, here quoted from Caldwell, *The Administrative Theories of Hamilton and Jefferson,* p. 20.

[66] This essay on the constant struggle for freedom is found in *Colección Palabras y Problemas,* No. 1 (Caracas, 1958).

the same thought when he called his farm "La Lucha Sin Fin." [67]
Similar views have been expressed by Germán Arciniegas, a former
Colombian Minister of Education, and Alberto Lleras Camargo,
who was elected President of Colombia in 1958. The attitudes
recommended by these men are realistic in the sense that their
efforts, whatever the immediate results, are never as futile as
those inspired by the political mirage of some desirable solution
standing between the principles of democracy and those of dictatorship. There is, after all, something to be said for the assumption
that "Latin America Moves Slowly Toward Stability," and that
"Under a sometimes turbulent surface, long-term economic and
political forces are working a change." [68] This change may be
hastened if the principles underlying it are understood.

[67] See Charles O. Porter, "The Struggle Without End," *The New Leader* (April 14,
1958).
[68] These are the title and sub-title, respectively, of an article by Adolf A. Berle, Jr.,
The New York Times Magazine, October 16, 1955.

CHAPTER VI

[WILLIAM S. STOKES *]

Democracy, Freedom, and Reform

in Latin America †

Democracy, Individualism, and Liberalism

Democracy—that political system in which the sovereign power of the state is vested in the members of the state as a whole—has produced inconsistencies and problems which every culture adopting the system has been obliged to face. The emphasis in democracy is on the individual. The individual shares power theoretically with all other individuals in the state. He is responsible for decisions that affect his own welfare. He also is responsible for decisions that affect the welfare of the community. Democracy clearly honors individualism, and it would seem to embrace

* William S. Stokes received his Ph.D. in political science from the University of California at Los Angeles. He served as Instructor and Assistant Professor at Northwestern University, and in 1946 went to Wisconsin University, being appointed Professor there four years later. He was a guest lecturer at the National War College, 1949, 1950, at the University of California, 1951–1952, and at numerous Latin American Universities. He has undertaken research trips to Latin America in 1941, 1942, 1944, 1948 and 1955. He is the author of *Honduras, an Area Study in Government* (Madison, Wisconsin, 1950), and two additional studies of his, *Latin American Politics*, and *Anti-Americanism in Latin America*, will shortly be published. He has published approximately seventy articles pertaining to his field of specialization in the leading historical and political science journals, and has also contributed sections to *Collier's Yearbook* and *Encyclopedia Americana*. He is at present Professor of Comparative Political Institutions at Claremont Men's College.

† Parts of this paper will appear in a forthcoming volume on *Latin American Politics* to be published by Thomas Y. Crowell Company.

equality as well. The large numbers of individuals in all modern nation-states make the practice of direct democracy impossible. All nation-states which have democratic forms employ representative democracy at the national level. If individuals believed sincerely in the principle of equality, they would select their representatives by lot. The evidence proves conclusively that individuals do not in fact believe that people are equal in talent, ability, training, experience, or virtue. They, therefore, restrict, limit, and control the number and kinds of individuals who are permitted to vote and to offer themselves as representatives.

Thus, some individuals are not permitted to vote, and a potential representative is not required to win their acquiescence in order to acquire power. More than that, the representative is not even required to win all the votes of the individuals who are permitted to participate in the political process. The usual requirement is that he should win a majority, but not a majority of all eligible voters. He is only required to win a majority of the votes of the individuals who choose to vote at the time and place set for the election. Latin Americans know as well as we do that in representative democracy, the representatives may in fact represent only a small percentage of the adult members of the state. "Majority government" may not, in fact, be government by majority at all.

When the representatives assemble and begin to exercise the power they have won, whom or what should they represent? If it is argued that they should represent the ideas and interests of those who elected them, how can they find out what are these ideas and interests? Individuals are infinitely complex and different in training, experience, attitudes, and values. If it is argued that they should represent the "general welfare" or "common interest," how can they discover what these things are? The evidence proves conclusively that, except for a very small number of great issues, individuals differ widely as to what they believe to be the "general welfare" or "common interest." If the representative proceeds to delegate power to executives or administrators, the problem is compounded. These individuals are not elected by the electorate nor are they any better equipped than the representatives to discover the "general welfare" or "common interest."

The Founding Fathers in the United States were aware of these difficulties and endeavored to control them through adoption of some of the principles of what was then called "liberalism."

The philosophy of liberalism was based on the observation that during many centuries of Western Civilization men lived in cultures characterized by rigidified class structure, concentrated political power, and controlled economic systems. Liberalism sought generally to free the individual from such restraints so as to encourage a maximum degree of vertical mobility from lower classes to higher classes, limitation of state power and increased sharing of sovereignty, and freer opportunity for individual initiative and self-expression in economic, social, and other fields.

This broad conception of liberalism took on important political connotations in the nineteenth and twentieth centuries, which can be summarized in these points: (1) specific limitation of the power of the state to deny the natural freedoms and liberties of the people; (2) positive guarantees of freedom of expression on issues of public controversy; (3) establishment of facilities by the state for peaceful adjudication of competing interests; and (4) development of institutional protections against tyranny, usually expressed through written constitutions, public law, and such devices for restraining power as checks and balances.

Liberalism, putting natural rights, individual liberty, and freedom in the forefront of the values of society, endeavors to correct and control the theoretical weaknesses of political democracy by establishing a system of limited government, in which the selected areas of governmental power are subject to checks and controls of various kinds. The leaders of the new states in Latin America understood the theories of democracy, individualism, and liberalism and incorporated these principles into many of their earliest constitutions.

The above conception of liberalism, of course, is no longer accepted by most individuals who call themselves "liberals" in the United States or in Latin America. Indeed, the principles of classical liberalism are attacked unremittingly, and some writters even label them as reactionary. The modern-day "liberal" tends to support responsible or disciplined political parties, strong executive government, federal centralization, and expanded governmental functions, especially in the fields of economic and social welfare.[1]

The Preservation of the Traditional Values of Hispanic Culture

Although the leaders of the new states in Latin America admired sincerely the achievement of political liberalism in the United States and England, which won some success in reconciling individual liberty and governmental authority, it was evident almost immediately that they would not, or could not, make the revisions and modifications in their social and economic institutions which would make individualism, democracy, and liberalism meaningful in the practical affairs of Latin American society.

Some of the most renowned and distinguished thinkers in Hispanic culture, noting the abyss that separated their theoretical goals of individualism, democracy, and liberalism from the observable facts of Latin American society, expressed a gloomy, negative, pessimistic view of their own age and of the future of Latin America as well. Many of these works are veritable classics, which have had a profound effect on the thinking of the Latin American elite and are still read today.[2]

In more recent decades, beginning early in the twentieth century, other Latin American intellectuals began to perceive that

[1] For democracy, individualism, and liberalism, *see:* William M. McGovern and David S. Collier, *Radicals and Conservatives* (Chicago, 1957), pp. 174; Luis Díez del Corral, *El Liberalismo Doctrinario* (Madrid, 1945), pp. 616; E. Aztiria, *El Balance en la Sociedad de Responsabilidad Limitada* (Buenos Aires, 1953), pp. 205; Francisco Ayala, *El Problema del Liberalismo* (México, D.F., 1941), pp. 112; José Lozano Muñoz, *Sofismas Morales, Políticos y Jurídicos* (Buenos Aires, 1947), pp. 250.

[2] See for example: Domingo Faustino Sarmiento, *Conflicto y Armonías de las Razas en América* (Buenos Aires, 1915 edition), p. 458; Francisco Bulnes, *El Porvenir de las Naciones Hispanoamericanas ante las Conquistas Recientes de Europa y los Estados Unidos* (Mexico, D.F., 1899), p. 282; Manuel González Prada, *Horas de Lucha* (Callao, 1924 edition), p. 362; Juan Agustín García, *La Ciudad Indiana: Buenos Aires desde 1600 hasta mediados del Siglo XVIII* (Buenos Aires, 1909 edition), p. 375; Alfredo Colmo, *Los Países de la América Latina* (Madrid, 1915), p. 661; Carlos Octavio Bunge, *Nuestra América* (Barcelona, 1903), p. 233; José Ingenieros, *El Hombre Mediocre* (Buenos Aires, 1917 edition), p. 250. Numerous volumes by Alcides Argüedas are also cases in point: *Los Caudillos Bárbaros* (Barcelona, 1929), p. 384; *Historia de Bolivia: los Caudillos Letrados, . . . 1829–1848* (Barcelona, 1923), p. 368; *Historia de Bolivia: la Plebe en Acción, 1848–1857* (Barcelona, 1924), p. 312; *Historia de Bolivia: la Dictadura y la Anarquía, 1857–1864* (Barcelona, 1924), p. 338; *Historia General de Bolivia, 1808–1921* (La Paz, 1922), p. 579; *Pueblo Enfermo: Contribución a la Psicología de los Pueblos Hispano-Americanos* (Barcelona, 1909), p. 255.

individualism, democracy, and liberalism had apparently resulted in values in United States culture which were contrary to their idealistic expectations. By comparsion of the most romanticized conception of their own values and the most debased conception of those of the United States, they began to develop an aggressive, positive, optimistic defense of the values of Hispanic culture.

It remains now to show that there exists a very substantial body of support for the traditional values of Hispanic culture which tends to obstruct the development of classical liberalism and which suggests other political theories as more logical, practical, and satisfying to Latin Americans. This can be done by examining the literature of the Latin American philosophers, essayists, historians, novelists, poets, and writers, usually called *pensadores*, with respect to their conception of the values of Hispanic and United States culture.

No one reading the works of the *pensadores* of recent decades can doubt the formidable intellectual influence of Rodó, Altamira y Crevea, Araquistaín, Pereyra, Vasconcelos, García Calderón, Ugarte, and others. The later writers of the highest status quote them again and again. Of all those who have defended the values of Hispanic culture against the cultural imperialism of the United States, however, José Enrique Rodó almost certainly has had the greatest impact. His best known work, *Ariel,* first published in 1900, probably has been read by all Latin American intellectuals. It is to Latin Americans in general what José Martí's *La Rosa Blanca* is to Cubans—a work known, quoted, loved, and uncritically accepted. Rodó's ideology, particularly as seen in *Ariel,* provides a core of values which one finds repeated in hundreds of later sources.

Rodó was a professor of literature at the National University in Montevideo. Aside from a trip to Chile to make a speech and a visit to Spain, Portugal, and Italy, where he died in May, 1917, he knew nothing of the world from first-hand observation. He never visited the United States, and there is nothing in his published works which would indicate that he had studied the history and culture of the United States in anything more than the most casual, superficial manner.

In *Ariel,* Rodó depicts the professor addressing his students for the final time. To illustrate his message, the teacher points to the graceful figure of Ariel as the symbol of reason, nobility, and sentiment in contrast to the invisible ogre, Caliban, insensitive, sensual, and stupid but possessed of the will to perpetrate horrors. Rodó defends the values of human solidarity, social aesthetics, and individual integrity and warns against the opposing tendencies of utilitarianism, materialism, positivism and individualism. He makes clear in *Ariel* who the Calibans of the world are.

In a broader sense, Rodó's ideology embraced the theory of Greco-Latin humanism with its emphasis on intellectual, romantic, and aesthetic idealism. His calm, dignified words reflected wisdom and quiet optimism at a time when Latin Americans were psychologically unnerved by the activities of the United States in international relations. The Monroe Doctrine and Manifest Destiny seemed not to have advanced the interests of the Latin American countries; the ease with which the United States destroyed Spain in the Spanish-American War was profoundly shocking; and Latin American republics were shortly to experience armed intervention by the United States. Rodó was describing an ideology which appealed to Latin Americans, an ideology which provided the foundations for an intense nationalism. It is obvious, of course, that his values could only be found, and then to a limited extent, in a small intellectual elite in the several Latin American countries. It would be grotesque to say that his values could be found in the disease-ridden, impoverished, illiterate masses in Latin America. On the other hand, it was in the elite that political power was concentrated.

Although modern-day *pensadores* realize that Rodó was not qualified professionally to analyze and criticize the values of United States culture, and many admit that his specific attacks were based on misconceptions, a large number of intellectuals continue to characterize the *yanquis* as the Calibans and Philistines of the earth. The *pensadores* frequently use the following words and phrases to describe the alleged values of Hispanic culture:

On mental ability and aptitude: intelligence; *capacidad;* "exuberant imaginative power;" "natural predisposition for speculative ideas;" "decided inclination toward artistic or aesthetic concepts;" superiority at jurisprudence, pedagogy, painting, history, poetry, oratory, art, literature, science.

On method of thinking: rational; irrational; superrational; through fantasy; intuitional.

On individual characteristics: courteous; free; bright; witty; sentimental; idealistic; "real" democrats; dreamers; artists; *dignidad;* moral; noble; honorable.

On group characteristics: "the idealistic generosity of our countries;" "realidad heróica;" "alma nacional;" "hazañas heróicas;" "conciencia nacional;" "spirit of the nation;" "soul of the 'people';" "a sentimental and exalted race;" "an idealistic culture;" "the cultivation of the spirit;" "the noble nationalistic spirit of our countries."

On cultural goals: holiness, truth, goodness, beauty, equity, justice, social justice, distributive justice.

Although these and similar words and phrases convey a value system frequently claimed in Latin America, it must not, of course, be assumed that the *pensadores* are blind to the realities of their culture. Many books of a highly critical nature have been published.

The following list of words and phrases can all be found in works of *pensadores* intent upon attacking United States culture, and, therefore, indirectly attacking individualism, democracy, and liberalism:

imperialistic
materialistic
utilitarian
cold
vulgar
immoral
conformist
contemptuous
barbarians
lustful
brutal
cruel
expansionist
loose morality of women

racist
lack of idealism
no soul
hostile to art
worship of money
passion for the dollar
superiority
Octopus of the North
Colossus of the North
crude
coarse
rude
stupid

The specific criticisms of major *pensadores* largely repeat the ideas suggested in this list. Rufino Blanco Fombona, distinguished

Venezuelan novelist and violent critic of the United States, rationalized his hatred because of this country's imperialism, customs, conception of life, incapacity for the fine arts, and lack of ideals. The great Mexican thinker, José Vasconcelos, opposed the food, mechanization, Protestant religion, cultural levels, and ideas on race, imperialism, and women. A minor Marxist writer, Enamorado Cuesta, called the *yanqui* a "bird of prey," a direct descendant of the pirates of the colonial period maintaining alive the ancestral instinct of the "blond beast" of Nietzsche. The same author quotes the American Marxist, Waldo Frank, approvingly on his conception of the national characteristics of the United States: 100 per cent Americanism, Ku-Klux-Klanism, colonialism, racial, religious, and ethnic discrimination, cult of the machine, conformism, distrust of originality and creativity in art and thought, vulgarity, etc. Elgüero refers to the "perfidious *yanqui*," and Sáenz seems to believe luck or providence has been on the side of the United States when he insists that this country achieved independence "without great battles, without mythological heroes, with very little shedding of blood."

Many more Latin Americans have visited the United States in recent decades than in the late nineteenth century and early decades of the twentieth century. It is seldom in the latest literature of anti-Americanism that one finds the *pensador* asserting that the United States is a cultural desert. Indeed, Sáenz, the most violent anti-American writing today, admits in a book published in 1949 that the United States ranks high in educational establishments, scientific investigation, journalism, libraries, and museums and galleries of fine arts. If anything, the recognition of the eminence of the United States in political, cultural, military, and economic fields has sharpened the danger of cultural imperialism, Elgüero warns. Ibargurén, writing in 1946, argues that in order to avoid suffocation by the United States, Latin America must become, and remain, free of the cultural, economic, and political influence of the United States. Indeed, among all the anti-American writers of the past and present there is a stated or implied assumption that in the Western Hemisphere there are "two Americas." When the *pensadores* use the term "nuestra América," they mean the America with a common language, common religion, and a common historical experience—things which have contributed to the development of common values. Alberto Wagner de Reyna, a Peruvian diplomat writing in 1954, concludes that culturally there is nowhere else to go. Latin Americans must preserve and develop the values they inherited from Spain and Portugal.[3]

Right Wing Deviations from Liberalism—Theories of the Equidistant or Third Force

In recent decades, Latin Americans have translated their disdain for the values of United States culture into an open repudiation of individualism, political democracy, and liberalism. They have developed and advocated theories more congenial to the social, economic, and political realities and values of Hispanic culture. One body of theories which deals with the role of government in society has come increasingly to be called the "equidistant" position or the Third Force. The origin of the Third Force ideology probably is to be found in the works of distinguished and influential political thinkers of the nineteenth century. Arturo Vilela, in a book published in 1953, which reviews the fundamental concepts of major nineteenth century thinkers, shows that whereas strong, centralized government dedicated to providing social and economic benefits for the masses was an almost unan-

[3] For complete bibliographical references to the section dealing with the preservation of traditional values of Hispanic culture, *see:* Stokes, "Cultural Anti-Americanism in Latin America," chapter in book to be published by the University of Kansas Press in 1959. The major *pensadores,* whose works can be consulted in card catalogues of major libraries are as follows: José Enrique Rodó; Rafael Altamira y Crevea; Luis Araquistaín Quevedo; Carlos Pereyra; José Vasconcelos; José María Vargas Vilá; Rufino Blanco Fombona; José Martí; Eugenio María de Hostos y Bonilla; Manuel Ugarte; Francisco García Calderón; Manuel Gálvez; Emilio Zurano Muñoz; Manuel de Oliveira Lima; Alfredo L. Palacios; Francisco Bulnes; Ricardo Rojas; Horacio Blanco Fombona; Roque Sáenz Peña; Jackson de Figueiredo; Max Henríquez Ureña; Tancredo Pinochet; Federico Henríquez y Carvajal; José Ingenieros; Ramiro de Maeztú; J. Enamorado Cuesta; José Elgüero; José Suárez Somoano; Bernardo González Arrili; Benjamín Fernández y Medina; Lucio M. Moreno Quintana; Gonzalo G. Travesi; Luis Enrique Osorio; J. Francisco V. Silva; Isidro Fabela; Francisco Caraballo y Sotolongo; Belisario Roldán; Fernando Ortiz; José Gaxiola; Fernando Berenguer; Salvador R. Merlos; Federico García Godoy; Vicente Sáenz; Alberto Cornejo S.; Teodoro Alvarado Garaicoa; Luis Alberto Sánchez; Juan Ortega y Medina; Enrique V. Corominas; J. Tudela; Miguel Angel Asturias; Blas Urrea (real name Luis Cabrera); Alberto Wagner de Reyna; Joaquín Gutiérrez; Baltazar Castro; Luis Gracián (real name Nestor Forero Morales); Carlos Ibargurén; Enriquen Patín; Alceu Amoroso Lima; Fernando Díez de Medina; Pablo González Casanova; Carlos Lacalle; Emilio Frugoni; José Luis Bustamante y Rivero.

imous concern of such thinkers, the values of representative government and individualism definitely were not.

As one reviews the very recent literature of thoughtful writers, such as Pierre Maxime Schuhl and Alberto Wagner de Reyna, and that of more aggressive, even violent, critics of liberalism, such as Julio Ycaza Tigerino, it becomes clear that, according to their conception of the nature of man and society, it should be the function of the state to establish and protect human solidarity, moral and spiritual ends, nationalism, and a "living together" of the classes. They propose a governmental structure characterized by order, discipline, and hierarchy under the guidance of strong, virtuous, moral, executive leadership, and disciplined parties or political organizations with functional rather than numerical representation.

The amorphous congeries of "rightist" thinkers agree on one position—that the values of Hispanic culture cannot be achieved under either capitalism and individualistic democracy or under Communism and totalitarian dictatorship. They, therefore, advance theories of the state which are "equidistant" between the "monsters that would waylay us," as Miguel Angel Ponce de León puts it. They propose a Third Position or Third Force, some writers openly using these terms and others not, although all support in general the same ideas.

Among the supporters of the Third Force must be included many "Christian Democrats" and other Catholic thinkers who advocate either the cooperative movement or the corporative state. A good illustration of the Catholic position is seen in Jackson de Figueiredo (1891–1928), renowned organizer and leader of the most important Catholic movement in Brazil in the twentieth century. Jackson de Figueiredo condemned individualism as a "terrible evil," opposed "Masonic and Judaic liberalism" because it led to "social injustice" and "political tyranny," repudiated tolerance, expressed a "fierce hatred" for democracy, and insisted that unless a powerful, central government were established, which would restore authority and discipline based on moral and religious principles, Communism would probably triumph in Brazil. Although the views of Alceu Amoroso Lima, who is presently the leading Catholic intellectual in Brazil, are more profound and philosophical and certainly less violent and extreme than those of Jackson de Figueiredo, they are not fundamentally different.*

Both *Integralismo,* which never acquired power in Brazil, and the *Estado Novo,* which did, were opposed to individualism, democracy, and liberalism. Plinio Salgado, the philosopher and leader of *Integralismo,* provided his followers with green shirts, arm bands, a salute (raised arm), a slogan ("God, Country, Family"), and an ideology which specifically repudiated capitalism, federalism, party organization, and parliamentary procedures. He proposed a centralized, unitary state, acting under strong executive leadership, which would guarantee social justice to all members of the "family" in accordance with the principles of Christian morality. The *Estado Novo,* the Constitution for which was drafted mainly by Francisco Campos, was announced by President Vargas in 1937. It was similar in doctrine and program to *Integralismo,* but it lacked dramatic ceremonials, and despite efforts to abolish political parties and unite the states in a unitary system under a powerful central government, it succeeded only in achieving a modest kind of authoritarian government or benevolent dictatorship dedicated to the special interests of the lower classes, mainly urban labor.

Father Félix Restrepo gave a memorable series of lectures in 1939 favoring the corporative state in Colombia. Gonzalo Restrepo Jaramillo, however, an open advocate of the corporative state since 1941, is undoubtedly the Catholic thinker with maximum intellectual influence in Colombia. Londoño and Vallejo, both writing in 1953, and Fernández and Silva, both writing in 1955, agree with Father Félix Restrepo and Restrepo Jaramillo on the desirability of the corporative state, preferably modeled on that of Franco Spain (Londoño) or on that of the European thinker, the Marques de La Tour du Pin (Silva). The ends of the state should be the establishment of "social solidarity" and the achievement of "social justice" through "compulsory unionism," "Christian economic planning," and cooperatives.

General Gustavo Rojas Pinilla, who seized power by force in Colombia on June 13, 1953, made speeches on May 1 and August

---

* On the basis of his article in this volume, however, one cannot detect hatred for democracy, or indeed extremism of any sort, on the part of Alceu Amoroso Lima. [Editor's Note]

7, 1954, which gave the impression that he supported certain aspects of corporativism. In early November, 1954, a Conservative, Félix Arango Vallejo, proposed a vague kind of Third Force, but President Rojas Pinilla rejected it. In January, 1955 an organization called *Movimiento de Acción Nacional* (MAN) was created, which was clearly a Third Force effort. President Rojas Pinilla forbade it to act in his behalf, however, and it died aborning. But on June 13, 1956, President Rojas Pinilla officially proclaimed the Third Force to be the philosophy and organization of his government and urged the establishment of a corporative state. He was ousted from power by force before it was possible to discover what effect the Third Force might have had in Colombian politics.

The eminent Chilean Catholic thinker, Alejandro Silva Bascuñán, expresses the conviction that "materialism," and "liberalism" are "dehumanizing" and impede the achievement of "social justice." Although he admits that "liberal individualism" is not as evil as Communism, both must be rejected and a corporate state established. It is interesting to note that Bascuñán asserts that there was warm sympathy for Jorge González von Marées among leading Catholics in Chile. Von Marées, regarded by many scholars as a Fascist, assuredly was a supporter of an authoritarian state and a planned economy. Other prominent Chileans writing along similar lines in recent years are Lorenzo Fernández Rodríguez, Jorge Lyon Edwards, and Diego Guillén Santa Ana.

The term "sinarquista" first appeared in Mexican political life in 1912 when a Mexican engineer, Tomás Rosales, wrote a pamphlet called *La República Sinarquista,* which contained the rudiments of a constitution for a political system. On May 23, 1937, an organization, not associated with the first one, was created by three lawyers and a farmer in León, Guanajuato. Possibly aided by an anti-Communist German professor at the University of Guanajuato, Hellmuth Oskar Schreiter, they called the organization the *Unión Nacional Sinarquista.*

The founders were devout Catholics who declared again and again in their newspaper, *El Sinarquista,* that it was their purpose to restore the Christian social order and oppose the Mexican Revolution, Fascism, Nazism, Communism, Liberal democracy, and the values of United States culture. In order to accomplish their objectives, they established an hierarchical, authoritarian organization with absolute, centralized power. The *Folleto para Jefes* (Instruction Manual for Leaders) makes crystal clear that *sinarquismo* opposed democracy in both theory and practice. All authority emanated from the leaders, all lower level officials were appointed, no issues were discussed or debated in the assemblies or meetings. An official song was adopted on October 17, 1940 ("Fe, Sangre, Victoria"), and other symbols devised: the salute (right arm across breast); the pass ("Viva Mexico!"); the flag (red with white circle with map of Mexico in the center and U.N.S. stamped on it); 2nd the arm band.

There is no doubt of the popularity of *sinarquismo* in the early years of its operations. It had a membership of hundreds of thousands. Some responsible Mexicans have informed the author that it probably had more than 1,500,000 supporters at one time. As the years passed, the publications of *sinarquismo* contained more and more criticism of Communism and the Mexican Revolution. On June 22, 1944, the Mexican Government suppressed *sinarquismo* and drove it underground because of alleged incitement to subversion in some of the movement's published statements.

A split in the leadership in 1945 was followed by changes in ideology. The majority segment now openly espoused the equidistant or Third Force theory. Although formerly opposed to voting, the leaders now formed a party, *Fuerza Popular,* and competed for public office. The Mexican Government outlawed the party, however, and it was unable to participate in the congressional elections of 1949. By the early 1950's, the movement had lost most of its appeal.

The *peronista* dictatorship in Argentina (1943–1955), with its ideology of *justicialismo,* the Third Force, *Doctrina Nacional,* or *Filosofía Peronista,* as it has been called, is the best known, most dramatic, and undoubtedly most influential "right wing" deviation from the principles of individualism, democracy, and liberalism ever to occur in Latin Amercia. It would be a great mistake to think of *peronismo* simply as a Western Hemisphere manifestation of Nazism, Fascism, or any other European political system. The ideas, sentiments, values, political principles, policies, and methods of government of *peronismo* can be traced far back in the history of Hispanic and Argentine development, and, of course, *peronismo* achieved its greatest power, influence, and popularity after the Nazis and Fascists were defeated in Europe. It would also be a mistake to treat *justicialismo* as the hastily contrived ideological expedient to justify casual dictatorship. Many who take this position assert that *justicialismo* as a term was not devised until the late 1940's, some years after the dictatorship had been operating.

The term *justicialismo* was always used but incidentally to describe the ideology, program, and methods of *peronismo,* as can easily be seen by examining issues of the official magazine *Mundo Peronista.* Moreover, just prior to the defeat of General Perón in 1955, one could have visited the *peronista* bookstore at San Martín 665 in Buenos Aires and purchased the packet of twenty volumes which described the various aspects of the history, ideology, program, and methods of the movement. None of the twenty titles contained the term *justicialismo* or *justicialista.*

Peronismo was a movement which sought to reassert the dominant traditional values of Hispanic culture. As such, logic and reality compelled it to oppose individualism, liberalism, representative democracy, limited government, capitalism, and Communism. Although the *peronista* state achieved its greatest support from the urban working classes, whose material interests it served, the purpose in using state power to benefit the individual was not to inculcate a spirit of materialism but to oppose materialism and utilitarianism and to encourage a regeneration of moral and spiritual values. Even after Perón quarreled with members of the Catholic hierarchy, he continued unceasingly to talk about Christian values, such as love, brotherhood, and living together in "equilibrium" or "harmony." Perón and the intellectuals who supported him had the most profound contempt for the materialistic and utilitarian values they associated with individualism and capitalism. It certainly was not their intention to develop or encourage such values. Many of the intellectuals the author talked to who early supported *peronismo,* such as Pablo A. Ramella, author of the important treatise, *La Estructura del Estado,* informed him that *peronismo* was attractive to them because it seemed to offer support for such moral ends as protection of the family, ethical standards and conduct as defined by the

Church and implemented by the state, and control of immorality through censorship of the media of communications.

The term *justicialismo* is frequently used synonymously with the end or objective of social justice. Perón insisted again and again that the masses of the people could never achieve social justice through either Communistic collectivism or capitalistic or liberal individualism. A state was needed which would harmonize and conciliate the interests of workers and management so as to encourage greater production and distribution for all, particularly for the humble classes. In his Labor Day speech of May 1, 1944, Col. Perón said: "We seek to suppress class warfare, replacing it by a just agreement between the workers and employers, under the shelter of the justice of the state."

Peronismo also sought to inculcate nationalism, which it described mainly in terms of love of country and race. The glorification of courage, heroism, and self-sacrifice in war and the advocacy of aggression in international relations appear in some *peronista* documents, but they were never translated into policies of the government.

In political organization and method, Perón was always clear, unequivocal, and emphatic. He sought, and guaranteed to establish, strong, centralized, executive government aided by a responsible or disciplined political party. Right from the beginning of the movement, he exalted authoritarianism as a working principle. He stated simply in 1944: "I believe that programs, as revolutions, should not be announced, but simply carried out."

What *peronismo* and other Third Force ideologies in general have sought—moral, spiritual ends, human solidarity, nationalism, abolition of the class struggle, economic planning, the welfare state, strong, centralized, executive government, responsible or disciplined political parties, and order and authority in society in general—are values that have had serious support from serious intellectuals and men in public life in periods much earlier than the last decade and half in Argentina. It is for this reason mainly that the author took *peronismo* seriously and continues to take it seriously, regardless of what individuals or political organizations may be in charge of the state in Argentina or elsewhere now or in the foreseeable future.

For example, one has only to examine Manuel Gálvez's forty volumes, not merely his well-known book, *Este Pueblo Necesita,* published in 1934, or even his *El Espíritu de Aristocracia y Otros Ensayos,* published in 1924, but his novels, prose, and poetry as well to discover almost every point in the *peronista* program. Alejandro E. Bunge was a Catholic, "revolutionary" professor who, since 1909, urged in his classrooms and in his writings, vigorously, unceasingly, convincingly, and with marked success, that a nationalistic "New Argentina" be created. He inveighed against foreign economic influence, he insisted that capitalism was "immoral," and he argued that private property must perform a "social function" under the leadership and guidance of the State. When Manuel Ugarte, famous Argentine literary figure, who published more than twenty books, explained in 1913 why he had renounced socialism, he put forth an ideology and program which paralleled the Third Force of Perón in striking fashion. In important statements made in 1915, 1919, and 1924, Ugarte made clear that the ideas he had expressed earlier were carefully thought through and were a fixed part of his philosophy. Works of other prominent Argentines, such as Héctor Raudón, Julio González, Cipriano Pons Lexica, Francisco Bayón, Luciano Catalaño, Mario Amadeo, and others provide an ideological foundation for *peronismo* which quite transcends a single political movement or administration, such as that of Perón from 1943–1955.

Arturo Frondizi, who won the Argentine presidential elections of 1958 in convincing fashion, published a major work in 1954, in which he described and defended his ideological position in considerable detail. One can dismiss many of his demagogic statements in the presidential campaign as the irresponsible products of partisan passion inflamed by the natural desire to win. The 1954 volume, however, the product of years of work and the most careful preparation, should be given thoughtful attention. In his presentation of ideology, Frondizi announces two main positions. First, he is convinced that Argentina's ills are caused by "foreign economic powers" and "imperialistic forces," mainly the United States, which are controlled by capitalistic monopolies. Foreign capital, he believes, "keeps us in spiritual dependence and subjection," and is dedicated to keeping Argentina from industrializing. In order for Argentina to achieve a "strong, national, independent industry," the state should nationalize the foreign "monopolies," and operate them as part of a program of "economic democratization" which includes economic planning and the forcible liquidation of the latifundia. Second, Frondizi thinks that the millions of people who are neither Communist collectivists nor capitalist individualists should form a "democracy" that is in between the two extremes. In order to do this, a "great force" should be formed made up of men with technical and scientific competence who are bound together by "democratic passion," "national mentality," and "revolutionary vocation." This "great force" should then attract the masses and rely on them and the armed forces to achieve the "social transformation." Frondizi, therefore, concludes that Argentina needs: (1) "a national, popular political party;" (2) "workers' forces;" and (3) "armed forces," all united for social and economic action. It would seem from this summary of Frondizi's political and economic philosophy that government in Argentina in the foreseeable future will reflect some, at least, of the values of the Third Force.

Finally, it should be noted that Fascist and Nazi ideology had significant impact and direct political influence in a number of Latin American countries in the 1920's and 1930's. It diminished in most countries in the 1940's and disappeared almost entirely with the defeat of the Fascist and Nazi forces in Europe.[4]

[4] For right wing deviations from liberalism—theories of the equidistant or Third Force, *see:* Julio Ycaza Tigerino, *Sociología de la Política Hispanoamericana* (Madrid, 1950), pp. 27–28, 105, 154, 158–159, 174–176, 281–313; Ycaza Tigerino, "El problema político de Hispanoamérica," *Revista de Estudios Políticos* (Madrid: septiembre-octubre, 1950), pp. 151–167; Alberto Wagner de Reyna, *La Filosofía en Iberoamérica* (Lima, 1949), pp. 35–98; Carlos Vaz Ferreira, *La Actual Crisis del Mundo desde el Punto de Vista Racional* (Buenos Aires, 1940), pp. 64; Pierre Maxime Schuhl, *Maquinismo y Filosofía* (Buenos Aires, 1955), pp. 122; Arturo Vilela, *Interpretación de la Historia Sudamericana* (La Paz, 1953), pp. 135–205; Manuel Moniz Falcão, *The Social Thought of Jackson de Figueiredo, A Brazilian Social Reformer* (M.A., Catholic University of America, 1938), pp. 12–55; Jackson de Figueiredo, *Correspondencia* (Rio de Janeiro, 1946), pp. 445; Alceu Amoroso Lima, *Pela Cristianização da Idade Nova,* Primeiro volume: *Teoria* (Rio de Janeiro, 1946), pp. 265; Carlos Mario Londoño, *Económica Social Colombiana* (Bogotá, 1953), pp. 13, 86–118, 133–143, 164–170, 190–215, 233–271; Gustavo Barroso, *Comunismo, Cristianismo e Corporativismo* (Rio, 1938), pp. 164; Gonzalo Restrepo Jaramillo, *La Crisis Contemporánea: Estudios Sociales* (Medelin, 1941), pp. 247; F. A. Vallejo, *Hacia una Sociedad Nueva* (Bogotá, 1953), pp. 249; J. M. Fernández, *Justicia Social: ni comunismo, ni propiedad absoluta, comunidad de bienes creados* (Bogotá, 1955), pp. 171; Alejandro Silva Bascuñán, *Una Experiencia Social Cristiana* (Santiago de Chile, 1949), pp. 19–36, 79, 169–176; Miguel Angel Ponce de León, *Los Monstruos que Acechán* (Holguín, Oriente, Cuba, 1951),

Left Wing Deviations from Liberalism—Aprismo ⊀

If space permitted, a series of case studies of left wing deviations from liberalism might be studied: the Mexican Revolution; the Cuban Revolution under President Ramón Grau San Martín, 1944–48, and President Carlos Prío Socarrás, 1948–1952; the Guatemalan Revolution, 1944–1954; or the *Movimiento Nacionalista Revolucionario* (MNR) of Bolivia, which acquired power with the military lodges by force in 1943, lost it in the same way in 1946, but came back by violence in 1952 and which continues to govern today. Instead, the author will have to content himself

pp. 35, 51–52, 67, 74–75; Lorenzo Fernández Rodríguez, *La Justicia Social Eterna* (Santiago de Chile, 1949), pp. 162; Jorge Lyon Edwards, *El Verdadero Sentido de la Democracia: Ensayo de introducción al estudio de la democracia cristiana* (Santiago de Chile, 1947), pp. 180; Diego Guillén Santa Ana, *Política Económica Sociología-Corporativismo* (Santiago de Chile, 1940), pp. 280, especially p. 272; José Gómez Izquierdo, *Problemas Fundamentales en la Ciencia Social Católica* (Quito, Ecuador, 1954), 134; Manuel Foyaca de la Concha, *Un Nuevo Orden Económico Social* (La Habana, 1947), pp. 110; Evaristo M. Pinón Filgueira, "El estado y la empresa," *Revista de la Facultad de Ciencias Económicas*, Universidad Nacional de Buenos Aires (octubre, 1950), pp. 956–973; Salvador Oría, *El Estado Argentino y la Nueva Economía* (Buenos Aires, 1944), pp. 13–17, 33; Abraham Fernández de Soto, *Treinta Lecciones de Sociología Católica* (Bogotá, 1952), pp. 342; Carlos P. Carranza, *El Mundo del Futuro ¿ capitalismo norteamericano o communismo ruso?* (Buenos Aires, 1948), pp. 220; Víctor Andrés Belaunde, *La Crisis Presente, 1914–1939* (Lima, 1940), pp. 101–102, 143–145, 162, 177–178, 190–199, 227–256; Remo di Natale E., *Revolución Agraria en Bolivia* (Cochabamba, Bolivia, 1953), pp. 103, 148; Andrés Ponte, *Como Salvar a Venezuela* (New York, 1938), pp. 320–334; Salvador M. Dana Montaño, *Justicia Social y Reforma Constitucional* (Santa Fé, Argentina, 1948), pp. 237; Confederación Regional Obrera Mexicana, *Memoria de los Trabajos Realizados por el Comité Central durante su Ejercicio del 1 de Agosto de 1943 al 31 del Julio de 1945* (México, D.F., 1945), p. 145; Ernest Hamblock, "The New Regime in Brazil," *Foreign Affairs* (April, 1938), pp. 484–493; David Nasser, *A Revolução dos Covardes* (Rio de Janeiro, 1947), pp. 268; Antonio Franca, *Años de Resistencia* (Rio de Janeiro, 1950), pp. 163; Plinio Salgado, *Como Nasceram as Cidades do Brasil* (Lisboa, 1946), pp. 166; Nemo Canabarro, *A Emancipação* (Rio de Janeiro, 1950), pp. 43–44, 355, 380–394; Getulio Vargas, *A Campanha Presidencial: Discursos* (Rio de Janeiro, 1951), pp. 665; Ricardo Silva, *Los Trabajadores ante los Partidos* (Bogotá, 1955), pp. 11–52, 121–123; 162–164, 254–255; Vernon L. Fluharty, *Dance of the Millions* (Pittsburgh, 1957), pp. 280–282, 305–306, 315; Mario Gill, *Sinarquismo—su origen, su esencia, su misión* (México, D.F., 1944); *Canciones y Corridos Sinarquistas* (México, D.F., 1940); Unión Nacional Sinarquista, *Orden* (various issues); Union Nacional Sinarquista, *México—1960* (México, D.F., 1941); Juan Ignacio Padilla, *Sinarquismo* (México, D.F., 1948); Nathan L. Whetten, *Rural Mexico* (Chicago, 1948), pp. 484–522; Luciano R. Catalaño, *Plan Argentino de Movilización Industrial* (Buenos Aires, 1943), pp. 36–39; Cipriano Pons Lexica, *La Cuestión Internacional Argentina* (Buenos Aires, 1946), pp. 106; Héctor R. Raudón, *Democracia: Valoración del Régimen Representativo* (Buenos Aires, 1941), pp. 181; Julio V. González, *Nacionalización del Petróleo* (Buenos Aires, 1947), pp. 3–6; Manuel Ugarte, *La Patria Grande* with the selection of *Aprismo* and a separate case study of Communism, which follows this section.

The *Alianza Popular Revolucionaria Americana, APRA,* the *Aprista* movement, or *Aprismo,* is an interesting and significant political ideology and movement in Latin America, although it never acquired supreme power in Peru, the country of its originator and its spiritual headquarters.

The APRA finds its earlier origins in Latin American protest literature of the late nineteenth and early twentieth centuries. Its development was hastened by the student movement in Peru,

---

(Santiago de Chile, 1939), pp. 11–26, 57–62, 67–77, 96, 114–118, 145, 195–204; Ugarte, *El Destino de un Continente* (Madrid, 1923), pp. 429; Ugarte, *Mi Campaña Hispanoamericana* (Barcelona, 1922), *passim;* Instituto Alejandro E. Bunge de Investigaciones Económicas y Sociales, *Soluciones Argentinas a los Problemas Económicos y Sociales del Presente* (Buenos Aires, 1945), pp. 5–7, 38; Manuel Gálvez, *El Espíritu de Aristocracia y Otros Ensayos* (Buenos Aires, 1924), pp. 166; Gálvez, *Este Pueblo Necesita* (Buenos Aires, 1934), pp. 133; Ministerio de Relaciones Exteriores y Culto, *La República Argentina ante el "Libro Azul"* (Buenos Aires, 1946), pp. 258; Salvador C. Vigo, *Reforma Constitucional Argentina* (Santa Fé, 1950), pp. 540; Juan D. Perón, *Doctrinary Principles of the Social Policy of His Excellency the President of the Republic, General Juan Perón* (Buenos Aires, 1947), pp. 32; P. Núñez Arca, *Perón, Man of America* (Buenos Aires, 1950), pp. 142; Perón, *Conducción Política* (Buenos Aires, 1951), pp. 198; Emilio D. Cipolletti, *Ante los Ojos de América* (Buenos Aires, 1947), 172; Eva Perón, *La Razón de mi Vida* (Buenos Aires, 1951), pp. 316; Atilio García Mellid, *Montoneras y Caudillos en la Historia Argentina* (Buenos Aires, 1946), pp. 176; Ernesto Vilches B., *Perón Visto desde Chile* (Santiago de Chile, 1947), pp. 86; L. Edward Shuck, Jr., "Distributive Democracy" in the Americas—An Analysis of the Perón Regime in Argentina (Ph.D., University of California, 1948); George I. Blanksten, *Perón's Argentina* (Chicago, 1953), pp. 280–305; Federico de Urrutia, *Perón* (Madrid, 1946), pp. 262; Raúl A. Mende, *El Justicialismo* (Buenos Aires, 1950), *passim;* Hernán Benítez, *La Aristocracia Frente a la Revolución* (Buenos Aires, 1953), pp. 461. Relevant criticisms of *peronismo* are: Alejandro Magnet, *Nuestros Vecinos Justicialistas* (Santiago de Chile, 1954), pp. 221; Ernesto E. Sammartino, *La Verdad Sobre la Situación Argentina* (Montevideo, 1950), pp. 394; Luis Pan, *Prensa Libre* (Buenos Aires, 1950), pp. 137; Carlos Sánchez Viamonte, *Utilidad de las Dictaduras* (Buenos Aires, 1947), pp. 278; Mario Martíns, *Perón: Um confronto entre o Brasil e a Argentina* (Rio de Janeiro, 1950), pp. 312. For the ideology of the incumbent president of Argentina, see: Arturo Frondizi, *Petróleo y Política: contribución al estudio de la historia económica argentina y de las relaciones entre el imperialismo y la vida política nacional* (Buenos Aires, 1954), pp. xxxvi–lxxiii. For Fascism and Nazism in Latin America, see: Hugo Fernández Artucio, *Nazis en el Uruguay* (Montevideo, 1940), pp. 151; Fernández Artucio, *The Nazi Octopus in South America* (London, 1943), pp. 248; Fernández Artucio, *La Organización Secreta Nazi en Sudamérica* (México, D.F., 1943), pp. 315; United States Department of State, *Documents on German Foreign Policy, 1918–1945,* Series D (1937–1945), Vol. V, *Poland: The Balkans: Latin America: The Smaller Powers,* June, 1937— March, 1939 (Washington, D.C.: Government Printing Office, 1953), *passim;* Luis Seguí González, *Política Migratoria e Infiltración Totalitaria en América* (Montevideo, 1947), pp. 146; Carleton Beals, *The Coming Struggle for Latin America* (New York, 1940), pp. 472.

which began in 1919. The leader and principal originator of *Aprismo,* Víctor Raúl Haya de la Torre, was deported from Peru on October 9, 1923. He proposed the APRA in Mexico City on May 7, 1924.

There is a vast literature about *Aprismo.* If newspaper stories are included along with books, pamphlets, and magazine articles, the list numbers in the thousands. Many sources, therefore, describe the maximum program, which is for all of Latin America, and the minimum program, which is for Peru alone. The maximum program is composed of five points:

(1) *Action against Yankee imperialism. Apristas* believe this is Latin America's most important problem. They believe that the imperialist countries, principally the United States, control the production and prices of Latin American industry and agriculture, and therefore determine what Latin Americans will earn. In order to resist the imperialists, the *Apristas* recommend that the wealth of Latin America be nationalized and that the entire area united into a political and economic union.

(2) *The political unity of Latin America.* It follows logically that *Apristas* would oppose the inter-American system, because they believe (a) it is dominated by the United States; and (b) it is made up of governments they call dictatorships.

(3) *The nationalization of land and industry.* The *Apristas* seek nationalization of land and industry, including foreign properties, with state ownership and operation of the means of production.

(4) *The internationalization of the Panama Canal.* The *Apristas* propose joint ownership and control of the Panama Canal by all the nations of America. Is Canada to be included? Would British, Dutch, and French possessions in the Western Hemisphere qualify for a share of the ownership and control? *Aprismo* is not clear on these points.

(5) *The solidarity with all peoples and all oppressed classes.* This is an emotional statement without specific recommendations for implementation.

The minimum program, which is designed for Peru alone, is found in a document adopted at the first national congress of the *Partido Aprista Peruano* in 1931. The *Apristas* view traditional Peru as a class state employed by exploiters to dominate and op-press the masses. They, therefore, make clear that they must capture the state, but do not indicate just how this is to be done. After it is accomplished, however, the individual must be subordinated to the group. The *Apristas* seem to believe in strict majoritarianism. At least there does not seem to be any recognition of the natural rights of man which classical liberalism insists upon to act as limitations on the powers and functions of the state. Instead, *Aprista* theory guarantees the state unlimited control over the individual. Specifically, the state should guarantee life, health, moral and material well-being, education, liberty, and economic emancipation of the working classes with the consequent ending of the exploitation of man by man.

Apristas call their state the *Aprista* state, school-state, anti-imperialist state, or simply functional democracy. By inference, they would permit opposition parties to organize and compete in politics. The author has the impression from interviews with *Apristas* that they would like to enjoy an institutional arrangement like that of the Mexican Revolution which wins, by rigged elections in the Mexican case, all the elections. On the other hand, the *Apristas* specifically express approval for the basic freedoms of speech, press, and assembly. In economic policy, the *Aprista* state seeks long-range nationalization, but with immediate nationalization of mining properties, especially vanadium and gold, which are mainly controlled by United States interests. The short-range economic policy is for the government to create new enterprises and institute a planned economy.

In foreign relations, the *Apristas* urge a defense pact among the Latin American countries to protect them from imperialism. They propose a complete separation of Church and state and a state monopoly over education. Most Catholic thinkers and writers consider the *Apristas* hostile to the Church. This is certainly the author's impression. Not only do the *Apristas* oppose the Church as an institution, but they also deny that individuals have natural rights which come from God.

There is a strong insistence running through most *Aprista* literature that the power of the state should be used to remake the values of society as a whole. Again and again the literature emphasizes morality, duty, heroic action, ideals, and brotherhood. *Aprismo* prescribes forty-eight rules of conduct for youth. It must be emphasized, however, that such moral or ethical norms are rationally devised and do not have a religious origin.

The maximum and minimum programs of the *Aprista* movement can be understood, in broad outline at least. Different people might draw different implications from the programs, of course. There is, however, another part of the ideology which is less easy to comprehend. It is called the space-time theory, but its meaning and importance escape the author. It has something to do with Marx's interpretation of history and Einstein's theory of relativity. Although all *Apristas* speak glibly about Marxism, the author has never talked to an *Aprista* who indicated that he understood any more about relativity than the author, which is nothing at all.

The *Aprista* movement is headed by a single chief of charismatic qualities, although Haya claims that this is not so. Busts, effigies, pictures, special publications, and ceremonies all honor Haya de la Torre. The cult of Haya seemed similar to the author in Peru in 1955 to that of Perón in Argentina, although the government of Peru restrained some of the enthusiasm along these lines.

The movement stresses mass public meetings, processions, and torch-light parades with a maximum use of symbols: the flag (a reproduction of *Indoamérica* in gold, surrounded by a gold ring upon a background of red); the condor, with four wings on either side, sometimes containing a five-pointed star either alone or with the letters APRA arranged to form a circle within the star; the salute (which consists in bringing the left arm up over the head, palm of the hand open, facing forward); the slogan ("Solo el aprismo salvará al Peru"); and the songs, the most popular of which is the *Cancionero Aprista*.

There is no doubt that *Aprismo* was influenced strongly by Marxism. Anyone who reads the major works of the movement will find Marx and Lenin and other Marxist socialists quoted frequently. Indeed, Kantor, who has written the standard work on *Aprismo* in English, says that ". . . *Aprismo* or Marxism-*Aprismo* is a combination of Marxian socialism and the reality of America." In addition, Eudocio Ravines, who knew Haya personally and was familiar with the revolutionary movements in Latin America, because he was once a Communist himself, insists that there is evidence that Haya was much impressed with what he saw in Nazi Germany and took from Nazism various ideas for his own use. Hierarchy, the power to command, the authority of a leader, marching ranks, and the salute Ravines believes come from Nazism.

A friendly, informal, amorphous kind of union or loose confederation exists among leftist and socialist parties and movements in Latin America. Sometimes such parties or movements are described as *Aprista* or *Aprista*-like parties. When one such party acquires power in a country, it welcomes leaders of similar parties from other countries not so fortunate and may even provide these people with money and positions in the government. When several leftist parties have acquired power, they tend to consult with each other and present a united front on certain issues of public international controversy. Some of the *"Aprista* parties"* include *Acción Democrática* in Venezuela, the *Auténticos* and *Ortodoxos* in Cuba, the *Partido Social Demócrata* and later, *Partido Liberación Nacional* in Costa Rica, the *Partido Febrerista* in Paraguay, the socialist parties of Chile, Argentina, Uruguay, the "liberals" of Colombia, and perhaps even the Government party of Mexico, the P.R.I.[5]

Communism in Latin America

No study of Latin America today can ignore at least mentioning Communism, because as an ideology it has attracted the support of some of the most distinguished thinkers and men in public life in Latin America, and as a political movement it has achieved notable successes from time to time. Communism in Latin America is like Communism everywhere else in the world in both ideology and procedure. The Communists speak Portuguese in Brazil, French in Haiti, and Spanish in the other eighteen Latin American countries, but they are all part of the international conspiracy to destroy capitalism and political democracy and to establish socialism and dictatorship of the proletariat ("people's de-

[5] For *aprismo*, see: Harry Kantor, *The Ideology and Program of the Peruvian Aprista Movement* (Berkeley and Los Angeles, 1953), pp. 163; Kantor, *Sources for the Study of the Peruvian Aprista Movement* (Gainesville, 1955), pp. 60; Luis Alberto Sánchez, *Haya de la Torre y el Apra: crónica de un hombre y un partido* (Santiago de Chile, 1955), pp. 475; Eudocio Ravines, *The Yenan Way* (New York, 1951), pp. 45, 89.

mocracy"). They take their orders from Moscow, and when the "line" changes, they change, instantly. Eudocio Ravines, distinguished authority on Communism in Latin America, writing in February, 1958, points out that at the recent Moscow Conference commemorating the Fortieth Anniversary of the Revolution, which was attended by more than 170 Latin American Communist leaders, the "line" was established that each Communist Party in Latin America was to be independent of the other and to look directly to Moscow for instructions. Previously, the main parties, such as those of Brazil, Argentina, Mexico, and Chile had competed for supremacy and control over the other parties in Latin America.

Communists in Latin America are atheistic as they are elsewhere and thus are not guided by moral principles of a religious nature, such as love, charity, mercy, truth, individual worth, or integrity in dealing with their opponents, or indeed, in dealing with one another. They are guided mainly by the Marxist-Leninist-Stalinist ethic of expediency. They thus believe that all methods, including violence, are legitimate to achieve their political ends.

It is a mistake to measure the strength of the Communist movement in Latin America in quantitative terms alone. Communism is always a minority movement and does not expect to acquire power by majority vote in any particular country. Nevertheless, there are many more Communists in Latin America than in the United States, their present influence is considerable, and their potential effectiveness is great indeed.

Examination of legislation dealing with Communism in Latin America would lead to the conclusion that the movement is non-existent or at least unimportant. In most of the countries, the Communist Party has been outlawed by legislation or by executive action. In other countries, criminal laws to protect the internal and external security of the nation and legal provisions relating to immigration, labor, the armed forces, education, political organization, and public administration affect Communists adversely. There are probably fewer legal or political restraints against Communism in Uruguay at the present time than in any other Latin American country, although they operate quite freely elsewhere, as in Mexico.

The Special Subcommittee on Security Affairs of the Senate Committee on Foreign Relations found that there were about 330,000 members of Stalinist Communist Parties in Latin America in the period from 1944 to 1947, which polled an aggregate of about 1,000,000 votes in national elections. It was estimated that by 1953, the total membership had fallen to about 200,000, with maximum membership by country being as follows: Argentina, 40,000; Bolivia, 2,000; Brazil, 60,000; Chile, 40,000; Colombia, 5,000; Costa Rica, 5,000; Cuba, 30,000; Dominican Republic, negligible; Ecuador, 5,000; El Salvador, 1,000; Guatemala, 500; Haiti, negligible; Honduras, negligible; Mexico, 5,000; Nicaragua, 500; Panama, 1,000; Paraguay, 2,000; Peru, 10,000; and Uruguay, 15,000.

Communist parties in Latin America developed rapidly around the time of the first World War and the Bolshevik Revolution. In Brazil, the Socialist Party was formed in 1916. By 1918, it had fourteen branches, and in 1921 it joined the Communist International and became the Communist Party of Brazil. The Chilean and Uruguayan Socialist parties joined the Third International shortly after World War I. Luis Emilio Recabarrén founded the Communist Party in Chile. In Argentina, Victorio Codovilla, an Italian born, naturalized Argentine citizen, along with José Penelón and Orestes and Rodolfo Ghioldi, founded the Argentine Communist Party. Julio Antonio Mella founded the Cuban Communist Party in 1925, although Antonio Rodríguez Feo, Manuel Martínez, Ambrosio Broges Figueredo, and Diego Vicente Tejere formed a Socialist Party in 1899. The Latin American Communist parties are always aided by the international movement, of course. For example, Manuel Cazón, the party name for a German Communist, a member of the Comintern delegation in Latin America from 1934 to 1938, aided importantly in the organization of Communist parties in Brazil, Argentina, Chile, and Ecuador.

A special word should be said about the Peruvian Marxist, José Carlos Mariátegui (1895–1930). His intellectual influence has been very great in Latin America in the past and is still important, although his published works are not impressive for their research and far from brilliant in literary style. He founded the daily newspaper, *Nuestra Epoca*, in 1918 to reflect his socialistic ideas. During the years 1919–1923, he was in Europe, mainly in

France, Italy, and Germany, and founded the first Peruvian Communist group in Rome with César Falcón and two other Peruvians. On his return to Lima, he took over the review, *Claridad*, wrote *La Escena Contemporánea* in 1925, edited the review, *Amauta*, for several years, and in 1928 published his major work, *Siete Ensayos de Interpretación de la Realidad Peruana*. His *Defensa del Marxismo* was published in 1934 after his death. Julio Portocarrero, one of Mariátegui's disciples, was the founder of the Peruvian Communist Party.

The record of Communist successes is impressive. In the important but little-known Osman case of the 1930's, it was revealed that the international Communist movement acquired valuable defense plans of the Panama Canal. In the post-World War II period, the Popular Socialist Party (Communist) won 196,000 votes in the congressional elections of 1946 in Cuba. A small country with about 6,000,000 population, Cuba guards the Windward Passage, the sea gateway to the Panama Canal, and is of vital importance to the security of the United States. Communists won about 500,000 votes in a single election in Brazil in 1947; they elected mayors, municipal councilmen, congressmen, and senators in a number of countries; they obtained cabinet posts in at least two countries, Chile and Cuba. The author has documented in detail their part in the Cayo Confites and Luperón episodes in the Caribbean and Central America in the post-World War II period and also their infiltration and final control of the Guatemalan government in the period, 1944–1954. These materials were published by the House Un-American Activities Committee in 1956 in a study entitled, *Soviet Total War*. In his research trip to South America in 1955, the author found much evidence of Marxism in most of the universities. Furthermore, it is clear that the labor movement is infiltrated in varying degree in most of the countries. There are almost without doubt Communists at some level of government in every country. Even the Army has been infiltrated in some instances, as primary evidence indicates in the case of Brazil. Many of the *tenentes* or lieutenants joined the Communist Party in the late 1920's and early 1930's, and Communist influence has remained a source of concern down to the present time in Brazil.

The evidence is overwhelming that Latin American Communists, as part of the international Communist movement, seek the establishment of Soviet-type governments in Latin America. But how? One by one or in a group after the United States is defeated by the Soviet Union? Fracaro, in a study in which Russian sources were used, takes the position that basic Communist strategy has taught for many years that there can be no successful revolution, followed by the creation of a Communist government, in any Latin American country unless an internal revolution has first been accomplished in the United States. In other words, the United States must first be rendered helpless before serious efforts are made to create Communist dictatorships of the proletariat in Latin America.

Much evidence supports this position, but the facts also show that international Communism is ready to seize power in a particular Latin American country at any time if conditions offer a reasonable possibility of success. The Cominform saw fit to permit their Communists to control Guatemala. The violence in recent years in British Guiana probably is a part of the pattern. The article, "Draft Program of the Communist Party of Brazil," published early in 1954 in the official Cominform newspaper, *For A Lasting Peace, For A Peoples' Democracy*, advocated revolution in Brazil. Ravines states that the issue was debated in earlier Comintern planning for Latin America. Dimitrov favored Popular Fronts everywhere, whereas Manuilsky supported armed insurrections in selected countries. Luiz Carlos Prestes led a Communist revolt in Brazil in November of 1935, which was probably planned in Montevideo. It was a serious effort. The 21st, 29th, and 3rd infantry regiments revolted in the states of Natal, Pernambuco, and Rio. President Getulio Vargas first declared a state of siege on November 26, and then on December 21 proclaimed a state of siege that existed for 90 days. The Communist effort failed, and Prestes was arrested on March 5, 1936.

Some Communist leaders in Latin America seem to believe that the objectives of their movement are to establish dictatorships of the proletariat in the Latin American countries in the foreseeable future. The author baited the famous Cuban Communist leader, Dr. Juan Marinello, in an interview in Havana on August 5, 1948, by suggesting that he and his Communist colleagues were wasting their time and energy in a cause that offered no hope for success and which was, therefore, in effect exploiting them. Marinello replied passionately that the Soviet Union would win against the United States in the near future and that we would live to see the day when he and the Communist Party were governing in Cuba.

On the other hand, in the period of the Cold War, Communists everywhere in Latin America above all other things have worked with or supported any party, coalition, person, or issue that was anti-American. Stated another way, their primary objective was and is to weaken, divide, and subvert the Latin American countries so as to make international action against Communism ineffective. In a word, their aim is to defeat the United States in the Cold War.

In the period from 1946 to the present, therefore, the facts demonstrate a continuous program to destroy or at least to weaken the sources of anti-Communist economic, social, and political power. It is logical that Communists should be anti-religious and focus their ridicule on any political programs which emphasize moral principles claiming a divine origin. In addition, they have reiterated constantly such themes as imperialism, warmongering, "McCarthyism," germ warfare, racism, "Defend the Rosenbergs," "Stop the bomb testing," and the like. Typical is an editorial in an Uruguayan newspaper which contended that the atom was not safe in the hands of the *yanqui* imperialists but was safe in the hands of Soviet socialism.

Foreign capital and United States companies have been the most frequently attacked by Communists in Latin America and perhaps are the most vulnerable, because Latin American lower classes are everywhere insisting on higher material standards of living immediately. Inasmuch as their demands have not been met as rapidly as they would like, and not at all in many cases, politicians have found the foreign company a convenient scapegoat. Moreover, the Soviet Union has no permanent investments in Latin America, whereas the United States has over $8,000,000,-000 invested in private companies.

The Communists in Latin America are largely an urban group and their leadership almost invariably comes from the upper and middle classes. Communist leaders, therefore, are likely to be educated and cultured people. Marxists have been influential in the student movement since its beginnings around World War I, as Gabriel del Mazo and others have made clear. In recent years, Communists have organized in the primary and secondary school fields. Children's and women's groups are one of their favorite targets. Communists have had conspicuous success in the trade union movement.

The Communists are well financed and very mobile: the United States Information Agency has reported that over 1,000 Latin Americans traveled to the Soviet Union for training or to attend Red Front meetings in Europe in 1953 as compared to 500 in 1952 and about 100 in 1950. They shift their main base of operations from one country to another depending on local conditions; it was Mexico in the 1930's and Cuba in the 1940's. Although many Communists left Venezuela, Cuba, and Guatemala for Mexico since 1954, Montevideo and Rio are perhaps more important bases for planning at the present time. Official testimony of the Immigration and Naturalization Service was presented to the House Agriculture Committee early in 1954 to the effect that about 100 Communists were entering the United States illegally every day.

Not only do the Communists endeavor to identify themselves with local patriotic groups, but frequently their principle of expediency leads them to support right-wing, nationalistic movements, which they might otherwise brand as Fascist. One approach they sometimes use is for one wing of the Party to support the dictator and thus win freedom of action, while the other wing of the Party blames United States imperialism for the dictatorship. For example, General Perón took Rodolfo Puiggros and González Alberdi, Communist "strong men," into his government in Argentina as advisers, at the same time that he was persecuting other Communists.

The Communists are quick to exploit crises, as was demonstrated in their participation in the riots in Bogotá in April, 1948. Many Communists from the United States, Europe, and various Latin American countries entered Bogotá in advance of the *Bogotazo*. Documents, published in Colombian newspapers, the authenticity for which the author cannot, of course, vouch, indicated that the Communists had plans for disrupting the Inter-American Conference. Arms and ammunition came into Colombia in large quantities, and the serial numbers on the material indicated that it had come from Venezuelan armories. It is assuredly true that President Rómulo Betancourt had some Communists on the payroll of his *Acción Democrática* government. Fluharty seems to believe that the Venezuelan government knew its arms were being sent outside the country in what has come to be known as the "Barranquilla Plan" for political violence, but defenders of *Acción Democrática* deny that this is true. The author raised the question of Communist participation in the *Bogotazo* of 1948 with many Latin Americans in South America in 1955, including some who were present at the time in a diplomatic capacity. Their evaluations depended on their own political positions, the "liberals" de-emphasizing the role of the Communists and the "rightists" taking the position that it was clearly a Communist-planned episode. In any event, it was violence of serious proportions, even for Latin America. Some parts of Bogotá were still in ruins in 1955.[6]

Concluding Remarks

Lord Acton contended that, "Liberty alone demands for its realization the limitation of public authority, for liberty alone is the only object which benefits all alike, and provokes no sincere opposition." Democracy is undoubtedly the most perfect political method of expressing liberty, if to political democracy one adds the natural rights of man and the concept of limited government as restraints on the powers of majorities. But theoretical conceptions are of little value unless they can be applied and used in society.

Latin Americans accepted the logic of individualism, democracy,

---

[6] On Communism in Latin America, *see:* Eudocio Ravines, "Communism in Latin America," *U.S.A.* (February 14, 1958), pp. 1–2; Robert J. Alexander, *Communism in Latin America* (New Brunswick, New Jersey, 1957), pp. 449; Vernon L. Fluharty, *Dance of the Millions* (Pittsburgh, 1957), pp. 96–98, 101–104; Alberto H. Niño, *Antecedentes y Secretos del 9 de Abril* (Bogotá, 1950?), pp. 159; Stokes, "For a 'Lasting Peace' in Latin America," Committee on Un-American Activities, United States House of Representatives, *Soviet Total War* (Vol. II, September, 1956), pp. 885–898; Eudocio Ravines, "Communism and Countercommunism in Latin America," *ibid.*, pp. 873–880; Serafino Romualdi, "The Appeal to Nationalism," *ibid.*, pp. 881–884; Victor Alba, *Historia del Communismo en América Latina* (México, D.F., 1954), pp. 150; William Z. Foster, *Outline Political History of the Americas* (New York, 1951), pp. 668. The author has collected a bibliography of Marxist and Communist literature, which is quite extensive. The above sources, however, are adequate for the section in this paper.

and classical liberalism in the nineteenth century, but they did not, for the most part, revise their social and economic institutions so as to permit the principles to operate. The author is aware, as all Latin Americanists are, of the magnificent statements of acceptance and defense of these principles by many thinkers and men in public life of the highest repute and greatest achievement— men like Benjamín Vicuña Mackenna of Chile, Nicolás de Pierola of Peru, Enrique José Varona of Cuba, Rui Barbosa of Brazil, and many others. Distinguished thinkers of the present day, such as Galo Plaza of Ecuador, Félix Palavicini and Gustavo Velasco of Mexico, Alberto Lleras Camargo of Colombia, and others speak and write in a somewhat similar way. The lawyers continue to produce volumes on constitutions and laws, which, though praising classical liberalism, unfortunately are more often than not, purely theoretical, even fictional, portrayals of the political life of many Latin American countries.

In the late nineteenth and early twentieth centuries, important numbers of thinkers began to perceive that liberty, and the political system best adapted to create and protect this value, was intimately a part of the psychological-sociological value structure of people, which in turn was produced by the force of tradition and by the experience of living in social and economic institutions. Some despaired on making this discovery, because the basic institutions of Hispanic culture were, and are, incontrovertibly more authoritarian than democratic. Others turned the truth in a positive direction: (1) by concluding, in part accurately and in part erroneously, that the principles of individualism, democracy, and liberalism had produced values more evil than good in United States culture, where such principles had their greatest practical application; and (2) by devising and advocating new political theories which reflected Hispanic values and which also provided the bases for realizing popular ideals and aspirations.

Such political theories or ideologies tend to restrict the initiative and participation of the individual in economic life, expand the functions of government, and centralize political authority, sometimes in an institution such as a party, or a combination of institutions, such as party, army, and labor unions, and sometimes, less frequently, in a single individual. Most popular, successful political movements—whether of the "right" or the "left"

—are openly and obviously deviations from individualism, democracy, and liberalism. Historical tradition, social mores or customs, the influence of family or church, accidental or emotional factors, and the effect of personalities all explain, in varying circumstances, why some individuals are "leftists" and others are "rightists." In the area of ideas, however, the insistence on moral and spiritual ends which have a religious origin and which, therefore, are based primarily on faith and only secondarily on reason, is what separates most sharply and most positively the ideologies of "left" and "right" in modern-day Latin American political theory. Programatically, both "left" and "right" are similar, as one can easily discover by making comparisons, such as a case study of the "leftist" government of Arbenz of Guatemala and the "rightist" government of Perón of Argentina. Furthermore, although the author stressed the fact that "right wing" ideologies identify themselves with the "equidistant" or Third Force philosophy, some "left wing" groups, such as the supporters of non-corporative and non-Church sponsored cooperatives, also use the term to describe their ideological position.

The heart of all of the great political ideologies in Latin America of recent decades, of course, is the insistence that government can better provide, through nationalization of the means of production or by direction, regulation, control, and planning of the economy, material standards of living significantly higher than those to which the masses of the people have been accustomed in the past. Those who agree with Lord Acton that when ". . . a single definite object is made the supreme end of the state," the state becomes "inevitably absolute," must conclude that the possibilities for individual liberty and freedom, whether expressed in economic or political areas, become less in Latin America. The author has discussed the possible consequences to individual liberty of various of the political ideologies current in Latin America with many Latin American thinkers. Their answer sometimes is that the price of restriction of individualism and liberty is not too high if economic standards can be raised. Others take the position that once the state has accomplished its objectives in the economic field, it can then reduce its functions and restore a greater degree of liberty and freedom for each individual to develop and express his talents and abilities as he sees fit. This optimistic prediction of the willingness of men to relinquish power once they have attained it is one which many individuals cannot share.[7]

In any event, it is the author's firm impression that "leftist" and "rightist" political ideologies will continue to enjoy in the foreseeable future greater popularity and success, in the sense of acquiring political power in most of the Latin American countries, than political ideologies which emphasize in any basic or fundamental way the principles of individualism, democracy, and liberalism.*

[7] For concluding remarks, *see:* John Emerich Edward Dalberg-Acton, *Essays on Freedom and Power* (Glencoe, Illinois, 1948), pp. 36, 40, 130, 163, 184; Augusto Iglesias Mascareno, *Benjamín Vicuña Mackenna: aprendiz de revolucionario* (Santiago de Chile, 1946), pp. 134; Alfonso Bulnes, *Errázuriz Zañartu: su vida* (Santiago de Chile, 1950), pp. 585; Domingo Amunátegui Solar, *La Democracia en Chile* (Santiago de Chile, 1946), pp. 465; Ricardo Donoso, *Las Ideas Políticas en Chile* (México, D.F., 1946), pp. 526; Jorge Dulanto Pinillos, *Nicolás de Piérola* (Lima, 1947), pp. 513; Alberto Ulloa y Sotomayor, *Don Nicolás de Pierola* (Lima, 1950), pp. 441; Enrique José Varona, *De la Colonia a la República* (La Habana, 1919), pp. 272, especially pp. 241–256; R. Nogueira, *Historia de Ruy Barbosa* (Salvador, Bahia, 1954), pp. 222; Galo Plaza Lasso, *Problems of Democracy in Latin America* (Chapel Hill, 1955), pp. 88; Félix F. Palavicini, *Política Constitucional* (México, D.F., 1950), *passim;* Gustavo R. Velasco, *El Mayor Peligro, el Estado* (México, D.F., 1950), pp. 17; Alberto Lleras C., *Un Año de Gobierno, 1945–1946* (Bogotá, 1946), pp. 398; Abelardo Londoño Marín, *Flavio Correa Restrepo: soldado sin coraza* (Medellín, 1957), pp. 412; José P. Barreiro, *El Espíritu de Mayo y el Revisionismo Histórico* (Buenos Aires, 1951), pp. 311; T. Alvarez, *Ciencia Política* (Santiago de Chile, 1953), pp. 355; J. Posada, *La Revolución Democrática* (Bogotá, 1955), pp. 156; B.A.M. Bambill, *Hacia la Realización de una Democracia Responsable* (Buenos Aires, 1953), pp. 343; A. L. Barbagelata, *Teoría del Estado* (Montevideo, 1953), pp. 228; F. Porrua Pérez, *Teoría del Estado* (México, D.F., 1954), pp. 412; Eugenio J. Gómez, *Problemas Colombianos* (Bogotá, 1947), pp. 331; Cecil Jane, *Libertad y Despotismo en América Hispana* (Buenos Aires, 1944), *passim.*

* The lack of agreement between this conclusion and that of Professor Hermens in the previous paper highlights, of course, one of the most hotly debated points in the field of contemporary Latin American politics. [Editor's Note]

CHAPTER VII

[PEDRO A. CEBOLLERO *]

Education for Freedom and Reform

THE FRAMEWORK

The approximately three hundred years of Iberian rule over American colonies constituted a school of absolutism and centralization. During this lengthy period, the colonists were deprived of most significant opportunities to practice political initiative. Viceroys, archbishops, captain-generals, *intendentes,* even upon occasion town mayors, were sent from Spain, or appointed by the crown from among resident Spaniards. The Latin American— flowering from the crossbreeding of Spaniard and Indian—was relegated to a position of subservience in his own land. The Indian fared worse. His lot was that of the medieval serf attached to the soil.

The political monopoly enjoyed by the Spaniards was matched by a similar monopoly over colonial trade. It was against the law for the colonies to trade with any nation other than Spain. Inter-

* Born in Puerto Rico, Pedro A. Cebollero received his higher education in the United States, earning his M.A. at the University of Chicago, and his Doctorate in Education at Columbia University. He has served as Assistant Commissioner of Education and Permanent Secretary of the Higher Council of Education in Puerto Rico. In addition, he has held the positions of Professor of Education and Dean of the School of Education at the University of Puerto Rico, Technical Assistant to the Ministries of Education of Venezuela and Panama, and Chief of Secondary Education, Pan American Union. He has been a visiting professor at the University of Texas, and at present is Professor of Education, UNESCO Center for the Training of Educational Specialist, Pedagogical Institute, University of Chile.

colonial trade was so beset with restrictions that, rather than running the gauntlet of customs and *alcabalas,* it was preferable to make shipments from one colony to another via Spain.

Naturally enough, the political inexperience to which the colonial status subjected the Latin Americans did not disappear when the colonies secured their independence. In fact, coming as it did before the Latin American countries were politically mature, independence gave rise to a long period of instability or, what was worse, to stability through dictatorships. The extent to which Latin America was unprepared politically for independence is revealed by the fact that the early leaders seldom had independence in mind when they started the revolutionary movements. To the surprise of the revolutionists themselves, Spain gave up the fight, more because of trouble at home than because of decisive revolutionary action in America. In many Latin American countries, independence was won by a group of revolutionists against the wishes of a majority of the population.

The ensuing period of instability or dictatorship also worked to prevent political education. Some countries, notably Chile, were fortunate in organizing a stable political situation as early as the middle of the nineteenth century, but the majority have suffered until recently from the evils that stem from political immaturity.

The ill feeling between Spaniards and Latin Americans to which the social and political character of the colonial period gave rise was carried to a high pitch by the wars of independence. This produced a revulsion against Spanish culture and prevented the development of an autochthonous one in Latin America, a culture which should have been based naturally on the cultural pattern of the mother country. The result was that, culturally, Latin America turned its eyes to France. The imitation of French models was apparent in literature, philosophy, business methods, recreation, manners, and, of course, education. The attempt to imitate a model rather than to work out a national culture was bound to fail. However, the failure has not been recognized by Latin Americans until quite recently. To the three hundred years of Spanish colonial life, Latin America added another century during which she was the cultural colony of France. But differences in language, civilization and national temperament hindered the adequate transplantation of an unadulterated French culture, and the result was a ludicrous parody.

The implications of these historical facts for the development of Latin America are too obvious to need further elaboration. Let us take a look now at a second set of considerations, namely, the one that springs from the social pattern of the population.

In contrast with the United States, Latin America had to deal with an Indian population which, in some countries, represents even today fifty per cent or more of the total population. The North American solution of organizing reservations did not appeal to the Latin Americans and, besides, proved wholly impracticable except in certain areas of New Granada. Hence, Latin America had to embark on an elaborate program of acculturation of the Indian. This process was accelerated by the practice of intermarriage. The crossing of the Spanish whites and the Indians gave rise to the mestizo who makes up, in the majority of the Latin American countries, a large proportion of the population. When Spaniards and Negroes intermarried, as happened in Brazil and the West Indies, the mulatto appeared, while the *zambo* was the cross between Indian and Negro.

The pure Spaniards eventually broke up into two groups, culturally if not racially different: the Spaniards born in Spain and the Spaniards born in America of Spanish parentage, who became known as *criollos*. In more modern times, other Europeans —notably Germans and Italians—have emigrated to Latin America. And more recently still, Orientals—Japanese, Chinese and Hindus—have swelled the Latin American melting pot.

At present, the coexistence of a Western and of an indigenous culture is one of the main barriers for national integration. The mass of Indian population is poor, underdeveloped and illiterate. The fact that many Indian groups do not speak the national language makes the task of acculturation doubly difficult. Herein lies one of the most formidable obstacles to universal education in many countries south of the Rio Grande.

The philosophical tradition of Latin America finds its roots in the Counter Reformation as personified by Ignatius de Loyola and in the libertarian ideas of the French Revolution. The spirit of Loyola—brought to Latin America by the Jesuits—was aristocratic and humanistic in its perspective. Its original purpose—the development of strong leadership among powerful groups that would stem the wave of cultural democracy inspired by the Protestant doctrines—produced an emphasis on the humanistic education of a few rather than on universal education. The result was a cultural minority, an aristocracy of letters. It was essentially a humanistic spirit, and it found a favorable climate in Latin America, where paganism, with its strong sense of hierarchy, was not extinct. In contrast, democracy is the product of early Christianity, rather than classicism and the closed society of the Middle Ages. It was strengthened by the value placed by the Reformation upon the individual and on individual self-culture. Where the tradition of classicism and the medieval closed society continue to exist in Latin America, dictatorships find a suitable hotbed. In fact, the efforts of Latin America to develop democratically and to adopt the ideal of universal education run counter to her philosophical traditions.

The lack of an autochthonous philosophy that will foment the effort to educate every child is evident. Where is Latin America going to get the stimulus for such a task? Can she find it in the democratic spirit? No, the democratic spirit is the consequence rather than the cause of universal education. How then is Latin America going to break the vicious circle? In our opinion the answer is to be found in the quest for economic rehabilitation. This natural aspiration will take the place of Christianity in providing the initial stimulus for universal education, which in turn will lead to democracy.

The ideals of the French Revolution are another ingredient in the political and cultural philosophy of Latin America. These ideals, along with French tastes in music, literature, manners and morals, were adopted as a part of the revulsion towards everything Spanish that was inspired by the wars of independence. Liberty, Equality and Fraternity were words to conjure with. They appeared in the national proclamations and were embodied in the constitutions and in the laws. In actual practice, however, social classes persisted, the chosen few continued to rule and the law of the jungle held sway. The noble sentiments that inspired the French revolution were—and in some places still are—beautiful shields that hide the ruthless rule of dictatorship.

Two additional elements contribute to the framework within

which educational development takes place. These two elements —modern influences on life and education, and social, economic and technological progress—are mutually supplementary.

European influence dates back to the colonial period. Reference has already been made to the factors that brought about the French influence in the Latin American countries. In addition, German influence was particularly evident in the organization of educational systems. Chile, for example, while taking the French educational organization as a model, especially in secondary education, entrusted the pedagogical reform to German scholars brought from Europe at various epochs. German influence was also felt in commerce and industry.

Emigration has had a large role in the development of Latin American life. Of course, Spanish emigration has provided the backbone of the population. After independence, emigrants from Germany, Italy, Czechoslovakia, and more recently, from China and Japan have arrived in large numbers. The influence of emigration has been especially felt in Argentina, Chile, Brazil, Uruguay and Peru. In very recent years, Venezuela too has received large numbers of emigrants from various European countries.

North American influence has been the result of three factors: economic penetration; Point Four programs; and the influence exerted through Latin Americans educated in the United States. The Point Four programs have assisted educational development in many countries. Likewise, many Latin Americans, educated in the United States, have brought back to their countries a wealth of new ideas and are rapidly becoming the leaders in education, medicine, engineering, and other phases of knowledge and endeavor.

Even if there are striking similarities in the nature of the social, economic and technological development of the Latin American countries, the rate at which changes become manifest varies considerably from country to country. There is evidence, however, that the concern for such development grows from year to year. In a speech delivered just before he took office, President Frondizi of Argentina explained that his main preoccupation was about economic prosperity, not because material values should take precedence over others, but because the development that increases the wealth of the country is indispensable for raising the standard of living of large groups of the population. He stressed the role of technical knowledge as well as the importance of science and of scientific research. "The social and economic development of a country," stated Dr. Frondizi, "is dependent in identical proportions on capital and know-how." In our times, he went on to say, technology and science have the "same influence on economic development that philosophy had on the political development of past centuries." Similar statements have been made recently by President Kubitschek of Brazil and other Latin American leaders.

Social and economic growth has been a factor in determining the stability of political regimes and in making it possible to secure permanent reforms in the field of education. However, there are still many countries that are a prey to frequent financial, economic or political crises that impede social evolution and, as a consequence, evolution and reform of their educational systems.

In contrast with the United States and with most European countries where the economic system is characterized by a robust industrial development, the economic systems of Latin America are predominantly agrarian, with an incipient tendency towards industrialization. As a consequence, the standards of living are still low, in spite of the progress made in the last decade, especially in the buying power of the working classes.

From the social point of view, a large mobility of the population is in evidence. Traditionally, there were only two social classes in Latin America: the landed aristocracy, and the destitute class, a good example of which is the Chilean *roto*. These two classes were static: there was no chance for persons of the lower class to rise above their level. Moreover, the groups of population were either rural or urban and remained so from year to year with very insignificant changes.

More and more, population movements, both vertical and horizontal, are now noticeable. On the one hand, groups of technicians, professionals, public and private employees, craftsmen, small merchants and manufacturers are rising to a higher social level. They constitute a middle class, which in the near future will probably overtake both the high and the low classes in number and in capacity for progress. There are numerous signs that this rising middle class will play an increasingly important role in the organization and leadership of their countries. It is interesting to note, in this connection, that in the majority of the countries of Latin America, the secondary school enrollment comes from this middle class in a proportion that increases from year to year. The probable effect of this phenomenon on freedom and reform in education is evident.

On the other hand, there is an increasing movement of population from the rural to the urban centers, a movement which we have characterized as horizontal, in contrast with the movement that gives rise to the middle class. Most of the Latin American cities have grown very rapidly during the last ten years, in part due to this migration from the rural areas. A case in point is the city of São Paulo, in Brazil, which has grown, in the last ten years, more than any other city in the world. This rapid growth aggravates the problem of housing, gives rise to slums and places a large burden on the public services of the cities, especially education.

Definite progress is being made in the promotion of a policy of interdependence and peaceful cooperation among the nations that make up the southern half of the Western Hemisphere. This is a clear break with the historic isolation of one country from another. The idea is gaining ground that the cultural integration of Latin America should be one of the important steps in strengthening continental solidarity.

THE MOVEMENT FOR REFORM IN EDUCATION

Among the factors to be reckoned with in an account of educational reform, the political organization of the country concerned is paramount. During the years just preceding and following World War II, a constellation of social and economic forces favored the organization of strong government in most of the Latin American countries. With only a handful of exceptions, the governments south of the Rio Grande could be classified as either dictatorships or semi-dictatorships. Some of these governments were progressive and compiled a good record of impressive attempts to pull out of the economic doldrums the countries over which they ruled. Others were plainly conservative and personal, with no interest outside of the self-preservation and enrichment of the leaders.

The last ten years, however, have seen a spectacular reversal. Most of the dictatorial governments have been swept away by popular movements, and have been supplanted by governments that either have been chosen in free elections or that have committed themselves to hold general elections as soon as possible. These new governments have attacked the problem of larger production and better distribution of wealth, and are actively studying the best means of exploiting the natural resources of their countries. At the same time, efforts are under way aimed at bringing about far-reaching reforms in popular education. The political pronouncements made by the chief executives show a growing concern with the problem of extending education to all children of school age and with the parallel problem of reducing and eventually wiping out illiteracy.

Several countries, among which Uruguay and Chile are notable examples, have reached a high degree of political maturity. These countries have reaffirmed the gains made shortly after independence, when the constitutions of France and the United States became the models for most of their supreme laws, when slavery was abolished peacefully and literacy was made a condition for the exercise of suffrage, and when equality before the law was decreed and all social privileges and titles of nobility were outlawed. Thus, some Latin American governments are reaching a stage in their political growth in which, to use Mead's words, "they have institutionalized the process of revolution."

It is significant that the quest for democracy is universal in Latin America. The word is surrounded by such a halo of respectability that even heads of state who in one form or another practice dictatorship, claim to be acting in the interest of democracy. There is, of course, a wide range in the extent to which true democracy has been achieved. In the tradition of all the social and political achievements of Latin America, democracy appeared in the constitutions long before it permeated the political and social organization of the countries. Historically, nations of Spanish origin have held the abstract idea of liberty on a higher plane of respect than the idea of democracy. But Latin American countries are rapidly realizing that these two ideals are inseparable and that either one is essential to the full realization of the other.

Within the frame set up by the historical, geographical, social,

economic and political considerations discussed in the first section
of this paper, education has evolved in Latin America from the
rudimentary school for the teaching of religion and the three R's
of the early colonial period, to the ideal—if not the reality—of a
school geared to the democratic and technological society of our
times.

During the colonial period there was no effort to make education either compulsory or universal. Sixteenth-century Europe
had not yet adopted such an ideal for itself, and hence could not
have been expected to realize it in America. In the larger centers
of population, a few separate schools for girls and boys were
organized. In the villages, the only education that existed was
connected with the churches and was in the hands of the priests.
It consisted mainly of religion and in a few notable instances,
European arts and trades. In this connection it is worth noting
the work of Bishop Vasco de Quiroga in Mexico and that of the
Jesuit missions in Paraguay and northeast Argentina.

Probably inspired by the *Utopia* of Thomas More, Bishop
Vasco de Quiroga organized the teaching of arts and trades in the
Mexican province of Michoacán. Each village had its own distinctive trade and it is interesting to note that the trades taught the
early settlers of these villages in the sixteenth century still flourish
in many of them and are being given new life through a school
for the promotion of adult education established in this area by
UNESCO a few years ago.

The Jesuit missions established a number of settlements for
Guaraní Indians in Paraguay and Argentina, where a practical
education for a better life, more efficient work, art-crafts and
recreation was organized. This experiment lasted from the latter
years of the sixteenth century until 1767, when the Jesuits were
expelled by the government of Spain from all its colonies in the
New World.

In harmony with the ideals of the Counter Reformation, many
secondary schools were established in colonial Latin America,
principally by religious congregations. When these secondary
schools grew, they tended to organize into universities. Thus in
1538, less than half a century after the discovery of America, the
secondary school established by the Dominican friars in Santo
Domingo was authorized to become the University of Saint

Thomas Aquinas. A second university was established in 1540 which disappeared shortly afterwards. In 1551 the Spanish government decided to establish universities in the capital cities of the two viceroyalties then existing in America: one in Mexico City and the other in Lima, Peru. These two universities were inaugurated in 1553. The University of San Marcos in Lima is considered the oldest in America, having functioned without interruption since it was founded, while the University of Santo Domingo and the University of Mexico have closed their doors for long periods. These and several other universities which came later were organized on the model of the medieval universities, with four faculties: arts, law, theology and medicine. The Universities of Salamanca and Alcalá in Spain served as models. With the exception of medicine, all disciplines were taught in Latin. In colonies with a large Indian population, such as Mexico, Guatemala and Peru, the universities started courses in the native dialects, especially for students of theology, who had to go out among the Indians as teachers or preachers. During the colonial period, a total of twenty-six universities were founded throughout Latin America.

Besides the universities proper, there were numerous theological seminaries, which in many cases were ahead of the universities in the teaching of modern philosophical doctrines. The last part of the colonial period saw the rise of different types of educational institutions, such as the School of Mining, founded in Mexico in 1792, the Academies of *Beaux-Arts* in Mexico (1783) and Guatemala (1797) and several other cities. In the eighteenth century the first public libraries were organized, and likewise, the Botanical Garden of Mexico, the Museum of Natural History and Botanical Garden of Guatemala, the Astronomical Observatory in Bogotá, and the Nautical School of Buenos Aires. Humboldt, writing in the beginning of the nineteenth century says: ". . . no city in the New World, the United States included, could boast scientific institutions as great and thorough as those of the Mexican capital," at that time the largest city in the Western Hemisphere (112,000 inhabitants as against 96,000 for New York). According to the same author, there was no botanical library in Europe which could compare with the one in Bogotá.

After the colonies became independent, the governments faced three fundamental problems: national economy, the relations between the Church and the state, and the problem of organizing public instruction. With the separation of Church and state in many countries, and with anticlerical programs in most of the others, primary and secondary education received a severe blow. In many of the countries this meant that the generous subsidies paid the Church were either reduced or eliminated altogether. The reduction of the educational services performed by the Church was the immediate effect.

Then began the fight to extend education and at the same time provide for the reconstruction of the countries from the effects of the wars of independence. In an effort to make provision for larger enrollments, first attention was given to reform of the methods of instruction. In the early years of this period, the principal innovation was the introduction of the Lancasterian method of monitorial instruction. This device seemed to provide a remedy for the urgent need to accommodate a larger number of pupils in the schools and for the dearth of trained teachers. Joseph Lancaster in person, invited by Simón Bolívar, was in Caracas in 1824, but before Lancaster came to America the method had been introduced by the Scotchman James Thompson who resided in Argentina, Chile, Peru and Colombia between 1818 and 1825.

The first normal school in Latin America was founded in Chile in 1842, by the Argentine teacher and statesman, Sarmiento. This was antedated by courses for the training of teachers in Colombia, Peru, Uruguay and Bolivia, which, however, were not properly normal schools. The efforts to extend public education were slowed down by the lack of funds. However, President Santander in Colombia was successful in doubling the number of schools in the country, from 500 to over 1000, in the decade from 1827 to 1837.

With the advent of independence, the universities established in the colonial period were very often in opposition to the movements for reform, and it was necessary to reorganize them. In general, an effort was made to wrest them from the control of religious bodies and to convert them into lay institutions. Most of the faculties of theology were discontinued and the teaching of this subject was entrusted to seminaries. Several new universities were founded: Buenos Aires (1821); Montevideo (1833); Chile (1842); Medellín and Cauca in Colombia (1843), and Costa Rica (1843). Separate schools of law and medicine were established in a number of cities.

The period from 1860 to 1890 was one of organization and stability. During these years the main concern was the increase in the number of schools to take care of the growing desire for an education which was the corollary of the rise of a middle class. Argentina, Chile and Colombia took the lead in this connection. The curriculum of the secondary schools slowly freed itself from the colonial tradition. While the humanities still held sway, there was a growing interest in the sciences, both social and natural. This change was stimulated by the philosophical doctrines of Comte, John Stuart Mill and Herbert Spencer. The number of schools increased appreciably, and the system of organization through laws and regulations advanced significantly. In fact, the theory of education and the laws relating to its organization have been since this period far ahead of the practice.

During the years of the twentieth century which preceded World War II progress in the extension of educational opportunities for all the children of school age had its ups and downs, in harmony with the phases of economic development. In theory, public education was considered a very important responsibility and it was given lip service in official pronouncements; in practice, the educational budgets were in the majority of countries lower than those of the other public services.

However, the number of both primary and secondary schools grew; teacher training institutions developed; and a great deal of attention was given to innovations in educational doctrine and method. Experimentation and research in education were started in Chile, Argentina, Mexico, Cuba; and a number of educational reviews were published. New universities were founded, the most important of which was the University of La Plata, in 1902, and the Universities of Mexico and Santo Domingo were reorganized. The movement for university reform, begun in Argentina in 1918, influenced other countries, especially Peru, where a similar movement was initiated which secured the participation of the students in the government of the university.

An impartial view of education up to the period of World

War II shows that, notwithstanding sporadic progress in a few directions, despite worthy movements for experimentation and the organization of some excellent schools in the larger cities, the accomplishments were far from satisfactory. For about twenty million children of school age and for over seventy million illiterate adults, no schooling of any sort was available. Besides this evident inadequacy in number, schools at all levels were woefully inefficient in organization, programs and methods of instruction.

In general, the existing schools limited themselves to the following tasks:

1) The teaching of reading, writing and the rudiments of arithmetic and very general and elementary notions of history, geography, grammar and science to those children between the ages of seven and twelve, who could come to school. The enrollment, as has been indicated above, was only a fraction of the school population. Two other factors combined to render the work of the primary school next to worthless: irregular attendance due to illness and distance of the homes from the school; and the need of numerous parents to secure any sort of gainful occupation for their children at the earliest possible age. The school generally did not concern itself with the situation of the children at home, and much less with the problems that were faced (or ignored) by the community as a whole. School lessons went on placidly in absolute ignorance or disregard of the fact that the children came to school without breakfast or lunch, that they were dirty and unkempt, that roads to the schools were impassable during many months of the year due to floods, that the parents emigrated frequently in search of better working conditions, and that home life was marred by intemperance and other vices on the part of one or both parents.

The pressure of school population forced upon educational administrators the need to organize the schools in two and sometimes three shifts, with consequent reduction in the time that the teacher could give to the children. A full year of school attendance thus became in fact one half or one third of a year.

2) Teaching a few trades and other types of manual work to a small number of pupils from the lower rungs of the economic ladder, between the ages of twelve and eighteen, who were

financially unable to continue their education in the humanistic secondary schools. This type of vocational or semi-vocational work was of little help even to those who took it. In the first place, the quality of teaching was very poor, the schools inadequately equipped and the time given to it ludicrously short. Old war veterans or superannuated widows were given jobs in these schools, more as a means of helping them financially than with the expectation that they would do much in the way of training their pupils. In the second place, the program of instruction had no relation to the economic demands of society: the pupils were taught anything that would keep them busy—sewing, making paper flowers and rag dolls, painting match sticks and dozens of other such insignificant tasks. If the useless items made in these so-called arts and trades schools could be put together they would probably make a pile as high as the Andes mountains.

3) Teaching secondary school courses to young men and women from well-to-do families, in preparation for university work in such careers as law, medicine, engineering and secondary school teaching. The program of these secondary schools had no reference to the lives of these students, for it was almost entirely made up of humanistic studies: languages, including Latin and Greek, history, literature, philosophy, logic and psychology, and a minimum of science and mathematics. For the student who found himself or herself unable to continue professional studies in the university after the end of the secondary school period, the education received was almost worthless. In many ways it was worse than nothing because it embittered the students and made them feel lost in a society that was radically different from the sheltered life of their secondary school years.

4) Training teachers for the elementary schools. The normal schools required only the completion of the six years of primary education; the length of the studies varied from three to five years; the enrollment consisted mainly of young women; the instructors were poorly trained; and the methods and materials of instruction were rudimentary.

5) University instruction in courses that lasted from five to seven years, depending on the type of studies followed, for such professions as law, medicine, engineering, architecture, pharmacy, and agronomy. Many universities also prepared young men for

the doctorate in philosophy and letters. No effort was made to prepare technicians, administrators or experts in such fields as economics and sociology. Very little if any attention was given to pure research.

Since the end of World War II education has enjoyed a period of extension and reorganization which has contributed greatly to the climate for freedom and reform in other aspects of public life. Education has advanced visibly in its four fronts: primary, secondary, vocational and higher. What is more important, it has recognized as its primary obligation to take cognizance of the social and economic problems of society and to lend its efforts to their solution. Most of the Latin American governments have realized that public education is, after all, a capitalistic enterprise and that sufficient funds are indispensable. School budgets have increased appreciably, even if they are still below that of national defense, a service of diminishing importance in the present Latin American situation.

International bodies, such as the Organization of American States and UNESCO have come to the rescue. Through direct efforts sometimes, and through the sponsoring of educational seminars and conferences in many instances, both of these organizations have joined forces with the Latin American governments and have assisted teachers' organizations in setting up long-range plans that cover the fields of illiteracy and adult education, primary and secondary education, vocational education and teacher training.

INTERNATIONAL EDUCATIONAL SEMINARS

Five international seminars have been held under the auspices of the Organization of American States and with the cooperation of UNESCO and the Latin American governments. The first Seminar of this series, held in Caracas, Venezuela in 1948, was devoted to a consideration of the general problems of rural education in Latin America. The main topic around which the discussions revolved was the concept of basic or fundamental education, which UNESCO was recommending as an answer to the problem of educating backward communities in underdeveloped areas of the world. In connection with fundamental education, the Seminar discussed the issues in teacher training, vocational education and education for peace and international understanding. This meeting was attended by delegates from most of the American countries, including the United States, and by representatives of the Organization of American States and UNESCO. The proceedings, in five volumes, have been distributed widely in Latin America.

The Seminar held in Brazil in 1949 analyzed the problems of illiteracy and adult education. Its organization followed the pattern of the Caracas Seminar and it was likewise attended by educators from all the American countries, as well as experts from UNESCO and the OAS. Shortly after the close of this meeting, the Pan American Union published a volume containing the studies presented at the Seminar, under the title *The Education of the American Adult,* which is the best available manual on the problems of dealing with the fight against illiteracy and with the programs of adult education in Latin America.

In compliance with recommendations made at the Brazil Seminar, two specialized institutes dealing with phases of adult education were founded shortly afterwards: the CREFAL, in the Mexican province of Michoacán, where workers in rural adult education are trained; and the Fundamental Education Press, at Washington, which has undertaken the publication of simple reading matter, in attractively illustrated booklets, dealing with agriculture, health, community organization, historical and geographical topics and other matters of interest to potential readers in the rural communities of Latin America.

In 1950 the third inter-American Seminar met in Montevideo, Uruguay. The central theme of this meeting was primary education. The Seminar faced the facts that even with an enrollment of approximately thirteen million children in the 350,000 primary schools in Latin America, there remained nineteen million children of school age for whom no educational facilities existed. The Montevideo Seminar was attended by eighty-five delegates from twenty American nations. Besides, there were observers from Great Britain, France, Italy, Switzerland and Syria, and experts from the Organization of American States, UNESCO and the Office of International Education. The program of work consisted of five main points: the organization of systems and primary school services; courses of study, curricula and methods; the problem of universal, free and compulsory primary education; teacher training; school textbooks and teaching materials. In other words, the task that the Seminar set itself was to find means to improve the quality of instruction for the thirteen million children now in school and to provide similar opportunities for the nineteen million who have no schooling whatsoever.

The problems of vocational education were considered in the Seminar held in 1952 at the University of Maryland in Baltimore. This Seminar contributed greatly to a common terminology on the subject and to the drafting of plans for the gradual organization of vocational work in Latin America. The teaching of vocational agriculture received paramount consideration, as was to be expected, since the delegates came from countries where an agrarian economy is predominant. However, a great deal of attention was also given to plans for the teaching of arts and trades.

The inter-American Seminar on secondary education was held in Santiago, Chile, in the early part of 1955. Of all the seminars held up to this time, this one has probably exerted the most influence. The plans studied in Montevideo for the establishment of a continent-wide system of free and compulsory primary education dealt mainly with the extension of primary education, financial measures and the reorganization of normal schools. Little attention was given to the reorganization of curricula and methods, even if these topics appeared in the agenda. This was natural in that almost every country has some excellent primary schools that may be taken as models in the formulation of national plans for extension of the school system. The situation in secondary education was very different. Three main evils in this connection had to be faced by the Santiago Seminar: the attitude that secondary schools were not a part of the educational ladder, but rather a separate school for the elite and therefore limited to the minority who were to pursue university studies; the method of teaching with emphasis on lectures; and the character of the programs, loaded with humanistic studies and having almost no reference to the problems of contemporary society.

At this Seminar a new definition of secondary education was adopted; the place of the academic high school within the field of secondary education was pointed out; the organization into cycles was discussed; a distinction was made between secondary education in general and humanistic studies; the relation of the secondary schools with professional education, on the one hand, and with university education, on the other, was established; and a set of objectives was proposed.

The fifth Seminar of the series that has given a new orientation to the educational work in Latin America has just closed at Washington, D.C., at the time when this report is being written (August, 1958). The main topic for discussion was the planning of education. For many years, Latin American educators have complained that educational reorganization was proceeding piecemeal and that, as a result, a lack of integration and coordination between the various services and levels of instruction was evident. The Seminar that met in Washington in the summer of 1958 considered measures to bring about a greater unification in planning. In a way, this Seminar comes as a climax to the various conferences on separate educational services; it will present a harmonious interpretation of the recommendations made separately in previous seminars and it will provide governments and educators with a blue print for an over-all attack on the problems of education.

Another joint enterprise of two international organizations in favor of Latin American education is Major Project Number One, undertaken by UNESCO with the collaboration of the Organization of American States. This project is another sign of the growing concern of the Latin American countries for the reform of their educational systems. It was adopted by UNESCO as a result of concrete action taken by the Latin American delegates at one of the recent general sessions of that international agency. The project has the following objectives:

1. To stimulate planning and development of education in general in the Latin American countries.

2. To further the extension of primary, free and compulsory education so that facilities will become available for all the children of school age.

3. To help with the study and revision of curricula and courses of study.

4. To contribute to the bettering of teacher training plans and to the programs for the improvement of teachers in service, and to promote the elevation of their social and economic status.

5. To assist in the preparation of specialists who will serve as leaders in the educational reconstruction of each country.

This program was launched in 1957 with the assistance of educational institutions of three types: a number of associate normal schools located in Colombia, Honduras, Nicaragua, Ecuador, Chile, Brazil and Uruguay; an inter-American center for rural education, located in Venezuela; and two associate centers of university study of education, located at São Paulo, Brazil and Santiago, Chile.

Scholarships provided by both UNESCO and the OAS make it possible for selected teachers with rural experience from Latin America to pursue a one year's course at the Inter-American Rural Center of Venezuela. These students get training as prospective instructors in rural normal schools and at the same time conduct research on the issues and problems of primary education in the rural areas of America. The associate normal schools in various countries will serve as testing grounds for the plans made at the Venezuela Center and for the investigation of local problems of rural education. The associate university centers at São Paulo and Santiago will conduct courses for the training of specialists and leaders in general education. These centers, which started their work in March, 1958, will offer specialization in such fields as Planning Organization and Administration of Education, Methods and Curricula, Orientation, and Teacher Education.

NATIONAL EDUCATIONAL ADVANCES

Under the spur of national public opinion and with the assistance from the international organizations to which reference has been made above, there are numerous indications that progress is being made in all the phases of educational reconstruction.

Many countries are carrying out detailed surveys of needs and resources. One such survey was recently conducted in Peru. The proceedings, published in several volumes, are an excellent guide for subsequent planning and reform. Aside from the purely statistical data on education, the survey includes a study of the geographical, demographic, cultural and economic factors. In the type of educational planning being done, the responsibilities of the federal government as well as those that pertain to private initiative, to local governments and to individual citizens are carefully mapped out. The plans are flexible enough so that they may be adapted to local needs as well as to future changes.

It is significant that the financial aspects are being studied in the light of the modern view that education is a national concern and a prerequisite for progress in other directions. National plans of education are no longer subordinated in many countries to the usual share of the national budget. Besides appropriations made in the federal budgets, the financial plans envisage provincial and municipal participation in the economic load, as well as the possibility of long-range loans, either internal or international, especially for capital investment such as school buildings and equipment. In order to insure a continuous and guaranteed income, necessary for current disbursements as well as for servicing loans, some countries have assigned, through legislation, a certain percentage of all the national income for educational purposes. This is a significant step and a clear break with the tradition that made school budgets a mere chapter of the federal budget voted annually or biennially by the national parliament. Colombia and Brazil have gone further than this by providing in their Constitutions that a certain percentage of the national income shall be earmarked for education.

The need for more financial assistance has brought about the reform of fiscal and administrative systems. It is giving impetus to better retirement and pension systems for teachers and administrators, more and better school buildings, a more satisfactory supply of teaching materials and textbooks, provisions for pupil transportation, and such special services as medical and dental clinics, school lunches, the providing of clothing and shoes and summer resorts for children.

The problem of illiteracy and adult education has been attacked vigorously. In most of the ministries of education, a department of illiteracy and adult education has been organized—a move unheard of up to now. Fundamental education missions are being organized, directed in many cases by graduates of the center established by UNESCO in Mexico, for the training of adult education workers. Several million pamphlets written for adults who have just learned to read have been printed by the Pan American Union and distributed, free of charge in most cases, throughout all of Latin America. New methods and special pamphlets for teaching reading to illiterates are emerging from a number of centers. Leaders are realizing more and more that since democracy in modern societies is fundamentally government by consent, the education of a competent citizenry is essential if consent is to be intelligently given.

The problem of a suitable supply of primary teachers is being attacked through the organization of more normal schools; through the preparation of normal school instructors at the inter-American center for rural education, located at Rubio, Venezuela; through substantial raises in the salaries of primary teachers, especially those who teach in isolated rural areas; through the establishment of systems of appointment and promotion based on merit; and through the provision of summer schools and other means for the in-service of teachers.

Curricula and courses of study for the primary school are developing along lines that follow a middle road between extreme pedagogical doctrines: those that take the child as the center for the organization of the teaching act, and those that take the community as the center. In regard to methods, Latin American educators have realized that many extreme notions currently in vogue are dangerous because they give the sensation of an illusory progress, and tend to the adoption of a "ritual" without much to show in permanent results.

While progressive educators in Latin America are convinced that the organization and administration of schools should be a cooperative enterprise, in which parents, school authorities, teachers and pupils participate, the rigidly centralized systems of education are proving an insurmountable barrier.

The most spectacular educational reform carried out in Latin America during the last ten years is to be found in the field of secondary instruction. The results have affected not only superficial aspects of methods, but the more fundamental principles of objectives and scope. The educational doctrine upon which the reforms are based gives a new meaning to the old humanistic approach, i.e. interprets the neo-humanistic task in a threefold direction:

1) Helping the student acquire a general culture interpreted as the acquisition of knowledge and the development of values

so that he may find his way in the modern world and face intelligently the problems posed by his social environment.

2) Assisting the student in the development of a set of skills, attitudes and ideals that will enable him to live a good life as a man and as a citizen in a democratic society.

3) Exploring the student's aptitudes and interests and guiding him so that he will prepare for and enter successfully into the field of professional or vocational activities.

There is a growing recognition in most of the Latin American countries that adolescents have peculiar needs and that the secondary schools should cater to these needs by studying and accepting as unavoidable the physical changes that accompany adolescence and providing for the wholesome development of those that are socially acceptable. In harmony with this new interpretation of the nature of the adolescent, the old uniform and rigid curricula that required exactly the same type and amount of work from each student are being replaced by flexible curricula and courses of study, so as to make the best of each child's endowment and provide an educational regimen fitted to his needs.

The preparatory character of the secondary schools, which made them the vestibule to the professional university courses, is being replaced by the modern interpretation that holds the secondary school to have as its chief aim the preparation of students for life as citizens and members of families, irrespective of possibilities for pursuing college work.

The list of the countries where reforms in secondary education are in progress includes most of the Latin American states. Space does not permit a full presentation of all; but a general idea of the scope and direction of the movement may be gathered from the highlights of a few representative countries.

BOLIVIA

Courses of study have been thoroughly revised. An interesting addition to the secondary curriculum is civic education, which includes a consideration of the social and economic problems of the country.

Prevocational education is introduced in the early years of the secondary school, and vocational courses are offered in the final years. This amounts to an adoption of the principle of the comprehensive high school. All students will attend the same school irrespective of their vocational objectives. Those who do not finish high school will gain semi-professional skills that will help them find some gainful occupation. These groups, together with those who follow the vocational courses, will provide the nation with skilled and semi-skilled workers possessing a basic cultural background.

At the end of the fourth year, the curriculum makes it possible for students to follow a course with emphasis either on the social sciences or the natural sciences. Both courses have a common core of fundamental studies and a diversified section that corresponds to one of the emphases mentioned above.

CUBA

The reform adopted in 1956 provides that secondary education will consist of two cycles, each of which will have a duration of three years: the elementary secondary years, and the superior secondary years. During the first cycle the curriculum will provide a general cultural education as well as prevocational courses. In the superior secondary cycle, students will be classified as to those who wish to follow a preparatory course in order to enter upon university studies, and those who prefer to follow vocational courses enabling them to enter higher technical schools or to take up gainful occupations. The students taking the vocational courses will be required to pursue a minimum of cultural studies that will round out the general cultural education started in the elementary secondary cycle.

The following types of superior secondary schools have been organized:

1. Institutes that will offer preparatory courses to students who propose to follow university studies.

2. Teacher training schools.

3. National schools of *beaux-arts* and schools of plastic arts.

4. Arts and trades schools, commercial schools, schools of journalism, schools for industrial and technological technicians.

Attendance at the secondary schools has been made compulsory, and pupils who fail to attend 75 per cent of the class periods are barred from taking the final examinations. A minimum of 130 days of work has been required of all secondary schools and the length of the class period has been fixed at fifty minutes. No student is allowed to repeat a course more than twice. Anyone who fails twice in four or more subjects is automatically suspended.

CHILE

The educational reform of the Chilean secondary schools is one of the most thoroughgoing. It is not limited to curricula and courses of study but includes also the organization and internal regime of the schools, the methods of teaching, the system of evaluating school work, the regulations regarding teaching personnel and many other technical details.

The introduction of the reforms has been a gradual process. The first step was the organization of an experimental secondary center in one of the schools attached to the Pedagogical Institute of the University of Chile. Through several years of experimentation, a plan was devised which has been extended gradually to a number of secondary schools throughout the country. Even if the reform, as pointed out before, includes almost all the phases of secondary education, the most significant changes relate to curricula and courses of study. The new secondary schools follow a curricula made up of two sets of courses: a set of integrating studies, called *Plan Común* and a set of studies which are not common to all the students, considerable option being allowed.

The integrating studies are made up of experiences, activities and knowledges that aim at satisfying the common needs and interests of the students and that try to promote the harmonious development of their personalities. An endeavor is made to train students in reflective thinking and to give them a fund of general culture that will allow them to take action and make intelligent choices in their daily lives. The optional courses aim at deepening and systematizing information and skills in harmony with the peculiar needs and interests of each student.

The optional plan is applied throughout the six years of secondary school. The scope and nature of the courses vary from year to year. For the students in the first and second years, the courses are described as "free activities." They aim at making possible the exploration of interests and aptitudes and at strengthening the techniques and skills acquired through the common courses. The students elect two optional courses in each quarter, so that by the end of the second year they will have experienced twelve different "free activities."

For students in the third and fourth years, the optional courses are called "directed activities." They consist of organized, systematic and methodic exercises related to the contents of the common courses. The process of exploration of interests and aptitudes is continued and intensified. The students elect two optional courses in their third year and three in their fourth year, and they are allowed to pursue these courses during two or three of the quarters that make up the school year.

In their fifth year, students elect four optional courses and in their last year they elect five. All these courses extend throughout the full year.

MEXICO

The movement for reform in Mexico began in 1951. It came to a climax with the organization of a National Conference for Secondary Education, the purpose of which was to study the state of secondary education in the country and propose changes that would make this type of education responsive to the demands of Mexican society.

The work of the Conference was carried out in three stages: in the first, a study of the problems facing secondary education was conducted; in the second, solutions were analyzed and planned in detail; in the third stage, a selection of the solutions was made on the bases of experimentation. From the nature of the work done in each, these three stages were called, respectively, investigation, planning and experimentation.

Planning was conducted on a national scale and consisted of three types of activities: a number of seminars held throughout the country and attended by teachers and other persons interested in the field of secondary education; regional round-table conferences, held in the state capitals and attended by the delegates to the seminars and other leaders especially invited, at which the conclusions and recommendations made by the seminars were examined; and finally, a national assembly, held at Mexico City, made up of representatives from the round-table conferences, educational authorities and professors from universities and other cultural centers. The national assembly was entrusted with the task of giving final sanction to the recommendations of the round-table conferences.

The proceedings of the national assembly served as the guide for an extensive reorganization of curricula and courses, organization, teaching methods, examination techniques, integration of courses and articulation of primary, secondary and higher studies. Curricula were modified through the adoption of compulsory and optional studies, a device very similar to the one utilized by Chile and which has been described above. Special courses of study were set up for students unable to stay for the duration of the regular secondary schools and also for adults interested in a shorter term. Provisions were adopted to make it possible for students to transfer from one type of school to another. Special periods were allotted to physical, social, recreational, aesthetic and other activities that train students in the wise use of their leisure time. Manual work was given a place in the program of all students, and child care and education for the home were made compulsory for the girls.

CONCLUSION

The movement for reform that has been sketched in the preceding sections has not been limited to primary and secondary schools. Universities have also undergone extensive reorganization that makes them more responsive to popular needs. This last stronghold of the privileged classes has come to recognize its obligation to the rising middle class. To the courses for the training in the classical professions—law, medicine and engineering—facilities are being added in a growing number of universities for training technicians and leaders in the natural and the social sciences. The philosophy of higher education has been permeated by ideas that aim at the transformation of the social and economic structure and that take into account the pressing social needs of society.

Latin America did not catch up with the changes in science and technology that took place immediately after World War II. This lag was not merely the result of the lack of a correct perspective of the direction in which the world was moving. To a larger extent it was due to the lack of resources, and to the isolation of the institutions of higher education from the great centers of scientific research, an isolation that was partly brought about by the War itself.

The situation described above is being corrected rapidly. Libraries are being enriched; laboratories are being expanded and equipped with the modern tools of study and research; and scholars from outstanding universities are being invited to collaborate. Such organizations as the Fulbright Foundation and UNESCO are contributing scholars and scientific equipment, and the governments are putting forth great efforts to make the universities true centers for teaching and investigation. Adult education programs are being organized wherever they did not exist and are being extended, where beginnings had been made. The departments of cultural extension, which is the name given to extramural work, are branching off into all the realms of human knowledge. Political science, especially, is studied vigorously and the forms of government that compete in the modern world are analyzed from the point of view of their ability to contribute to the happiness of mankind.

The extension and reform of education to which reference has been made in this paper are bringing about the liberation of the human spirit in Latin America. This liberation is the groundwork for freedom and democracy. The movement is already bearing fruit: the roll call of countries that have transformed their regimes from dictatorships to democracies is impressive. The political climate is no longer healthy for those few countries where the evolution is not complete. To the extent that the movement for reform in education takes root, to that extent will the Latin American citizen be able to exercise intelligently the right to give his consent for the actions of his government. This is the only road to the perpetuation of democracy and human dignity.

CHAPTER VIII

[WENDELL C. GORDON *]

Freedom and Reform in Urban and

Industrializing Latin America

A high and rising standard of living is necessary if a people is effectively to take advantage of freedom. This paper is chiefly concerned with the role of industrialization in providing the material basis for the effective acquisition of freedom; and, of course, industrialization is occurring in a setting of population increase and urbanization. So, it is desirable to relate the population and urbanization developments with that of industrialization.

Latin America is in ferment. It is on the threshold of (if it is not already well advanced in) a period of explosive population increase, economic growth, and cultural change. The region and its problems deserve more attention than they are currently getting from United States students momentarily obsessed with the Soviet Union.

POPULATION TRENDS

Rate of Growth: About the year 1500 the population of what is now Latin America was probably somewhere within the range

---

* Wendell C. Gordon received his B.A. from Rice University, his M.A. from the American University, and his Ph.D. from New York University, the last in 1940. In the same year he joined the faculty of the University of Texas, and now holds the rank of Professor of Economics. He has traveled extensively in Europe and Latin America, and contributed articles to the leading journals in his field. His books include: *Expropriation of Foreign-Owned Property in Mexico* (Washington, D.C., 1941); *The Economy of Latin America* (New York, 1951); and *International Trade: Goods, People and Ideas* (Austin, 1958).

of 10 to 16 million (in spite of La Casas' belief that the Conquest killed between 15 and 20 million Indians).[1] However, by the end of the colonial period Latin America may well have contained a smaller proportion of the world's population than had been the case in 1500. The low figure for 1750 may have been roughly 1.5 per cent. The relative stagnation continued during much of the nine-

ANNUAL RATE OF POPULATION INCREASE
(Per Cent)

	1953–56	*1950–56*
Argentina	1.9	
Bolivia	1.2	
Brazil	2.4	
Chile	2.6	
Colombia	2.2	
Costa Rica	3.9	
Cuba	—	
Dominican Republic	3.4	
Ecuador	2.7	
El Salvador	3.4	
Guatemala	3.1	
Haiti	1.2	
Honduras	3.0	
Mexico	2.9	
Nicaragua	3.4	
Panama	2.7	
Paraguay	2.9	
Peru	2.2	
Uruguay	1.5	
Venezuela	3.1	
Latin America:		
Middle America		2.7
South America		2.4
United States	1.8	
World:		
Africa		1.6
Asia		1.7
Europe		1.6
		0.8

Source: United Nations, *Statistical Yearbook, 1957*, p. 35.

[1] Victor Audera, *La Población y la Inmigración en Hispanoamérica* (Madrid, 1954), p. 24; Lewis Hanke, *Bartolomé de Las Casas* (The Hague, 1951), p. 57.

teenth century, but in recent years the situation has changed. During the period between the two World Wars (1920–40) the population of the world grew at about the rate of .75 per cent per year while the population of Latin America was growing by some 1.73 per cent per year.[2] In more recent years, as the table "Annual Rate of Population Increase" indicates, Latin America has been growing in population at the rate of about 2.5 per cent per year. The growth rate is even higher in some of the countries of the Caribbean and Central American region. The Latin American growth rate is much faster than that for the rest of the world. The figure for the world as a whole seems to be about 1.6 per cent while for the United States it is 1.8 per cent.

Present Population: As the accompanying table on "Population" indicates, the population of Latin America has now reached a figure approximating 183 million. The population of the world is, perhaps, 2,737 million. These two figures indicate that the Latin American population is now 6.7 per cent of the world total which contrasts with the 1.5 per cent of circa 1750.

Within the last few years the population of Latin America has surpassed that of the United States which is now over 10 million less than that of Latin America. Moreover, there is every indication that the Latin American population edge over the United States will increase steadily in the next few decades.

The table headed "Population" also gives estimates for the various Latin American countries for the most recent year possible, generally 1957. Brazil is by a considerable margin the most populous of the countries with 61 million inhabitants; Mexico is next with 31 million; Argentina follows with almost 20 million.

Population density is, however, most pronounced in four of the countries of the Caribbean–Central American region. Haiti has over 300 inhabitants to the square mile; El Salvador has some 173; Cuba 145; and the Dominican Republic 141. No other Latin American country even approaches 100 people to the square mile, and the average for the region is only 24. The United States has about 57 people to the square mile, which is somewhat over the world average of 53.

Cities and Urbanization: Not only has the population in Latin

[2] Kingsley Davis, "Future Migration into Latin America," *Milbank Memorial Fund Quarterly,* XXV (January, 1947), 59.

POPULATION, 1957

	In Thousands	Per Square Mile
Argentina	19,674	18
Bolivia	3,272	8
Brazil	61,268	19
Chile	7,119	25
Colombia	13,227	30
Costa Rica	1,034	54
Cuba	6,410	145
Dominican Republic	2,698	141
Ecuador	3,897	37
El Salvador	2,268	173
Guatemala	3,430	82
Haiti	3,390	318
Honduras	1,739	40
Mexico	31,426	41
Nicaragua	1,288	23
Panama	960	34
Paraguay	1,601	10
Peru	9,923	23
Uruguay	2,668	37
Venezuela	6,130	17
Latin America Total	183,422	24
United States	171,299	57
World	2,737,000	53

Sources: *Informaciones Económicas* (Pan American Union), January, 1958, p. 6; *Statistical Abstract, 1957*, p. 937; *Statistical Yearbook, 1957*, pp. 21–35.

America been growing apace in recent years but also that growth has gone on in a more pronounced manner in the cities. It is of course difficult to find a completely satisfactory measure to indicate the degree of urbanization. But one simple, perhaps too simple, possibility is to do nothing more than state the population of the largest city as a percentage of the national population. The table attempts to do this for the various Latin American countries for 1900, or some date shortly thereafter, for 1940, and for the latest date obtainable.

In all cases the concentration of population in the largest city was more marked in the more recent year than it was in 1900. Also, in all cases, the degree of concentration seems to be greater now than it was in 1940. In a few instances, however, it was not higher in 1940 than in 1900. In Ecuador there is the possibility of a non-conformity because the identity of the largest city changed during this period from Quito to Guayaquil. In the case of El

PER CENT OF POPULATION OF COUNTRY IN LARGEST CITY

	1900	*1940*	*1955/57*
Argentina (Buenos Aires)	16.4	18.5	18.5
Bolivia (La Paz)	3.1	8.5	10.2
Brazil	3.8 (Rio)	3.8	5.0 (São Paulo)
Chile (Santiago)	10.4	19.0	19.0
Colombia (Bogotá)	2.6	3.7	8.5
Costa Rica (San José)	8.9	10.6	12.4
Cuba (La Habana)	13.1	13.8	18.9
Dominican Republic (Ciudad Trujillo)	2.5	6.1	9.2
Ecuador	6.1 (Quito)	5.2	9.0 (Guayaquil)
El Salvador (San Salvador)	6.2	5.6	8.5
Guatemala (Guatemala City)	4.7	5.0	8.6
Haiti (Port-au-Prince)	4.5	4.0	5.8
Honduras (Tegucigalpa)	3.0	4.0	5.8
Mexico (México)	2.8	7.4	13.9
Nicaragua (Managua)	5.9	9.4	11.7
Panama (Panamá)	14.4 (1919)	17.7	19.9
Paraguay (Asunción)	8.7	8.7	13.1
Peru (Lima)	2.6	7.4	10.1
Uruguay (Montevideo)	30.3	32.4	31.9
Venezuela (Caracas)	3.3	5.8	16.3

Note: This table probably understates current urbanization somewhat. The national population figures are generally 1957 and the city figures 1956.

Sources: Kingsley Davis and Ana Casis, "Urbanization in Latin America," *Milbank Memorial Fund Quarterly*, XXIV (April, 1946), p. 3 (of reprint); *The South America Handbook, passim;* Raúl C. Migone, *Inter-American Statistical Yearbook*, 1942 (New York), pp. 67–76; *Statesman's Yearbook, passim.*

Salvador, the data are probably for some reason or other non-comparable. Except for the minor exceptions of El Salvador and Ecuador there is remarkable homogeneity in the pattern. Population concentration in the largest city has increased apace and consistently.

The increase of Buenos Aires would be more marked if various of the suburbs were included. Buenos Aires has, of course, long since outgrown the city proper. It is about the only case of a Latin American city with a significant suburban area that adds to the proper population of the city as do, for example, the suburbs of New York.

Notable among the examples of growth is Mexico City, which

POPULATION OF SELECTED CITIES

(Approximately, 1956)

Argentina:	Buenos Aires	3,641,000
Bolivia:	La Paz	335,000
Brazil:	Rio de Janeiro (Federal District)	2,895,000
	São Paulo	3,069,000
Chile:	Santiago	1,348,000
Colombia:	Bogotá	1,180,000
Costa Rica:	San José	128,000
Cuba:	La Habana	1,211,000
Dominican Republic:	Ciudad Trujillo	248,000
Ecuador:	Guayaquil	350,000
	Quito	210,000
El Salvador:	San Salvador	194,000
Guatemala:	Guatemala City	295,000
Haiti:	Port-au-Prince	195,000
Honduras:	Tegucigalpa	100,000
Mexico:	Mexico City	4,227,000
Nicaragua:	Managua	151,000
Panama:	Panama City	191,000
Paraguay:	Ascunción	210,000
Peru:	Lima	1,000,000
Uruguay:	Montevideo	850,000
Venezuela:	Caracas	1,000,000
United States:	New York	7,800,000
	Chicago	3,700,000
Great Britain:	London (Greater)	8,300,000
	(County)	3,300,000
Germany	Berlin	3,400,000
France	Paris	2,800,000
Spain	Madrid	1,600,000
U.S.S.R	Moscow	4,800,000
Portugal	Lisbon	790,000
Japan	Tokyo	6,900,000
India	Bombay	2,800,000

Principal source: *Statesman's Yearbook, passim.*

held under 3 per cent of the nation's population in 1900 but 14 per cent in 1956. Another important case is the growth of Santiago, Chile, from 10 per cent to 19 per cent in a similar period of time. Havana has grown from 13 per cent to 19 per cent, Bogotá from 3 per cent to 9 per cent, Caracas from 3 per cent to 16 per cent. The conclusion is unambiguous. The capital cities in the larger countries have experienced during the last fifty years a very substantial increase in their relative importance on the national scene.

Also of interest is a comparison of the concentration of population in the large cities of Latin America with the concentration elsewhere, particularly in the United States. In absolute size no Latin American city approaches New York. But Latin America has three or four cities of roughly the size of Chicago. It is difficult, nevertheless, to make a meaningful comparison of the concentration of population in the largest city as between the United States and the Latin American countries. The United States has almost as much population as does all of Latin America. New York City has under 5 per cent of the population of the United States. Mexico City, with 4 million people, is perhaps the largest Latin American City. The population of Mexico City is under 2.5 per cent of the Latin American total; but it is 14 per cent of the population of Mexico. Who is bigger than who depends a lot on what is compared with what.

Brazil, with a population of 61 million, is in somewhat the same position as the United States. Big as New York City is, it contains only 5 per cent of the population of the country. In Brazil, even though Rio de Janeiro and São Paulo are each cities of about 3 million, one of them represents only 5 per cent of the national population. Haiti is a country with a fantastic concentration of population in agriculture. But it is a smaller country, and 5.8 per cent of the population in Port-au-Prince may not be evidence of much urbanization. On the other hand 12 of the 20 Latin American countries have over 10 per cent of the population in the largest city; and 6 of them have virtually 20 per cent. This is noteworthy concentration of population in the largest city. At least it is a type of concentration that is bound to color the national political and economic arrangements in the shadow of an ascendant capital.

Study of urbanization should, however, call for an effort to assimilate data on population in general in the cities—not just in one city. The accompanying table, "Measure of Urbanization,"

MEASURE OF URBANIZATION

	Latin America	United States City Proper	Metropolitan Area
The Five Largest Cities			
(1) Composite population	14,953,000	17,403,000	29,461,000
(2) Per cent of population	8.2%	10.5%	17.9%
Cities over 1,000,000			
(1) Composite population	19,344,000	17,403,000	44,439,000
(2) Per cent of population	10.5%	10.5%	26.8%
The 65 Largest			
(1) Composite population	30,500,000	39,400,000	68,272,000
(2) Per cent of population	16.6%	23.8%	41.2%
Cities with a Population over 100,000			
(1) Composite population	30,500,000	44,300,000	83,065,000
(2) Per cent of national population	16.6%	26.8%	50.3%

Note: It has been estimated that for the world as a whole in 1930, 11 per cent of the population lived in cities with a population in excess of 100,000. W. S. and E. S. Woytinsky, *World Population and Production—Trends and Outlook* (New York, 1953), p. 122.

Source: Computed by author from miscellaneous sources.

gives some comparative data on the concentration of population in the cities in Latin America and in the United States. Most Latin American cities do not have an extensive metropolitan area distinct from the city proper. However, this is not entirely true and it is a weakness of the table that it has not been possible to give the same sort of two-fold classification for Latin America that has been attempted for the United States. Nevertheless, on the basis of this data the generalization seems justified that Latin America is almost as well endowed with great metropolitan centers as is the United States. (This comparison has added force if one remembers that the population of the United States is roughly the same as—or slightly less than—the population of Latin America.) But the amount of population in middle-sized cities is relatively less in Latin America than in the United States. One might say Latin America is cosmopolitan but not urban.

The United States population is 64 per cent urban.[3] But probably if comparable data were available for Latin America as a whole an urbanization coefficient under 30 per cent would emerge. A figure for Mexico for 1940 has been estimated at 35 per cent. But comparable figures for countries such as Bolivia and Peru, not to mention the Caribbean countries, if available, would certainly bring down the average considerably.

Allocation of Productive Effort: The population of Latin America is, then, increasingly urban. The importance of this development would be difficult to overestimate. Nevertheless the

ECONOMICALLY ACTIVE POPULATION, 1950 APPROXIMATELY

	Total (In thousands)	Per Cent in Agriculture	Per Cent in Manufacturing
Argentina	6,446	25.2	22.2
Bolivia	1,048	63.0	10.5
Brazil	17,118	60.6	13.0
Chile	2,155	30.2	19.0
Colombia	2,880	61.0	5.1
Costa Rica	272	54.8	11.0
Cuba	1,972	41.5	16.6
Dominican Republic	826	46.7	5.7
Ecuador	1,237	49.4	23.9
El Salvador	653	63.0	11.2
Guatemala (1940)	1,066	73.1	12.8
Haiti	1,747	83.5	5.0
Honduras	647	83.5	5.9
Mexico	10,585	53.6	11.9
Nicaragua	330	67.6	11.2
Panama	263	50.5	8.6
Paraguay	425	53.0	16.0
Peru (1954)	3,285	62.5	17.5
Uruguay	—	—	—
Venezuela	1,706	41.3	10.1
Total (of countries for which data is given above)	51,596	54.3	13.9
United States	60,037	12.2	26.8

Source: *Statistical Yearbook, 1956*, pp. 55–9, is the chief source of data. Other sources include Nacional Financiera (Mexico), *Informe Annual, 1957*, p. 35.

[3] People living in towns of over 2,500 inhabitants are classed as urban. *Statistical Abstract, 1957*, p. 20.

population is still predominantly rural, and the continued importance of agriculture is indicated by the accompanying table on the "Economically Active Population."

In Latin America 54 per cent of the working population is in agriculture. This compares with only 12 per cent in the United States. This data is merely further confirmation of the oft-noted phenomenon that countries with highly developed, prosperous agricultures have a relatively small proportion of the population in agriculture. The Argentine figure, the lowest in Latin America, of 25 per cent is further evidence. The countries where agriculture gives the barest livelihood have the largest proportion of people on the land. Note the 83 per cent figure for Haiti.

Sociology of Urbanization: Mexico City may be taken as an example of the difficulties that arise as a by-product of rapid urbanization. The following comments are largely paraphrased from a statement on the problem of urban concentration in Mexico City prepared by the Banco Nacional de México.[4]

Mexico City is faced by a growing problem as the result of shortage of housing and public services. No adequate provision has been made for the very substantial population increase that has occurred in recent years.

This rapid population growth has been accompanied by the concentration of population in urban slums. "The area of *jacales* or shanties, clustered around industrial suburbs, completely lacking running water, electricity, and sewage facilities, contain 11% of Mexico City's population." In addition, overcrowded apartment houses account for only 12 per cent of urban land area but for 34 per cent of the population. Also:

so-called "proletarian" zones, characterized mainly by inadequate construction, contain 14% of the city's inhabitants. In an intermediate class of dwellings, generally old and poorly maintained, which covers 36% of the city area, live another 27% of its people. The first class residential districts occupy 36% of the city's land, but provide dwellings for only 14% of its population.

In addition to the problem of inadequate housing, the city is faced with a serious problem resulting from congestion in its transportation facilities. Downtown Mexico City is a nightmare of transportation bottlenecks. There is every reason to expect that

[4] *Review of the Economic Situation of Mexico,* March, 1958, p. 8.

this problem will get much worse as the number of vehicles and the number of people increase further.

One effort by private enterprise to do something about this problem has involved the construction of so-called "satellite cities" or suburbs intended to be completely autonomous. Planned as co-ordinated community centers, generally around manufacturing plants, they contain residential, commerical, and industrial units. In these communities communication and public utility services have been adequate in the beginning. But the difficulty has been, especially in the Mexico City area, that the city has grown up to these satellite cities, surrounded, and absorbed them. It has done this to San Angel, Coyoacán, and Tacubaya. In addition, lack of water is one of the chief problems in the valley in which Mexico City is located. And as long as the satellite cities are located in the valley of Mexico, they contribute nothing to the solution of the general water problem. They constitute, on the contrary, an additional drain on the already inadequate supply. Also the satellite cities draw on the same meager resources of electric power as does Mexico City. In this setting the satellite cities do not seem to represent a solution to the urbanization problem. "The problem is aggravated by the fact that the impetus to urban expansion, rather than being diffused, appears likely to continue concentrated in the present centers of growth."

The Banco Nacional statement then concludes by recommending effort to develop "a widespread program of regional economic development" in an effort to diffuse the growth away from Mexico City and also away from the other present centers of population such as Guadalajara and Monterrey.

Strikingly similar situations undoubtedly exist in connection with the urbanization going on elsewhere in Latin America.

ECONOMIC GROWTH

Latin America has embarked on a period of major economic growth. Much time, effort, and planning have gone into this effort in recent years. However, since it is probably true that the really pronounced growth is still a thing of the future, it is worthwhile to look at such data as are available in an effort to obtain as accurate a picture as possible of the current state of this development.

Social Statistics: As the accompanying table on "Social Statistics" indicates, the infant mortality rate is still very high in the region. Life expectancy is low. Per capita food consumption measured in calories is low. A study of the Food and Agriculture Or-

SOCIAL STATISTICS [1]

	Infant Mortality Rate [2]	Expectation of Life at Birth in Years— Male (or M&F)	Net Food Supply per Person in Calories per Day
Argentina	62.4	56.9	2,840
Bolivia	106.1	—	—
Brazil	171.0	49.8	2,340
Chile	112.3	49.8	2,490
Colombia	104.2	—	2,730
Costa Rica	104.6	55.7	—
Cuba	—	—	2,730
Dominican Rep.	68.3	—	—
Ecuador	118.0	50.4	—
El Salvador	76.7	49.9	—
Guatemala	88.7	43.8	—
Haiti	—	32.6	—
Honduras	54.9	—	2,030
Mexico	83.3	37.9 (1940)	—
Nicaragua	79.6	—	—
Panama	54.7	50.5 (1942)	—
Paraguay	93.2	—	—
Peru	94.5	46.1	—
Uruguay	73.0	—	2,810
Venezuela	69.5	—	2,280
United States	26.0	67.4	3,100

Notes: (1) In most cases data is for 1955 or 1956.
(2) Deaths of infants under 1 year of age per 1,000 live births.

Source: *Statistical Abstract, 1957*, p. 937.

ganization has indicated that it considers a reasonable minimum calory food consumption per capita to be 2,550 to 2,650 calories per day.[5] Several of the countries listed do not come up to this minimum. And most of the countries not listed would probably not reach the minimum if the data were available.

In addition the disease problem continues serious. The inci-

[5] Food and Agriculture Organization, *Proposals for a World Food Board and World Food Survey* (Washington, 1946), Part II, p. 11.

dence of various contagious diseases is very high in Latin America. Yaws, for example, is widely prevalent in the Caribbean countries. The death rate from cancer and heart disease is relatively low, but only because so many people do not live long enough to contract these diseases.

The millennium has not yet arrived in Latin America. Nevertheless the situation is by no means as discouraging as the social statistics might indicate.

Production and Income Data: The sketchy data of the table on "Real Per Capita Product" is still sufficient to indicate a sub-

REAL PER CAPITA PRODUCT
(1953 equals 100)

	1938	*1947*	*1954*	*1955*	*1956*
Argentina	86	108	103	105	—
Brazil	—	84	106	108	—
Chile	—	86	97	92	—
Colombia	—	80	106	104	—
Cuba	82 (1939)	111	105	119	—
Ecuador (94 in 1950)	—	—	107	106	109
Guatemala	—	119	95	104	114
Honduras	73	87	98	98	—
Mexico	61 (1939)	90	105	112	—
Paraguay	—	88 (1950)	96	—	—
Peru	—	80	103	110	—
United States	59	84	97	102	103

Source: *Statistical Yearbook, 1956,* 472; *1957,* p. 485.

stantial development in recent years. The same is true of the data in the table on "Industrial Production." These statistics do not indicate that Latin American growth is sensational by comparison with the rest of the world. But it is reasonable to expect that the growth of a region that is just beginning to flex its muscles will be modest initially. Economic growth is a cumulative process that seems to be slow in gathering momentum.

The data on growth in real per capita product indicate substantial increases during the last decade in Brazil, Colombia, Mexico, and Peru. In fact, growth in those countries seems to have been at least as rapid as growth in the United States. Per capita product in Argentina does not seem to have risen at all during the last ten years. Also, significant increase does not seem to have occurred in Cuba or Chile. However, if one looks at the last twenty years instead of merely at the last ten, growth in real per capita product would seem to have been substantial in all the countries listed.

INDUSTRIAL PRODUCTION
(1954 equals 100)

	Earliest Year for which Data Available	1948	1956
World (1)	—	73	116
United States	44(1929)	78	107
Argentina	59(1937)	105	117
Brazil	58(1944)	68	112
Chile	33(1929)	70	104
Guatemala	83(1946)	91	115
Mexico	61(1939)	81	130
Peru	62(1945)	65	122(1955)

Note: (1) Excluding U.S.S.R. and associated countries.

Source: *Statistical Yearbook, 1957,* pp. 114–39.

Growth in the chief unlisted country, Venezuela, has probably been substantial, but one may guess that the average citizen has not benefited much from the increase.[6]

The data on industrial production in the last ten years corroborate the evidence derived from the real per capita product figures. The growth in Brazil, Mexico, and Peru has been pronounced. It has been modest for Argentina. However, in the case of Chile it looks as though there had been a rather substantial increase in industrial production which is not reflected in the per capita product figures. The reason for this is not immediately obvious.

Both the per capita product figures and the industrial production figures suggest a generalization of some importance. There is no observable pattern of geographic concentration so far as the more rapidly developing countries are concerned. Mexico and Brazil, two of the more rapidly developing countries, are about as far apart as it is possible to get in Latin America, and one has a Span-

[6] *The New York Times,* April 1, 1958, p. 4. This failure of the bulk of the population to benefit materially from what should have been a wonderful opportunity provided by the large receipts from oil would seem to be a result of the behavior of the Marcos Pérez Jiménez dictatorship.

ish background and the other Portuguese. Also it would be hard to build a case to prove that dictatorship facilitates development. Brazil and Mexico have been about as free of the heavy hand of dictatorship as any countries in the region.

Wages: Information on what is happening to wage levels also should be significant as indicating what is happening in the area of well-being to the great mass of the population. Both the data on real per capita product and the data on national income and product leave something to be desired in this regard. They do not tell whether the improvement in level of living is widely spread among the population or whether it is highly concentrated among certain groups of the government officials, the new industrialists, and the army.

In addition, data on wages are difficult to obtain. Nevertheless some clue as to the situation may be obtained from data on minimum wages. In Mexico, the minimum wage varies from state to state and within each state there is a different minimum for city and rural workers. In Mexico City the legal minimum wage for 1958–9 is 12 pesos per day, about 96 (U.S.) cents. For rural workers in the Federal District it is 10.5 pesos.[7] This compares, but very, very roughly, with a $1.00 an hour minimum wage in the United States.

Of course the philosophy underlying this system of wage setting is that major differences between wages in different sectors of the economy have existed and correspond somewhat to cost of living differences. At any rate, for the nonce, the official view seems to be that it is better to respect these differences than to fight them. The whole system of minimum wages might otherwise have broken down. But in the long run such differences are probably undesirable. They create irritations between different economic groups and make planning difficult. Wage comparability is desirable, if it can be obtained, for it can make a significant contribution to social harmony and orderly planning.

Venezuela provides a striking example of lack of wage comparability. The wage paid to workers in the oil industry is substantially higher than that paid in general in industry and agriculture. It has been said that, in consequence, the oil industry is able to monopolize such of the labor force as it desires—to the detriment

[7] *Hispanic American Report* (December–January, 1957–1958), p. 647.

of other industrial sectors. This might be better put, however, as follows: the disproportionately high wage paid in the oil industry —the inequity of it—demoralizes the whole labor force of the country.

The solution of the problem is not obvious. The wage in the Venezuelan oil fields is, no doubt, lower than the wage paid for comparable work in the oil fields of the United States. Lowering the wage in Venezuela to correspond with the prevailing wage in the rest of the economy is not the solution. And yet these wage relations will not become satisfactory (they will not become relations that "people can live with") until there is effective wage comparability among the three groups: (1) the oil field worker of a certain skill in the United States, (2) his peer in Venezuela, and (3) the worker of equivalent skill in other sectors of Venezuelan industry. The proposition can be and should be generalized: genuine, meaningful wage comparability is necessary if people are to live in reasonable harmony with each other.

But our stated goal, at the beginning of this discussion of wages, was to ascertain whether the mass of the population was sharing in the fruits of the industrial development. The comments made up to now have helped little to answer that question. Data on the point are not generally available for Latin America as a whole, but some significant study of the problem has been made for Mexico in particular.[8] An important conclusion of the Mexican investigation seems to be that the rise in the level of living of the mass of the population has been modest by comparison with the profits accruing to the new class of industrialists. Probably there was similar distortion in connection with the early burst of industrialization in the United States during the last half of the nineteenth century. Nevertheless one may be excused for wishing that there were a better way for industrialization to proceed than via great disproportionality in the distribution of the gain from the rising national income.

On this note we may now turn to a brief discussion of at least one or two major policy issues connected with the effort to raise the standard of living in Latin America.

[8] United Nations, Economic Commission for Latin America, *Economic Survey of Latin America, 1951–1952*, p. 88.

POLICY

As was stated at the beginning of this paper, a high and rising standard of living is necessary if a people is effectively to take advantage of freedom. The "reforms" with which this paper is primarily concerned, then, are the policy measures in the economic area which will tend to raise the level of living.

The social statistics indicate that in many aspects of health and human welfare Latin America is not well off. On the other hand the data on industrial production and income indicate that things are stirring in the region. One may surmise that an industrial revolution of considerable magnitude is going to occur in Latin America in the next few decades and that it has already begun. But such a development is not foreordained and certain. Some rather intelligent human guidance will not be amiss to help the process along.

Sources of Data: Much useful information on the economic resources and development possibilities of various of the Latin American countries is now available in a series of publications being issued by the Bureau of Foreign Commerce of the United States Government.[9] Providing much the same sort of data on a frequent, but intermittent, basis is the *World Trade Information Service,* also prepared by the Bureau of Foreign Commerce. Similarly, the International Bank for Reconstruction and Development has done a series of country studies.[10] In the different Latin American countries various agencies such as *fomento* or development corporations and central banks prepare annual and occasional reports on development problems. On the whole there is a mountain of data available and the quantity is growing apace.

Country Size: I should like next to discuss certain selected measures which may make an important contribution to establishing the climate in which a major amount of industrialization can occur.

Recently various Latin American leaders have expressed concern about the European Economic Community. Some fear it will lead to the loss of Latin American markets in Europe. On

[9] See, for example, United States, Department of Commerce, *Investment in Peru, Basic Information for United States Businessmen* (Washington, 1957).

[10] See, for example, International Bank for Reconstruction and Development, *Report on Cuba* (Washington, 1951).

the other hand there has been talk of the possibility of a Latin American Common Market:

The Latin American countries ought to try to form regional markets in various combinations in order to encourage industrialization and overcome the obstacles set up by narrow and weak markets, such as prevail in most of the countries. This effort is necessary in order that efforts may not be duplicated, in order to facilitate the effective use of scarce resources, and, above all, in order to secure the advantages of a controlled market. Regional markets represent steps directed toward strengthening the economic unity of this area and they will serve to facilitate gradually a greater measure of integration.[11]

Latin American economic development has just about reached the point where the small size of the countries when juxtaposed with international barriers to trade will make a real hindrance to further development. Up to now there has been very little trade among the Latin American countries—very little intra-Latin-American trade. In past decades this has probably been about as much because of poor transportation arteries as because of trade barriers such as tariffs. But with improvement in transportation, trade barriers will carry an increasing share of the blame. And the growing Latin American industrial plant will miss a real opportunity if the industry of each country is limited to that country's markets.

In general, countries of small size, and the Latin American countries are small, in a world of trade barriers do not provide a very attractive setting for industrialization. The local market is frequently not large enough to provide an outlet of reasonable proportions for a manufacturing plant of efficient size. Or the market is not large enough to provide justification for plant expansion from one plant to two, or from two to three, or from three to four. These are steps that must be passed in industrial expansion and they are very difficult steps to take in an economy of small size.

A light-globe manufacturing plant in Colombia will provide an example of the nature of the difficulty. It has been said: "The capacity of the smallest mechanized plant is such that three months' operation would fulfill Colombia's present demands for

[11] Ricardo Torres Gaitán, "El Mercado Común Latino-Americano," *Cuadernos Americanos*, XVII (January, 1958), 29–41.

a year." [12] What is to be done in a case of this sort if trade barriers effectively limit the sale of Colombian light-globes in Venezuela and in Peru. Of course in such situations many Latin American countries have sponsored industrial plants either much too large for their market or much too small for efficiency. Probably the sponsorship of plants too large for their market has been the more common phenomenon. This is bad for morale, bad for the spirit of the people in the industry and bad for the attitude of the people toward their country's industrialization program. Industry morale is not likely to be high in a setting where plant capacity is a third utilized, and the workers and managers can see the consequent waste and ineffective use of resources. Taxi drivers in the capital city then have, also, as one of their chief gossip topics the inefficiency of the industrialization program. The chief tidbit of knowledge of the country's economy that the foreign tourist goes home with, then, is likely to be some aimless gossip about the "foul-up" in the industrialization program. The Colombian steel mill at Paz del Rio seems to be such a case, but the number of examples could, no doubt, be multiplied many times.

The existence of a free trade world would help to solve this problem. But other things may be done which are well within the competence of the Latin American countries to do for themselves.

A customs union of the whole Latin American area, comparable to the European Economic Community, is the immediately obvious step for them to take. Other possibilities include the fusion of the countries of the area into three or four much larger countries. This latter step might have to be taken over the dead bodies of some foreign fruit and oil companies.

The fusion of the Latin American countries into a few much larger countries would, of course, make the population of the individual country larger. It would reduce the populationwise dominance of the capital city. Just conceivably these developments could also make a significant contribution to political stability in the region. And political stability would in its turn provide a more auspicious climate for industrial development and for individual freedom.

[12] International Bank for Reconstruction and Development, *The Basis of a Development Program for Colombia* (Washington, 1950), p. 93.

Surely a stable political climate is more conducive to business expansion, including an inflow of foreign investment, than are unimplemented laws favorable to investment. Colombia in recent years has been beset by chronic civil war. The country has been in chaos. Fighting has raged in the countryside. And yet a certain type of foreign observer can be so entranced with the fact that the laws of a despotic government are ostensibly favorable to foreign investment that he will say something like the following: "Americans here [Bogotá] who are familiar with Colombian laws and practices governing foreign investment say this nation has [1953!] the healthiest climate for foreign investment of any South Ameican country, and probably one of the best in the world." [13]

The set of conditions which would be most favorable to industrialization, to business generally, and probably to foreign investors too, would be stable governments in countries of sufficient size to offer reasonably large markets. Of course the genuinely larger markets that free trade in the whole of Latin America, if not in the whole world, would give would be even better.

Barriers to Trade: A major element in the method being used to encourage industrialization in Latin America is misdirected. It is the idea that internal industrialization can be encouraged by barriers to competing imports. The trouble with this approach is that none of the Latin American countries, with the possible exception of Brazil, is large enough to support a major industrialization program in a world of trade barriers. Basic dependence on the domestic market for sales outlets means in many cases that it is either impossible to establish a plant of efficient size in the first place or, and this is a more important point, difficult to time the stage when it is desirable to expand the national industry from, say, two plants to three. In addition there is the great truth that industrialization is a process which involves something more than the development of a few isolated, selected plants. The development of an industry, any industry, involves not only the central plant itself but also a complex of related service organizations. It also involves a nucleus of a group of people with an assortment of skills. The evolution of technical skill in a group of people is not a process that proceeds in any very satisfactory manner in a one

[13] *Houston Post,* September 3, 1953, sec. 5, p. 9.

plant setting. There needs to be a large group of people, and many of them with conflicting viewpoints and different approaches to the same problem, to provide the basis for a significant development.

As was said above, no one of the Latin American countries except possibly Brazil is in a position to provide such a setting. A *sine qua non* for a significant degree of industrialization in Latin America is, at the least, a removal of trade barriers—rather than the emphasis on their use which has characterized the programs up to this time. But even more effective for this purpose would probably be a series of major political fusions which would leave at the most only three or four countries in the Latin American area.

Instead of reacting with such alarm (e.g., Miguel Cuaderno) to the European common market—the underdeveloped countries should form a common market of their own.

But someone who is reasonably knowledgeable in these matters, like Raul Prebisch, may say: "In Latin America, reality is undermining the out-dated scheme of the international division of labour. . . ."[14] Prebisch does not switch to the other extreme and advocate wholesale use of trade restrictions to encourage industrialization. But many Latin American writers do exactly that. The Banco Nacional de México states:

For Mexico, high tariffs are essentially defensive. They mean the protection of infant industries during their formative period. They mean defense of the nation's international balance of payments against excessive expenditures on foreign luxuries, assuring the maintenance of adequate exchange reserves and enabling the nation to meet its international obligations. They make it possible for the country to spend scarce foreign exchange upon imports critically needed for development. . . .

The practical efficacy of protective tariffs for the encouragement of industry was historically demonstrated in the case of the United States. Mexico has now entered a period of industrialization similar to that experienced by her northern neighbor in the Nineteenth Century, although unfortunately without the advantage of a similar vast market. During such a period, a rational Mexican tariff policy can be an eco-

[14] United Nations, Economic Commission for Latin America, *The Economic Development of Latin America and Its Principal Problems* (Lake Success, 1950), p. 1.

nomic resource of the highest usefulness for the stimulation of industrial progress.[15]

Diatribes against the classical position on free trade (and comparative advantage) are frequent among the Latin American economists. They point out, quite correctly, that in a world of free trade the lagging country is at a disadvantage when it attempts to catch up because of the economic power of the more advanced countries. They then argue for tariffs, etc., as devices for protecting infant industries. It is this latter extension of the argument which does not follow. Yet, there is just enough truth in this sort of assertion to make it an attractive rationalization of a quite misguided policy—the extensive use of trade barriers such as tariffs, quotas, and licenses.

The truth of the matter is that the problem exists in just the form conceived by Raúl Prebisch and the Banco Nacional. But the trouble with the argument is with the unimaginative policy tool taken over from Friedrich List, Alexander Hamilton, Joseph Chamberlain, and Senator Reed Smoot.

(1) Certainly domestic producers need some assistance against the cutthroat competition of older, financially stronger companies in the more developed countries. (2) Certainly a combination of pure competition and free trade cannot be trusted to implement economic development in the underdeveloped countries. (3) Certainly some measures that will encourage the importation of machinery rather than Buick cars are desirable.

If trade barriers such as tariffs and quotas were the only way to accomplish the desired results, one would be forced to use them. But trade barriers mean goods scarcity during the period of transition. They mean that people whose basic need is goods will have less goods and higher priced goods while they starve themselves into a capacity for greater production. If there is any reasonable alternative to this procedure, it should be used—and, there is a reasonable alternative.

Alternative Policy: An attempt to construct the broad outlines of a more desirable system follows.

First, the system should be as simple as possible. The general rule in planning should be that the system of controls needs to be

[15] *Review of the Economic Situation of Mexico,* March, 1958, p. 7.

simple if the government is to have any faint idea what it is doing. A government attempting to encourage industrialization by a combination of a tariff structure with several thousand different rates, an import quota system involving the licensing of thousands of different importers on the basis of scores of different criteria, a foreign exchange control system which is fantastically complicated and probably corrupt as well, miscellaneous embargoes, assorted discriminations (some for political reasons on the basis of national origin), all of these things confuse, they do not facilitate, planning.

Planned interference with the economic process may occur at one of three stages. It may occur at (1) the production stage; it may affect (2) commerce—in the broad sense; or it may occur at (3) the consumption stage. It is the thesis of this writer that all of the commercial controls should be eliminated. They are the ones whose effect it is most difficult to judge. If you want to encourage a piece of industrialization the thing to do is to encourage it in some positive way, that is to say at the production stage, in a manner that makes it at least halfway likely that the desired development will occur. The negative assistance that is given by such measures as tariffs gives little assurance that the desired development will actually occur. Even if the development does take place, there may still be difficulty in inducing the enterpriser to emphasize large production rather than high unit profits and small volume. There may be difficulty in getting him to appreciate that the real purpose of the aid he has been given is to get more goods produced. Latin America is replete with cases where tariff protection granted on the basis of the infant industry argument has merely facilitated local producers in price gouging and profit making in a setting of limited production.

Controls to encourage production should occur at the production stage of the economic process. Controls to influence consumption patterns should occur at the consumption stage. Controls at the commercial stage, the effect of which it is so difficult to judge, should not be used for either of these purposes.

The chief problem at the moment would seem to be to suggest a workable pattern of controls to encourage production, that is to say a workable alternative to the infant industry tariff. Social capital (such as dams, highways, electric power projects, etc.) should probably be built outright by the government using its own funds, chiefly revenues raised by a tax system that takes money from the people who are most likely to spend it in a way that seems undesirable. That is to say, take the money from the people who would spend it to finance the import of Buick cars—a progressive income tax will do this. Another possibility is planned allocation of bank credit so that it gets into the hands of people who will use the money to finance desirable development projects. "Qualitative control" of the use of borrowed funds is necessary in this setting. To keep this process from being unduly inflationary, the tax system should be geared to take enough money away from people to prevent the inflationary effect. The tax system in conjunction with bank lending can also be made to serve much better the purpose for which exchange controls and quotas have been used. That is, they can guarantee that the people who are left with purchasing power are the people who will use it in the desirable way. The people left with purchasing power are those who will use it to import machinery rather than Buick cars. But at the same time everyone should have a free choice with what purchasing power he has to decide whether he wants to make his purchase at home or abroad, whether he wants to buy a luxury or a necessity.

In the absence of an international currency, I am tempted to say that the problem of the international balance of payments should be solved by a system of freely fluctuating foreign exchange rates. Anybody can then buy abroad who will pay the free market price for foreign exchange. Such a system avoids the difficulties involved in the exhaustion of foreign exchange reserves and the undesirable uncertainties of by-fits-and-starts devaluations. But there is not space here to discuss the manifold implications, most of them desirable, of a system of freely fluctuating rates. Suffice it to say that the problems which tariffs, quotas, licences, and exchange controls are intended to solve can be better solved by qualitative control of the identity of the individual who has effective purchasing power within the country, using bank credit policies and tax policies as the chief tools. Then, the man who has the most purchasing power in the domestic currency is the one who will be most able to import—that is to say, buy on a free foreign exchange market such foreign exchange as may be had; essentially under any system of foreign-exchange-rate setting, that is no more nor less than what the country's exports bring.

Barriers to People: Development is encouraged by the absence of barriers to effective interchange among people. It is discouraged by barriers. Isolation contributes to stagnation. This is an important consideration indicating the weakness of trade restrictions as devices for encouraging development. But another aspect of the problem of international barriers should concern us for a moment. The Latin American countries have very significant administrative barriers to the international movement of people. I am tempted to make the generalization that the American countries (the United States should be included in this list, but the behavior is probably costing the Latin American countries more because they are smaller countries) place more petty annoyances in the way of the traveler than do the European countries. That this does anybody any good is doubtful. Probably the purpose of many of the restrictions is to establish a control that makes it possible for a frightened dictator to check more effectively on whether his political enemies are traveling. But this type of usefulness hardly provides a justification for such controls if the matter is looked at from the viewpoint of the general interest.

Latin America can use during the next few years a tremendous amount of interchange of technical information. All measures that will facilitate this interchange are desirable. This of course does not mean that the Latin American countries should copy foreign or United States ways. But it does mean that they should want to have available to them as much information about those ways as possible and as much range of choice as possible. Then the Latin American planner, or the average citizen, will be in a better position for making his own decisions.

An Argentine, Alberdi, almost a hundred years ago advocated as a policy for his country: "To govern is to populate." He wished to encourage the migration of skilled Europeans to his country. Such a policy now on a grand scale could be good for both Europeans and native-born Latin Americans. The more productive economies that would result should benefit both groups.[16]

The population implications for Latin America of free inter-

[16] Another part of Alberdi's views which involved scorn for the Indian and willingness to see him die off is not defended here.

national movement of people may well be a substantial increase and greater heterogeneity in population. Both of these developments could have most desirable implications provided the various elements effectively fuse. Latin America's population of 24 per square mile is well below the United States average of 57. Latin America could well obtain a substantial increase in per capita productivity as a by-product of the population increase. At any rate, population increase resulting from migration or natural increase is at the moment no threat to Latin American welfare. Greater heterogeneity in the population, especially if the elements are well mixed, could stimulate everybody concerned. One of the reasons Latin America has lagged behind the United States in development may be because Latin America has been less of a melting pot: culturally, racially, ideologically.

EVALUATION

Of course the use or non-use of many policy tools not discussed above may influence industrialization. But, in general, one can fairly say that encouragement to industrialization should be positive rather than negative. (It should take the form of an engineering report on how a project can be implemented rather than the form of an import restriction to keep competing goods out.) The developing countries should have the greatest possible range and latitude in their decision making. They should not be protected from foreign competition, but they should have access, on the other hand, to wide markets for their own produce. And people should be free to come and go and to make their contributions when and where they choose. Freedom of action, implemented by a high and rising standard of living, is the essence of freedom.

That the Latin American population is rapidly rising and urbanizing is in part a result of the industrialization, in part a problem for industrialization to solve. Production must rise yet more rapidly if it is to provide for a substantial increase in per capita income. At the same time, the rising population in the cities will in time to come provide the skilled labor force to support the industrialization process.

CHAPTER IX

[RICHARD N. ADAMS *]

Freedom and Reform

in Rural Latin America

Basic Concepts of Freedom and Reform in Rural Latin America

In order to avoid metaphysical and moral issues that cannot be elucidated or resolved in the present chapter, I want here to restrict the use of the term "freedom" to political and religious freedom, i.e., the right to have a voice in one's own government and to worship as one chooses. This restriction does not, I believe, do an injustice to more philosophical usages, but it does exclude such dubious freedoms as the liberty to steal from one's neighbor or to ignore all incest prohibitions. It thus avoids freedoms that might lead to the dissolution of a community. It does, however, include some of the major issues over which revolutions have been staged, and towards which some reforms in history have been directed.

* Richard N. Adams received his M.A. and Ph.D. from Yale University, the latter in 1951, after undergraduate work at the University of Michigan. He has held a Social Science Research Council fellowship for a year's work in Peru, and has worked for the Institute of Social Anthropology of the Smithsonian Institution and the World Health Organization. Since 1956 he has been a Professor of Sociology and Anthropology at Michigan State University. He has done extensive field work in all of the Central American countries, as well as Panama, Peru, Chile and Bolivia. His major publications include: *Culture Surveys of Panama-Nicaragua-Guatemala-Honduras* (Washington, D.C., 1957); *Un Análisis de las Creencias y Practical Médicas en un Pueblo Indigena de Guatemala* (Guatemala City, 1952); *Change in the Andes, the Story of Muquiyauyo* (to be published in 1959 by the University of Washington Press, Seattle).

Reform is less abstract a term than freedom. Since ultimate freedom is an ideal state, real freedom is a relative one. Reform, however, is an actual process. Many of the activities of contemporary governments are called reforms, and are said, from time to time, to have freedom as one of their goals. Whereas one may seek more freedom, one actually reforms a government, a land tenure system, or something else.

The question here is what, in the lives of the rural peoples of Latin America, is the significant relationship between freedom and reform, between a relative state and an actual process? Let us consider four possibilities: (1) reform as an actual process may be a means by which freedom is relatively increased; (2) reform may be a means by which freedom is decreased; (3) reform may be a method by which the means for achieving relatively more freedom are kept accessible; or (4) reform may be a method by which these means for achieving freedom are restricted or kept shut. In the first two instances reform is a means of increasing or decreasing freedom. It would probably be correct to say that the contemporary peasants of Communist China are effectively having their freedom reduced by reforms, whereas the townspeople of France did gain wider freedom of action due to the reforms of the French Revolution. The second two situations do not propose that reform is a device by which the amount of freedom is changed, but rather that reform is a device by which the accesses to freedom, through whatever channels, are either kept open or shut. There are, then, two divergent roles of reform: one whereby it is an actual changer of the degree of freedom, and another in which it is a means of permitting freedom to be sought by whatever means possible. It will be the thesis of the present essay that while contemporary reforms in Latin America frequently restrict freedoms, and less frequently enlarge them, their most important role is as a mechanism by which access to freedom is maintained.

Let us distinguish between two very different kinds of rural Latin Americans: the independent aboriginal Indians on the one hand; and the peasants, laborers, and town dwellers who are part of the rural-urban complex of contemporary Western civilization on the other. The aboriginal groups are to be found principally in interior South America, but there are scattered survivals in Central America and Mexico. These aborigines have had varying contact with Western peoples and have at certain points taken over various Western culture traits. But they remain economically, socially and culturally independent of the Western centers.

The other kind of rural population is that which is part of the Western tradition, whether still culturally divergent although surrounded by it, as is the case with many of the Indian communities of Meso-America and the Andrean highlands, or historically derived from it, as are the Neo-American communities. These rural peoples are essentially part of city civilizations; their lives and activities are premised upon the existence of larger trade and production centers, both within their own national boundaries and beyond them. It is the presence of this kind of rural population that has given rise to theories concerning the "folk" societies and cultures. These groups patently do not have the independence of the aboriginal groups; and yet, they do not manifest many of the characteristics of the city dwellers. Folk-urban theorists, unfortunately, placed them on a continuum between the tribal societies at one end and the urban at the other, thereby obscuring the all important fact that they are a part of the city civilizations, a complementary necessity to the city, and therefore quite distinct from independent tribal societies.

There are some communities or population groups that superficially provide a problem of classification, but on closer inspection they are easily placed. There are indigenous populations that have been somewhat ignored by the moving Western civilization, so that they give the appearance, when first encountered, of being independent of this civilization. Such is the case with some isolated highland Andean communities (in the Department of Apurimac, Peru, for example). Whether these communities are actually independent of the urban centers and the civilization of the nations that contain them is almost an academic question. Consistently ignored, they have tended towards ever intensifying isolation; but movements within them are of national concern. They must, therefore, be included as a part of the city civilizations. Another problem is presented by the lowland indigenous groups that move within the orbit of the city civilizations for varying periods. Some of the Amazonian tribes that turned to rubber tapping, and thereby underwent profound social change, seem to have operated within the city system for a time, and then returned to their independent status. To the degree that groups become dependent upon city-oriented activities, they may be said to have moved out of the first rural condition, and to have become encapsulated or surrounded by the city, even though their individual members may never have seen an urban center.

Freedom and Reform Among the Independent Aboriginal Groups

At the time of the Spanish conquest most of South America was peopled with societies of Indians. These societies were organized principally on a kinship basis, sometimes of extraordinary complexity, and on territorial identification. By and large, the Indians were agricultural or semi-agricultural peoples, depending in part upon the products of horticulture and in part on hunting, fishing and gathering. In the extremities and isolated interior were to be found groups entirely without agriculture. Through the course of postconquest history these tribes have been exterminated, pushed back or assimilated; few remain today.

Without resorting to Rousseauian dreams, it is still abundantly evident that these tribes enjoyed a very real degree of freedom, more extensive than that which could obtain in city civilizations. While periodically in conflict with other tribes or communities, the individuals politically had a direct voice in their government, and did not suffer from stressful alternatives in religious matters. Indeed, it is not incorrect to say that in most cases organized political control was absent. In its place, order in the society was maintained through observance of kinship and economic exchange obligations, by respect for traditions and concern with public opinion and supernatural sanctions. Political control approaching a kingship situation was found only in limited regions, usually those under considerable influence from the much more highly developed societies of Meso-America or the Andean highlands. For the most part, however, the head of a community was a person regarded as the most capable, and adherence by the members of the populations to his suggestions and directions depended upon their respect for him. Most of these societies were, in a real sense, prepolitical.

Freedom for many of these tribes was restricted principally by natural obstacles, and by other tribes that might, from time to time, decide that a raid was appropriate. But there was no consistent and progressively destructive threat to their freedom except through contact with other groups. While such a menace was endemic prior to the conquest, the arrival of the Neo-Americans provided a new and deadlier enemy that made the situation assume epidemic proportions. The advent of the white man brought about multiple forms of restrictions. The aboriginal response to the activities of soldiers, missionaries, and men interested in exploiting the natural resources of the lowlands was varied. In most instances it was not realized until much too late just what intercourse with the white man entailed. Over the course of the centuries, however, repeated ill effects in the form of disease and warfare decimation, slave traffic, and reduction into mission settlements with concomitant restrictions on hunting and traditional practices conveyed a lesson that was taken to heart by various surviving peoples.

Some communities disintegrated completely, either disappearing or surviving to the present time as little more than poverty-stricken appendages to Neo-American settlements and therefore constituting a part of the city civilizations. Some communities have repeatedly tried to move back and literally avoid further contact with European centers. From time to time a few arrows are let loose at available Europeans, but evasion is preferred to contact of any kind. And some societies have even given up, overtly preferring social suicide to producing more children for assimilation into the new cultures. In a few instances, the Neo-European nations have felt that some sort of salvation for aboriginal groups was warranted and have afforded them a degree of protection from the more haphazard exploiters. Even these cases involve a limited tolerance of the aboriginal culture and reflect a significant restriction on freedom. They are only a variant of incorporation into the realities of a dominant city civilization.

The rationale is frequently employed by Neo-Europeans, especially missionaries, that contact with Western civilization is, in fact, freeing the aborigines from the "ignorance" in which they were living, from the "superstitions" that made them fearful of certain actions, and introducing them to the wide ranging advantages of Western civilization. In the opinion of the present writer, this borders on sheer nonsense and is a difficult position to maintain since these Western advantages have seldom been unprejudicedly evaluated by aboriginal peoples free to make the choice and possessing a clear view of the ramifications. The argument sounds too much like the rationale behind the newly established "People's Republics" of eastern Europe and the Far East.

Freedom in the political sense, then, has a very special meaning in these societies which generally lack political organizations and in which administrative functions are carried out by neighborhood groups, by bands of family or related families with head men. One cannot, within the context of the aboriginal cultures, separate their political freedom from their entire way of life. The same may be said of the religious practices. The religion is, also, tied in with many other activities. One can see how freedom could be reduced by somehow forbidding the Indians their religious and political activities. But one could hardly extend them more freedom than they have now.

Reform activities in the aboriginal societies are of two types. There are, first, overt changes in the rules of conduct undertaken by members of the society in response to problems they face. It is a common misconception, found even among some ethnologists, that change is uncommon in tribal societies, and that inventions (and reforms must be considered as social inventions) are rare. The fact of the matter is that inventions are probably frequent but that for various reasons they may not be capitalized upon. Few Westerners have spent a long enough time living with the lowland tribal groups of South America to provide us with a meaningful estimate of the frequence of social invention. Where a certain Christian belief has been accepted by members of some communities under the prodding of missionaries, the acceptance itself can be seen as a reform effort, although the specific ramifications and images of the new belief may vary considerably among the Indians. Perhaps the most famous kind of reform efforts that have something of an internal quality, in that they are sponsored by people who are recognized members of the society, are the so-called nativistic or revitalization movements that crop up from time to time in the course of the breakdown of aboriginal societies. Movements of this kind are better known in the United States, where the Ghost Dance occurred, and in Melanesia, where a series of such reactions to contact followed World War II. Records on these reform efforts in the Latin American aboriginal populations are skimpy, and few of them have been satisfactorily recorded.

A reform urge was definitely manifested in the religiously inspired migration of some nineteenth century Guaraní speaking peoples towards the Atlantic Ocean.[1] While little known, it seems that there was a large scale movement of these peoples in search of a "land without evil." Another such effort was the insurrection led by Santos Atahuallpa in the montaña of Peru in the middle of the eighteenth century among the missionized Indians.[2] This led to the death of many missionaries and, coupled with the later expulsion of the Jesuits, left the efforts of many years of mission work little to show beyond the decimation of the Indian population.

The second significant type of reform activity among the independent aboriginal tribes is that sponsored by outsiders for the benefit of the Indians, although the nature of the benefit is always defined by the outsiders. Here again the religious mission activities, as seen by the missionaries themselves and by the members of the Christian population that support them, are pertinent. These activities are undertaken in the conviction that they are "good for" the Indians. This type of reform activity marks the initial incorporation of the independent tribes into a socio-cultural system of the rural-urban type. To the extent that missionizing is successful (without exterminating the native population), the missionized segments in fact become part of the rural-urban system. As we will see shortly, this kind of reform is typical of the city civilizations: a change is pursued by members of one segment in the interests of what they believe to be the benefit of the members of another.

Among other significant reforms are those instituted from

[1] See Alfred Métraux, "Migrations Historiques des Tupí-Guaraní," *Journal de la Société des Américanistes de Paris,* XIX (1927); James B. Watson, *Cayuá Culture: A Study in Acculturation and Methodology,* Memoir Number 73 of the American Anthropological Association (Menasha, Wisconsin, 1952), pp. 51–54.

[2] See Julian H. Steward, "Tribes of the Montaña: An Introduction," in *Handbook of South American Indians,* Vol. 3 (Washington, D.C., 1948), pp. 511–513.

time to time by laws as well as by individual endeavors aimed at protecting Indians from excessive exploitation by Neo-Americans. Included in this category would be the now famous work of Rondon of Brazil, the reservation system established for the Cuna of Panama, and some of the attempts at Indian legislation by many other countries of the hemisphere. Unfortunately, in many cases the definition of what was good for the Indian closely reflected the needs of the Neo-Americans: the extensive efforts since the time of Bolívar to destroy the Indian community afford one such instance, just as the mission pattern of reducing a jungle population to living in larger nuclear communities constitutes another. The efforts of the colonial Jesuits in Paraguay, and elsewhere, were overtly directed at protecting the Indians from the depredations of the colonists *and* imposing what was "good" for the Indian upon him.

Reform of this kind has been the doubtful privilege of the Indian since early in the history of White-Indian relations. It is hard to argue that it has in any fundamental way led toward greater freedom. Nor can it be held that, in most cases, it has been designed with freedom as a primary goal. Rather, these reform efforts have been but single steps in the acculturation, assimilation or general elimination of the Indian as an Indian, and their basic purpose has been to create a working adjustment between civilizations. Indeed, insofar as the aboriginal independent tribes are concerned, the instances in which reform has been directed at something that might be called freedom are those which were nativistic efforts or insurrections against white control. These have not usually resulted in more freedom, except for limited periods. The very goal of missionizing is to restrict freedom of religion, and the purpose of most Neo-American activity is to reduce the political sovereignty of the Indian. Since the degree of freedom available to the Central and South American independent Indians can hardly be imagined to be greater than it is, almost any contact with other societies is bound to reduce and not enhance it.

However, the presence of these reforms, religious and secular, has some meaning in terms of whether the aborigine has any choice at all in the course of his transition into the city civilization. Granted that the societies as integral entities break down under the impact of the West, the reforms sometimes turn out to be a way by which the society can make the transition to Western civilization and gain access to the freedoms of that way of life. So, even though a reform effort may substantially reduce the areas of free action of aboriginal peoples, it does hold a door open for the achievement of freedom within the context of the new culture to which the members of that society are shifting.

Controls Among Rural Peoples of the City Civilization: Internal Relations

An extensive treatment of the aboriginal independent tribes smacks somewhat of futile moralizing; Western civilization is expanding, and the world's two billion people now approach three. Of greater significance are rural peoples who are an intrinsic part of this expanding population. The Indian and mestizo of rural Latin America, the subsistence agriculturalist, the farm laborer, the migrant planter, the village craftsman, and the country shopkeeper form a very important part of the total Latin American population. Whereas there is a conflict of the two independent and traditional ethical systems at stake in the case of the autonomous aborigines, freedom and reform are specifically part of the Western tradition, and therefore a consideration within that context is appropriate.

Any community is organized as a compromise between the necessities for internal, day-to-day operation, and the demands and needs that relate the community members individually and collectively to the outside. This is equally true in independent aboriginal societies and in rural Western societies. But in the latter there is a profound difference in that the outside elements are, in themselves, a series of related social, economic, and political forces. It is thus realistic, in city civilizations, to distinguish the varied complexes of outside factors from those operating within the rural portion of the whole. This is not to deny for a moment that the two are interrelated and that to consider one alone gives a badly distorted picture. In order to examine the status and nature of freedom, however, it is convenient to consider separately those restraints on action that are due to the internal organization of the rural community, and those that are directly due to relations that ramify from the city toward the communities and from a community toward the outside world.

Inside the rural community there are, as among the aboriginal groups, many forms of social control that are embedded in familial kin, and voluntary group relationships. Our concern is not with these, but with the organized control that can be termed political. The nature of rural political organization over most of Latin America can be classified into four general kinds of systems. While usually exclusive of each other, there is some overlapping or blending. There are: (1) the corporate community system; (2) the cacique system; (3) the farm system; and (4) the civil system. We will describe each of these briefly.

Corporate communities[3] consist of well defined groups of people with collective interest in the maintenance of community integrity. In almost all cases, these communities are composed of peoples of an Indian tradition, and have maintained their structures (although these have undergone a series of alterations over the centuries) as something distinct from community structures elsewhere in their region.

Historically many characteristics of these systems can be traced to Iberian influences, but functionally they operate with a high degree of autonomy. Of particular importance is that their form of the community structure is distinct from the official, constitutionally accepted, organization as set forth in the nation's municipal code. The local organization sponsors the activities which the members of the corporate community feel it necessary to undertake. Functionaries are recruited and selected in accordance with local traditional means; and prerequisites for office are also traditionally recognized. The political organization of these communities is usually only one complex of many that set them culturally apart from others of the country. Just as the political structure is distinct and semiautonomous from the national system, so also is the entire culture. It has been pointed out elsewhere that the total breakdown of this political organization usually marks the ultimate disintegration of these communities as distinct cultural entities.[4]

[3] This term is borrowed from Eric Wolfe, "Types of Latin American Peasantry: A Preliminary Discussion," *American Anthropologist*, Vol. 57, No. 3 (June, 1955), pp. 452–471. Wolfe was concerned with a classification on economic principles rather than political, but his corporate community is phenomenologically the same as ours.
[4] See Richard N. Adams, *Cultural Surveys of Panama-Nicaragua-Guatemala-El*

While corporate communities can most readily be identified as those surviving in the traditions of the Central Mexican, Mayan, and Andean pre-Columbian civilization, it is important to recognize that there have been "incorporations" in recent years. One of these that has received considerable attention in the Andean area is Muquiyauyo, a central Sierran community of Indians and mestizos. It should be noted that Muquiyauyo is not the only community to have passed in recent decades into the corporate status, although evidence suggests that it has been a leader within its region; it should also be noted that it is culturally far more mestizo than Indian, and that the corporate character was achieved through disengagement from the indigenous heritage.[5]

Muquiyauyo had operated essentially under the sort of civil system that will be described below. Then, in the first decades of the present century a series of steps was taken that culminated in the establishment of a separate community government. This administrative organization, which paralleled the previous civil hierarchy, accomplished through the efforts of community members various projects for civic improvement. It managed to hold together community-owned lands, and in effect transformed the community into a capitalistic unit. This type of intracommunity structure is a far cry from most of the surviving corporate indigenous communities of the Meso-American and Andean regions, but from the point of view of political organization, it enjoys the same kind of autonomy from national government control and influence that they do. National government leaders are perfectly aware that variant organizational activities are under way in the corporate communities; but they tolerate these processes so long as they do not undermine what degree there is of national unity, and so long as the communities meet the government's demands for tax payments, recruits for the army, labor supply for the growing agricultural and industrial enterprises, agrarian produce for the expanding cities, and votes for needy politicians.

Salvador-Honduras, Pan American Sanitary Bureau, Scientific Publication No. 33 (Washington, 1957); and "La Ladinización en Guatemala," in *Integración Social en Guatemala,* Seminario de Integración Social Guatemalteca, Publicación Numero 3 (Guatemala City, 1956), pp. 213-244.

[5] See Richard N. Adams, *Change in the Andes,* American Ethnological Society (in press, University of Washington Press, Seattle).

Civil communities do not change to the corporate type very readily. In fact, such an occurrence is contrary to the increasing involvement of Indian communities in the general nationalistic development. But, in a case like that of Muquiyauyo, it is not a step backward, as it provides a path for local progress under local leaders.

The second type of political control within the local community is what we are calling the cacique system. It may be a mistake to employ this worn term here, but it fits so well that its use may be excused. In the cacique system, a single individual within a given community occupies a position of political control through the exercise of extraordinary powers. The usual cacique gains his position not only through his great personal influence within the community, but also by his effectiveness in serving as a link between the community members and the outside. He may be the local labor recruiter and vote organizer, and at the same time the person recognized locally as the one to turn to if a loan, good advice, the settlement of a dispute, or help in evading the police is needed. He is something of a ward heeler as well as a headman and representative to the outside world.

To the cacique, then, the community members look for internal order and for guidance in external relations. From him they also expect aid in understanding the demands of the outside and in escaping excessively onerous pressures. The cacique system may arise when a corporate community organization proves not entirely satisfactory for dealing with the national government. The two systems may merge, with the corporate organization continuing to function in regard to matters that do not concern the outside world. Caciques may arise, however, in any community that, for cultural or other reasons, is isolated from the national socio-cultural system. They permit a community to maintain effective internal operations in the face of outside demands through the tacit allotment of extraordinary powers to a single individual to act in the name of the community. While this leader may not be liked personally, he is strongly respected for his influence with outsiders.

Caciques are found in communities of many ethnic colors. A surviving Pipil Indian community in El Salvador has an important cacique, although he is gradually being replaced by a straight civil system. A Black Carib community on the north coast of Honduras has its principal governmental focus in the person of the cacique. An hacienda community in highland Peru, for some years now under an effective development program, is tending to develop a cacique system, with the individual in question being one who lived for years outside the community and therefore understands better the aims of the national development personnel. Caciques are often pictured by outsiders as little dictators, as bosses, and in some cases there is much truth in this. However, their significance can only be understood in the totality of their roles, one of which is that of protector (at times inadvertently so far as the individual cacique is concerned) of the local socio-cultural system. The official position that a cacique may occupy in the community ranges from some formal post, such as mayor, to simply the status of an "elder statesman" who oversees political activities and, frequently, makes sure he gets his "cut" from any activities that seem remunerative. The cacique system is not all sweetness and light for, as Friedrich has illustrated in regard to the Tarascan area, there may be contending factions behind different individuals for the privileges of power.[6]

The large farm system is the third to be considered here. This differs from the corporate community in that its internal structure is imposed upon it by the form of farm management system that it used. The farm system involves a permanent resident community, sometimes of a variant ethnic or socio-cultural population, sometimes simply Ibero-American. This population is essentially organized along a farm labor basis. Real control and decision-making powers stem from the farm owner or administrator, and are carried through channels to the work force. Changes within the lines of authority are usually made at the discretion of the management. Of course, if a given intermediate foreman fails to keep effective control over those under him, he loses his position and the extra salary and privileges that go along with it.

The farm and cacique systems are similar in that the major focus of power (in one case the farm management, in the other

<hr>

[6] Paul W. Friedrich, "A Tarascan Cacicazgo: Structure and Function," in *Systems of Political Control and Bureaucracy in Human Societies,* American Ethnological Society (Seattle, 1958), pp. 23–29.

the cacique) acts as the intermediary between the outside world and the farm. If a farm laborer is wanted by the national police for some crime, it is up to the management to locate the culprit and send him out. If the farm laborers need special help, they turn to the management. But while there are parallel functions between the farm managers and the cacique, the structure is quite different. The cacique owes his position to a delicate balance of outside and inside pressures. The farm owner stands in a legal position with respect to the farm and its labor that the cacique does not enjoy. The cacique can lose his position simply by losing his influence. In the farm system, power inheres automatically and permanently in the owner and administration. The development of agrarian labor unions in some areas in recent years has done much to change the nature of the farm system, but for the most part farm communities continue to be essentially different in structure from the others discussed here. In some areas the municipal governments are more and more taking over legal responsibilities from the farm owners, but even in these cases the fundamental activities of the community are shaped by the political power of the land owner.

The final type of local political and administrative organization is by far the most important in terms of the number of communities working within it. It is the political and administrative organization that is sponsored by the state, usually through a municipal code and other decrees and laws regulating public life. Latin American countries are generally centralized in their political systems, and one aspect of this is the national level formulation of the patterns under which local communities govern themselves. While the specific patterns vary from one country to another, there is a local territorial unit designated as the "district" or the "municipality" (for convenience, we will use the last term in the present discussion). This unit has within it at least one nucleated center, where the municipal governing structure usually has its headquarters. Comprising this governing structure are a mayor, a municipal secretary, a fiscal, a treasurer, a town council of aldermen and, in addition, assorted varieties of employees. Depending upon the country, the constitution, and the present incumbent government, the local officers may be elected by the residents of the municipality, or they may be appointed by a superior provincial, or state, or even national functionary.

The basic pattern of local government in Spanish America has a long and honorable history, but in recent decades its importance has been increasingly subordinated to interests of the growing national capitals. This trend has often been accompanied, paradoxically, by the institution of local elections. But, in order to understand the functioning of the municipality, one must keep in mind that it is fundamentally the local subdivision of the national governmental system, not an independent community government. The basic functions of the municipal government are set for it by the national government, not necessarily by the needs of the local population. To put it in an extreme form, the the municipality is regarded more as a tax collecting agency of the national government than as an articulate assembly of local residents. Whether or not, then, there are local elections for municipal officials has limited significance. The municipal electoral procedure is of importance only in that particularly lively political activity within the community may be the sign of discontent or of the effective campaigning on a national scale of a previously obscure contender.

The meaning of local control at the municipal level is illustrated in an exaggerated way in Honduras. The municipality in Honduras holds elections for local officials. But the national administrative code stipulates that some areas are too important to entrust to locally elected officials; these are designated as districts. A district is a region of financial importance, such as a port or the banana growing areas of the north coast. Districts do not enjoy local franchise and the officials are appointed by the national government. Thus, local democracy is tolerated where it will do no harm. But, as one district official expressed it, the country cannot afford to have its district officials spending half the year playing politics in order to get the vote. They have the serious responsibility of collecting taxes and maintaining the *status quo* so that the extraction industries and ports of entry can continue to pour their taxes into the national treasury.

Under the Spanish colonial system distribution of the land was often controlled through the representatives of the crown. Land was allotted to Indians in Peru on the basis of civil status, age and sex, and theoretically, reallotments were made periodically. The interest of the central authority in land tenure systems has continued through the centuries. One of Bolívar's first decrees embodied the endeavor to eliminate the rights of Indian communities to hold land collectively. With the advent of the century of the common man, concern with land has turned to attempts to provide some for each family. In recent decades Mexico has expropriated most extensive hacienda holdings and instituted the *ejido* system; Guatemala and Bolivia have attempted agrarian reforms, and Peru is trying to find a way to release some of its indigenous communities from age long attachments to absentee land holders. Land reform laws have inevitably included clauses setting up modes of control. These involve new elements in the local hierarchy of government, such as the *ejidal* committees of Mexico and, for a time, the agrarian committees in Guatemala. Such committees are legally constituted by the national government, as are the civil municipal organizations, but frequently for limited periods they wield more power than regular channels of local administration, since they have access to land for distribution and the authorization of the central government to press expropriation. Where this sort of committee is established, the community affected still remains basically within the system previously established by the central government. The change has not been in the source of authority, but rather in intermediary agencies.[7] Agrarian committees do, however, undermine what semblance of local self-rule had previously been permitted.

Before leaving this subject, it should be pointed out that both corporate and cacique-headed communities may bear outward features of similarity to the civil administrative structure. To identify a community as being of one or another type, there must be knowledge of precisely how power is, in fact, exercised, and how the men who play the dominant roles achieve their positions and maintain them.

Influences Over the External Relations of City Civilization Rural Peoples

Turning now to the external relations of the communities, we find ourselves in a broad field that can probably more easily be

[7] See Richard N. Adams, compiler, *Political Changes in Guatemalan Indian Communities,* Middle American Research Institute, Tulane University, Publication No. 24 (New Orleans, 1957), pp. 1–24.

classified for present purposes in terms of areas of concern. We will distinguish four such areas for discussion here: the economic, the political, the religious, and the welfare.

The rural communities of Latin America vary considerably in the degree to which they are economically dependent upon the city centers. It is hard to find one that is not in some way so dependent, be it ever so small. Even Indian peasant communities that appear to be culturally autonomous usually rely upon basic metal tools, like the machete or hoe, on the availability of cash wages that may be earned on distant farms in years of scarcity, and on production directed in some part for an external market. Generally, dependence is quite high. This is particularly true in the Meso-American Indian communities which Sanford Mosk [8] and others have shown to be highly commercialistic and tied in with the national market. The same situation prevails among the isolated regions of the Andean highlands, where production for subsistence is more standard, and obligations to the outside world are often paid in labor. Even in these areas, an expanding population is finding its outlet in the cities and on commercial haciendas.

Economic considerations not only restrict the freedom of action of the rural Latin American, but formally direct his activities: he is pummeled by the market on the one hand, and the climate on the other. There is some buffer from the first, however, because of the subsistence nature of much of the farming. A poor market may make a bad year, but it will not always drive a man from the fields. Working on a subsistence level, many farmers in Latin America can last out a poor season or even a depression, although none would regard these conditions as satisfactory. The rural laborer is not in such a position. When the market goes down, so do his wages. Although he may produce a little on a subsistence basis, it is never enough, and he is always dependent upon outside earnings.

Politically there are various ways in which the rural community is dependent upon and brought into relationship with the outside world: funds and technical help for civil improvements usually must be sought from the outside; legal decisions on disputes are often carried beyond the local justice of the peace;

---

[8] Sanford Mosk, "Indigenous Economy in Latin America," *Inter-American Economic Affairs*, VIII, No. 3 (Winter, 1954), 3–25.

and pay for the school teachers (as most schools are run by the central government) comes from national sources. In return, the local dweller may be called upon from time to time to get into a truck with his fellows and attend a political rally or vote in the approved manner at the nearby provincial capital; and he will be expected to pay taxes on certain activities and properties. Political demands are not infrequently enwrapped in economic demands, so that to separate one from the other is artificial.

Religious obligations of the rural inhabitants were eroded by the anticlerical reactions that set in over much of the continent following independence. From time to time, however, the presence of a priest or a Protestant missionary has led to a flurry of activity. Most of rural Latin America is Roman Catholic today, and in much of it Catholicism is maintained without strong help from the clergy. As will be noted shortly, this is a reason behind some of the reform movements afoot. Religious ideology, however, whether immediately bolstered by an organized church or not, is generally Christian, and ties with that tradition provide a basis for further religious activities within the rural areas. It would not be far from the truth to say that while formal church activities may not be of great concern to many, the saints, Christ and the Virgin are regular inhabitants of the countryside. Christianity seeps from the pores of the countryman in the form of reliance upon the Virgin, fear of the devil, dependence upon the saints in healing or bringing certain events to pass, and in simple expletives.

The final corpus of outside influences and demands made upon the countryman we include under the general category of welfare. Here we find those activities, stemming usually from the national government, that concern formal education, public health, agricultural extension and similar matters in which the wealth of the state and the technical knowledge of outsiders may be placed (sometimes under pressure) at the disposal of the rural dweller. Beyond these extension type activities there is also, of course, the enactment of an increasing number of health laws pertaining to sewage, medicines, the treatment of foods, and other related matters. Municipal systems often include posts of "public health inspectors." These and similar offices, assigned to aldermen, involve little more than collecting the tax on sales of medical supplies, or perhaps overseeing the occasional slaughtering of livestock.

As the central government's concern for the people as a whole grows, however, welfare activities become increasingly demanding. Major among these to date has been the matter of education. Although literacy is still low in many of the countries, there has often been a public school system, and in recent years great steps have been made to extend education. Some communities have resented the fact that in the interests of education children are removed from the home, and thereby are lost as an economic asset for work in the field and domestic chores. This problem is much more serious in Indian communities than among mestizo populations, but it is by no means absent in the latter. Tied into the welfare activities are periodic collections of money or materials for improving the school house, building a new clinic, or whatever it may be.

This very hasty summary of the more common kinds of ties that relate rural communities to their city centers in the rural-urban civilization of Latin America makes it clear that the rural dweller certainly does not enjoy the degree and kind of freedom found among the still independent aboriginal tribes. Among the political systems described earlier, the corporate communities appear to enjoy the greatest relative amount of freedom. In point of fact they may at times be under more restraints than the others since their members must observe the rules both of the national society and those of their own differing traditions. But they have made the choice to remain, at least in part, within their own traditions. The individual in the corporate community has much closer access to and control over his immediate leaders. For those dwelling under civil administration, control is exercised many miles away in a provincial or national capital; and in the cacique and farm systems, being on good terms with the local boss may be a critical factor. Essentially, however, the corporate community can simply ignore the leader that is considered inept. While this can sometimes be done with a cacique, to do so is more perilous; and it is more difficult still under a farm system. In the civil system, of course, it cannot be done without threatening revolution.

Reforms for the Countryman

If the above is an overview of some of the aspects of freedom among the rural peoples of Latin American civilization, what of reform? We have, obviously, already touched upon it in a number of connections. The establishment of a contrary, corporate government in the community of Muquiyauyo was a case of internally sponsored reform. Welfare efforts from the central government are clearly reforms of a kind, and efforts to strengthen religious dogmatism or to change individuals from one faith to another are also in the nature of reforms. In reviewing these few cases, the distinction evident among the independent aboriginal tribes is seen to be present here too. There are reforms that are sponsored from within a rural community and there are others sponsored from the outside.

Let us look first to an internally sponsored reform, the case of Muquiyauyo. While at the time of his field study the writer encountered various assertions that the town's development of an autonomous community organization was the result of consistent and purposeful steps in that direction, a study of the records did not entirely support the claim. Rather, the reform in village organization in Muquiyauyo can almost be characterized as haphazard. Over a period of at least sixty years the members and leaders of the community were faced with problems in dealing with the central government and the outside in general. Their quest for answers to these problems led them gradually, step by step, to a point where the creation of an autonomous organization was one, perhaps the only, way out of a difficult situation. While the Muquiyauyinos deserve every credit for what they in fact achieved in the way of free action in the face of increasing centralization of government, it would be a mistake to believe that they did it solely under the banner of a preconceived sixty-year plan for freedom.

Moreover, in the Muquiyauyo situation, the addition of community organization to the regular civil government amounted not, in point of fact, to a reduction of restrictions upon the members of the community, but the imposition, by their own choice, of an increasing number. However, from the point of view of the residents, these further restrictions were actually a step toward free action, for they thereby gained protection against domination in certain matters by the central government. Whether or not freedom was achieved in this matter becomes a matter of point of view. Patently many Muquiyauyinos believe that they now can exercise a degree of freedom not to be found among many other neighboring communities.

Examination of externally imposed reforms involves one, however, in a still more difficult problem, arising from the fact that the countryman is seldom given a choice in the matter. Most reforms of the past one hundred years did not derive from the rural population itself. Even in those cases where a rural population was very active, reform was most frequently the brainchild of a literate or city oriented group. Where there are exceptions to this general statement, the reforms frequently assumed the shape of revolutions, and were usually a part of a greater revolutionary pattern.

Let us, for purposes of discussion, limit ourselves to three kinds of externally derived reforms: agrarian, religious and welfare. The first of these, under one guise or another, has been of mounting concern throughout much of Latin America, although it has been of most significance in Mexico, Guatemala and Bolivia. In Mexico the agrarian reform was part of a total social revolution, and years were required for its implementation after the military action of the uprising had terminated. Similarly in Bolivia, agrarian changes came in the train of a sweeping revolution that also involved nationalization of the major mines, disbandment of the army, and even an attempt to nationalize the entire education system, including the universities. In Guatemala, too, the agrarian reform arose as a development subsequent to a significant revolution. While it did not follow immediately and was itself a partial cause of a reaction to the excesses of the revolution, it was identified with broad revolutionary activity, and cannot easily be extracted as an independent event. Unless we attribute revolutions in their totality to the peasant and small town peoples, we cannot ascribe the agrarian reforms in these situations to an uprising of the peasants.

In fact, while there was in limited regions some peasant activity that pointed toward an interest in agrarian reform, actual attempts at improving the *status quo* were sponsored by members of the urban-rural intelligentsia. This paper cannot undertake to estimate to what degree these reformers were involved with international leftist preferences, and to what degree they were idealists, set upon "freeing" their rural fellow countrymen from what they perceived to be bondage and restrictive labor and living conditions. It is the writer's impression that there were varying proportions of both elements involved. The issue, however, concerns not the motives of individual leaders; fundamentally at stake is agrarian reform in its total context, involving an attempt in many parts of the world to alleviate the limitations endured by the peasant because of his low productivity, isolation from city influences, poor income, and other conditions associated with the term "underdeveloped." To see Latin American agrarian reforms apart from similar movements in Egypt and elsewhere in the world is to miss their meaning. They are as much efforts on the part of the urbanites to advance their own political and economic positions as they are attempts to better the condition of the rural inhabitant. The issue is one of nationalism as much as it is goodness of heart. If one reads closely the rationales of the men who have championed agrarian reform, the peasant pictured has two faces: on the one hand he is downtrodden but righteous, poverty stricken but wise, subject to feudal toil but seeking the light of a new day, and so on; on the other, his economic ignorance is retarding the national development, his antiquated traditions are responsible for the backwardness of the nation, and he is incapable of handling his own economic future without government guidance. One wonders if the printed and spoken words refer to the same peasant. In fact, of course, there is truth in both faces, even though the two together fall far short of the whole truth.

Agrarian reform, then, while aimed on the one hand at improving the peasant's economic situation, is also a vested interest of certain nationalistic groups who see the peasant as holding the country down. Add to this a third element, that of a few reformers affiliated with international Communism who hope to utilize the peasant in shattering the current social system, and the relation of agrarian reform to freedom takes on an entirely different hue.

Another kind of reform now under way in Latin America is

religious in nature. It involves the efforts of both major branches of the Christian Church to win adherents. While there are representatives of other world religions in Latin America, they have not come as proselytizing reformists. Among the Christian churches, the Roman Catholic is, of course, dominant in the area at present. Almost a century of varying degrees of anticlericalism and heightened attentiveness to material considerations, preceded by such acts as the expulsion of the Jesuits in the latter part of the colonial era, have reduced the Church today to a condition of extreme weakness. By the beginning of World War II, many parishes had been without a priest for decades and there ware significant elements in the clergy itself that proved inadequate to their tasks. In some areas, particularly in Indian communities, religious observances were maintained in spite of absence of the clergy and the general deficiencies of the Church. Elsewhere, priests with insufficient resources were doing their best to serve the needs of an expanding population. Some countries had enacted laws prohibiting the entrance of additional priests, thereby compounding the difficulties of the Church.

Reforms sponsored by the Catholic Church, essentially directed at rekindling a faith which through years of insufficient attention has tended to become dormant, have been undertaken in a number of ways. Seminaries have been bolstered, political groups that promise the Church more freedom of action have been supported, and foreign missions have been set up in regions where local bishoprics were too poor to minister to the needs of the population. From the point of view of the rural peoples, all of this has sometimes entailed a good deal of activity that can best be characterized as reform. Religious sodalities are now being sponsored and strengthened and traces of colonial religious practices, such as the *cofradias,* are being suppressed. The local clergy is being spruced up with more Europeans and North Americans, and the seminaries are thus being prepared to turn out more effective national priests. Above all, the efforts of the Church aim at preserving the dominant position of Catholicism that has been characteristic of the past.

The Protestants, for their part, see their efforts also in the nature of a reform. They are concerned, however, not with the strengthening of a Church, but with bringing light to a population that they consider to be dwelling in the darkness of a rival religion. Missionaries, indeed whole groups of them, undertake to live in rural communities and to convert the members of the population to their particular brand of Protestantism. Protestant reforms demand a good deal more, psychologically, than do the Catholic. Not only must the background assumptions of Catholicism, traditionally carried on even in communities where priests have not effectively worked for decades, be given up, but smoking and drinking, both habits of considerable antiquity among rural populations, are often placed beyond the reach of the good *evangélico*.

Both Catholic and Protestant reformers have decided that religious reform is not enough, and have long since taken to enhancing their activities with efforts at social welfare. Protestant missionary activity is often combined with medical work, the introducing of agricultural improvements, and the establishment of schools. Among Catholics, as parish priests generally have little training in such matters, welfare work is most often carried on by Catholic Action groups and missonaries.* The rivalry between Protestant and Catholic missionaries in the Latin American countryside has, obviously, its paradoxical aspects. One Protestant of many years residence in a tropical community complained that the work among the Indians demanded cooperation between him and the local Franciscan priest, but that the latter would have none of it. "We both have our feet on the same Bible," said he, conveniently forgetting that miles away in the highlands his Protestant colleagues were trying to eliminate the Catholic religion.

The reasons behind reform efforts in religion do not seem to be any more closely related to freedom than do those in the agrarian field. Again, the argument is that the rural resident will be better off.

While welfare reforms are involved in both religious and agrarian activities, they are also sponsored as ends in themselves. At the outset they have the same concern with nationalistic de-

* The National Catholic Rural Life Conference, under the Executive Directorship of Monsignor L. G. Ligutti, has also in recent years been extremely active in working for reform in rural Latin America. [Editor's note]

velopment as the agrarian reforms; indeed, the latter could for certain purposes be regarded as a special case of welfare effort. Welfare goals also embrace, among other considerations, public health programs (including the attempted eradication of certain endemic and epidemic diseases, environmental sanitation, maternal and child health, rural clinics, and the like), agricultural development and extension programs, improvement of education facilities, bettering the quality and financial remuneration of teachers, and introduction of new vocational alternatives through special schools. Once it becomes known in the countryside that the government is making serious efforts in the direction of improving conditions in these areas, it is fairly common for community leaders to appear in the capital city with requests for specific types of aid for their local regions. If funds are available, these requests are granted; usually, they must be rejected because the funds are already destined for welfare activities planned by the city dwellers.

The resistance on the part of many countrymen to change sponsored by outside programs is incomprehensible to many welfare workers. Resistance stems in part from the natural inclinations of any social order to continue to function in channels familiar to it. It also can be attributed to the fact that not infrequently the reforms envisaged by the city dwellers as "good" and intrinsically leading toward a better life, strike the rural dweller as a real restriction on his customary activities. Agricultural credit is appreciated, but the control exercised by the credit agent over the crops planted and the fertilizers used is not welcome. Medical services are frequently accepted, but changes involved in environmental sanitation habits are bothersome. It is useful to have one's child know how to add, subtract, read and write, but the time lost in helping in the fields may be regarded as a serious disadvantage. This all derives from the seemingly inevitable fact that the reforms are designed by city dwellers and therefore involve what is perceived by them as good.

Welfare reforms, taken as a whole, seem as little directed toward the issue of freedom as are the others here discussed. The justification advanced for them is that they will offer better conditions of life to the rural inhabitant, enabling him to enjoy the good things of Western civilization. Whether these good things start with reading *The Federalist,* Karl Marx or a comic magazine has not been very well worked out.

CONCLUSIONS

This brings us to the crux of the issue of contemporary rural reform movements in Latin America. With few exceptions, they are not and have not been concerned with freedom as a goal, except in the most indirect and idealistic sense. The agrarian reforms and the other welfare reforms, whether sponsored by the government or a religious missionary group, do not have the achievement of freedom as their overt rationale. The argument given for these activities is that they provide a better life for the rural dweller, and that they contribute to the progress of the nation. The principal place where freedom enters, and here sheerly on a propagandistic note, is on the posters of a political party or movement that, with or without revolution in mind, advertises itself as better than other political parties.

The general spread of industrialization, of international exchange of goods, of city dwelling interests, of nationalism, and concern with the raising of national incomes and standards of living are seen as more important issues than freedom in Latin America today. Even the national Indian Institutes, now functioning in most of the major nations with significant aboriginal populations, are not concerned with extending freedom to the Indian, but rather with incorporating him into the national life. The rural dweller who resists setting up an outhouse, or having his home sprayed with DDT, or who rejects agricultural credit because he does not want supervision of his crops, is expressing his desire for freedom as he knows it. From the nation's point of view, however, this fellow is an obstacle in the way of national development, a broken cog in the wheels of progress. On the other hand, the countryman who happily submits to the various sanitary and agricultural regulations destined to prolong his life, preserve the nation's fast dwindling food supply, and conserve the topsoil, is not necessarily achieving greater freedom thereby. He is, in fact, restricting his activities.

Perhaps the only refuge for the concern for freedom in reform activity is in the political sphere. After all, the world's population *is* approaching three billion, and sanitation, food production, and education are problems that must be solved. But differences may still enter into deciding whether solutions will be sought under one kind of political system or another. Even though the rural peoples of Latin America find themselves under many pressures, they are not intentionally going to sacrifice themselves as human beings in order to make way for a new kind of world.

Seen in this light, the reforms are not significant because they are providing Latin Americans with greater freedom, but because they are providing a way by which the degree of freedom that is already enjoyed can be maintained in a changing world. If these reforms are not pressed upon the rural populations, the power in political action will slip into the hands of those who will be willing to promise the sky so as to reorder the universe in the name of a nineteenth century German philosopher. The rural populations of Latin America face the problem of accepting reform in the face of concomitant restrictions on their freedom; failing this, they will become the unwitting tools of extremists with reforms that make contemporary efforts look like child's play.

In a sense both the rural inhabitants of the city civilization and the surviving aboriginal tribes are the targets of reforms designed to alter profoundly their societies. Whereas the tribal Indian is destined to become the rural and urban citizen or die, the ruralite is, over the next generations, going to be drawn closer and closer to the city. It is today impossible to say whether the man who dwells in a small Indian community by night, and works as a city laborer by day is more "rural" or "urban." The fact of the situation is that the way of life of all rural peoples is changing, and if it is to change in keeping with traditions of freedom, it must submit to the pressures of reform, whether from within or without.

Reform for the surviving aboriginal tribes and for the Western ruralite differ somewhat. For the former it almost inevitably leads to a reduction of freedom in terms of the system familiar to them, whereas for the latter it may or may not provide some wider realms of action, depending upon the nature of the reform. For both, however, reform is a means by which adjustments are being made to a newly emerging social order that calls for the dominance of a national system within an international context. Looked at from this point of view, the reforms provide a way for the ruralites of both backgrounds to have access to the kinds of freedom that still characterize most of Western civilization and that have been effectively obliterated behind the various curtains of iron, bamboo and propaganda. The virtue of reform in Latin America lies not in its ability to increase freedom, for in fact it does not always do so; rather, it is to be found in its role as a way to maintain freedom to the degree that it now exists in the Western World.

CHAPTER X

[RUSSELL H. FITZGIBBON *]

Uruguay: A Model for Freedom and

Reform in Latin America?

Uruguay's Unique Position in Latin America

The concluding sentence of a volume I wrote on Uruguay
(prepared for the most part about five to six years ago) read: "It
is in the role as a grand exemplar of democracy that Uruguay's
challenge and her opportunity lie for the second half of the twentieth century and perhaps for all the decades beyond."

Was that conclusion too optimistic? Has Uruguay provided by
now a sad demonstration of the inability of a democratic state—
traditionally regarded as Latin America's most democratic—to
preserve hard-won and admirable advantages to the individual in
the face of intricate and perhaps selfish political and economic

* Russell H. Fitzgibbon began his teaching career as an instructor at Hanover
College in 1924. In 1933 he received his Ph.D. from the University of Wisconsin,
and three years later joined the Political Science Faculty at the University of California at Los Angeles, where he now holds the rank of Professor and has twice
served as chairman of his department. From 1944 to 1945 he was a staff member of
the Office of Inter-American Affairs. He has lived, traveled, or done research in
fifteen Latin American countries, and during 1951 lived in Uruguay and Argentina.
Besides numerous articles published in leading journals and reviews, he has written
a number of books, among them: *Cuba and the United States, 1900–1935* (Menasha,
Wisconsin, 1935); *Visual Outline of Latin American History* (New York, 1938);
Uruguay, Portrait of a Democracy (New Brunswick, New Jersey, 1954). He has also
served as editor of *Global Politics* (Berkeley and Los Angeles, 1944), and *The Constitutions of the Americas* (Chicago, 1948).

pressures in a complex world? Is Uruguay facing bankruptcy, political anarchy or impotence, or psychological civil war?

Any analysis of freedom and reform in Latin America can well —no, must—take a long look at Uruguay. That country, South America's smallest, has been variously called Latin America's "Utopia," "a laboratory for social and economic experimentation," "South America's first welfare state," "the Switzerland of the Americas," and other intriguing epithets. Those labels deserve critical appraisal before we accept them at face value. The philosophical implications of the congruence of freedom and reform are nowhere more meaningful than in Uruguay.

Historical Background

Let us look briefly at the course of Uruguayan development which led to the assumption that that country had become a paragon, at least among the lands of Latin America.

In the colonial period Uruguay had little distinct personality of its own. It was simply an appendage of the vast area across the Plata, economically, culturally, and psychologically tributary to Buenos Aires, and at times a bone of political and territorial contention between Spain and Portugal or their more direct agents, the Viceroyalties of La Plata and Brazil. Montevideo was but a raw frontier settlement with none of the glamour or wealth of the larger and older Spanish cities in the colonies, even of Buenos Aires, which was a relatively late claimant of the title of metropolis.

The process of winning Uruguayan independence was not the cleancut thing it was with, say, Chile or Colombia. It was more a product of politics than of decisive battles. When independence came it had humiliating conditions attached to it and for many years the intervention of Argentina and Brazil was almost as flagrant as it had been in the late colonial era. Early in its period of independence Uruguay began to be torn by domestic political dissensions which were as pointless as they were persistent. Various writers have called attention, with at least the implication of approval, to the longevity of Uruguay's major political parties, Colorado and Blanco, but it must be remembered that for many years in their early life they were little more than feuding factions which brawled pettily and ceaselessly through the pages of mid-nineteenth-century history and across the plains and in the cities of Uruguay. It was a dreary business and one which offered little promise of better things to come.

Indeed, most of the nineteenth century saw the record of Uruguay written in about as undistinguished fashion as that of any Latin American country. There was not even the distinction of outstanding dictatorships, bad or good: Uruguay produced no Rosas, no García Moreno, no Díaz, no Guzmán Blanco.

Uruguayan Transformation: The Generation of Batlle y Ordóñez

Then, in a relatively short time, say a generation, Uruguay made a remarkable transformation. It is easy to oversimplify the explanation and assign all the credit to one man. As I have written elsewhere, "Probably in no other country in the world in the past two centuries has any one man so deeply left his imprint upon the life and character of a country as has José Batlle y Ordóñez upon Uruguay." That evaluation can still stand. Neither Napoleon nor Hitler, Atatürk nor Gandhi influenced a single country as much or as variously as Batlle did his own beloved Uruguay.

One consequence of the dramatic entrance of Batlle onto the Uruguayan stage was to clarify and solidify the ideological differences between Blancos (officially, Nationalists) and Colorados, differences which earlier had been at most uncertain or inchoate. The Colorados became much more strongly stamped as a liberal party and the Blancos as conservative, though the latter party did not thereby become Catholic-oriented: such a role was reserved for the small but respected Unión Cívica. The growing gulf between capital and *campo* was reflected politically by Colorado tenderness for Montevideo and simultaneous gravitation of Blanco strength to the rural *estancias*. Colorados soon undertook to monopolize a championship of labor, though such monopoly was in later years challenged from various party directions by Communists, Socialists, and the Unión Cívica.

In some degree, though perhaps less certainly, speedily, and pointedly, the spectacular changes which Uruguay experienced over the turn of the century would have come anyway. The country was ripe for an awakening by late in the nineteenth century;

it lacked the obstacle of a large unassimilated and perhaps partly unassimilable alien ethnic group; it had favorable climatic, topographic, and other features. But Batlle was initially a catalyst and later a captain of the ferment and change which came to Uruguay. The ten or a dozen years following approximately 1905 saw Uruguay experiencing a social and economic revolution of a very real sort. It was the first such reorganization of life and activity that any Latin American state had undergone, antedating by several years the far more highly publicized Mexican revolution. Some of the Uruguayan changes were good, others were perhaps questionable or at least premature, but the net result was to make the government more democratically responsive and a significant fraction of the people more politically conscious and articulate than in any other country of Latin America.

The Interlude Between World Wars

The decade of the 'twenties saw experimentation continuing in Uruguay, most notably with the modified *colegiado* or plural executive. The experiment, surely one of the most novel in all Latin American political experience, had to be on a modified basis because Batllista forces were compelled to compromise by a hostile majority in the Constituent Assembly of 1916–17. In brief, the compromise called for a popularly elected presidency (Batlle had favored doing away with the office entirely) and in addition a popularly elected, and independent, nine-man National Council of Administration. Although the functional line of demarcation between the two agencies was not entirely clearcut, the president was given primarily a political role and the National Council an administrative one. The bifurcated executive machinery which resulted from the constitutional compromise of 1916–17 was not entirely satisfactory and it was a major contributing factor to the *coup d'état* engineered by President Terra in 1933. On the whole, the decade of the 'twenties was not a time of great world-wide pressures, either political or economic, even though in certain European countries reconstruction following World War I was prolonged and painful and in Germany was never satisfactorily completed prior to the economic breakdown at the end of the decade. But in general the War touched Latin America relatively little, Uruguay scarcely at all.

The colonial nature of Uruguay's economy did mean that the depression would inevitably bring profound repercussions to the small and essentially agricultural country on the Plata. The Terra coup of 1933 thus had two primary bases: the President's political dissatisfaction with the independent National Council of Administration and the hammer blows to the national economy caused by the drying up of foreign markets for wool and meat. Uruguay was one of the many Latin American countries in which irregular changes of government in the early 1930's were induced by economic stress.

In the 'thirties Uruguay, along with other economically colonial countries, was primarily concerned with the long, uphill struggle to recover foreign markets. In the political sphere the exacerbations of the Terra dictatorship were gradually erased, although the awkwardness of the "half-and-half" Senate, one of the expedient prices Terra had had to pay for support from the Herreristas (as the closely reined followers of Luis Alberto de Herrera, the dominant Blanco chieftain, were called), remained until amended out of the constitution in November, 1942. The curious composition of the Senate, written into Terra's Constitution of 1934, was another instance of Uruguay's readiness to experiment. The provision permitted each of the first two parties in every election's voting to have half of the Senate membership; all other parties were excluded. On a practical basis this meant that, at least temporarily, the Senate would include only Terra's brand of Colorados and Herrera-dominated Blancos, in equal numbers; it was, of course, an open invitation to tie votes.

World War II and Uruguay

The impact of the Second World War on Uruguay differed in a number of significant ways from that of the First. For one thing, the shock and scars of the depression, preceding World War II by only a few years, were not matched by any similarly economically and psychologically upsetting experience in the period just before the earlier War. The tensions of the depression were scarcely eased before those of the Second War were upon Uruguay.

In the second place, the demands of World War II, both economic and psychological, upon even neutral states were much greater than had been true of the First War. The Second War, although both were "World," was much more nearly a total conflict than the first. The damage to shipping by both surface and undersea craft was greater, and the Second War was less than four months old before a dramatic incident had brought belligerent action to the very port of Montevideo. The economic effects were still more drastic, if perhaps less spectacular. This was true even before the United States was involved in the War. Goods were in short supply and the trading lines and habits of Uruguay had to be considerably revised. All of this bred a psychological awareness of war over and above whatever would have come anyway to a literate, cosmopolitan, and sophisticated people.

Third, the fantastic and successful efforts of the Nazis to align, control, and use the loyalties of the *Auslandsdeutsche*—Germans abroad—were felt in Uruguay as in almost dozens of other countries, and of course had no counterpart in pre-World War I propaganda. This sinister impact was doubtless the more apparent in Uruguay because of its small size and population and because of the fact that across the Plata the larger and more powerful Argentina was governed by regimes after mid-1940 in which potential sympathy for, if not active collaboration with, the Nazis posed its own threat to Uruguay. This threat was compounded by the alleged Nazi sympathies of the Herreristas, who almost invariably took anti-United States and perhaps pro-Nazi positions because of the reverse stands assumed by the dominant Colorados. Even though we, too, were objects of Nazi propaganda and sabotage, it is difficult for us in the United States to realize, so great is the contrast in our area, population, and strength from those of Uruguay, how paralyzing the effects of this propaganda barrage might have been were it not for the staunchness of democratic faith and devotion maintained by the Uruguayans in that time of crisis.

The end of World War II brought a context in which worldwide elasticity of the spirit was sadly lacking. In considerable degree the whole world was morally exhausted. This was true even of Latin America, an area which the War had directly touched relatively little. Uruguay shared that Latin American reaction.

The forging of the United Nations at San Francisco in the spring of 1945 was characterized by a hard realism which contrasted strangely—and perhaps prophetically—with the idealistic atmosphere which surrounded Wilson, Smuts, and their colleagues (Clemenceau, Lloyd George, and others to the contrary notwithstanding) at Versailles a quarter of a century before. The guns of World War II had scarcely ceased echoing before the wary wartime alliance between the Soviet and the West (whose wariness was so vividly revealed in Churchill's postwar volumes) began to disintegrate before the erosion of new East-West suspicions which the exigencies of the military alliance had so poorly concealed. Talk of "World War III" began to be heard, and of course "the Cold War" was a phrase that quickly became almost trite. The eruption of the Korean conflict a few years later simply served to crystallize and intensify international tensions and irritation.

All of this murkiness of world atmosphere certainly served Uruguay badly. That little country had achieved a notable maturity and sophistication but, in large measure because of its small size, it was basically at the economic and, in degree, the psychological mercy of the outside world. As a craft sailing on international waters Uruguay simply did not have the tonnage, as a figurative United States or Soviet or other vessel would have had, to escape a considerable buffeting by stormy seas.

The Reinstated Colegiado

The election of Andrés Martínez Trueba as President in 1950 paved the way for the return, in undiluted form this time, of the *colegiado* by constitutional change in 1951. The shape of the *colegiado* in this second experiment with it was such as to freeze the two major parties in fixed proportions of membership on the National Council and to exclude all other parties from membership in it. That two-thirds of the seats were to go to the party polling the largest vote and the remaining third to the party with the next largest vote would mean, in practical terms, the indefinite and all but automatic presence on it of six Colorados and three Blancos. In this respect it represented a denial of the useful principle of proportional representation,* although the minor

---

* For a powerfully expressed disagreement with the aptness of the term useful in regard to proportional representation, see the essay in this volume by F. A. Hermens. [Editor's Note]

parties still had access to the two houses of the Congress. The details of the reform which established the *colegiado* revealed a tender political consideration for both the Independent Nationalists and the minority wings of the Colorado party which accorded but poorly with any basic respect for such parties as Unión Cívica and the Socialists, for example. Expediency required the disguised concession made to Independent Nationalists and Independent Colorados—"it was the price paid," I have written elsewhere, "for political support from those two subordinate party groups." The Independent Nationalists (or Blancos) were an offshoot of the main Blanco party, but the peculiarities of Uruguayan electoral laws compelled them to operate as a legally distinct party, though the various fractions of the Colorados are all gathered under the rubric of the one party (despite their ideological and political differences) and combine their votes for the single slate with the highest separate vote. Independent Nationalists have differed from the old-line Blancos in that they are more conciliatory and, especially in terms of foreign policy, more moderate.

Any detailed examination of the course of Uruguayan history in the present decade would need to focus much attention on the role of the *colegiado* in the years since it has been reinstituted. It has been alleged—and I use that phrasing advisedly—that it bears a considerable responsibility for the difficulties that Uruguay has experienced in the past half dozen years, both economic and political. Hence it needs at least a brief examination in terms of its philosophical and political impact on contemporary Uruguayan public life.

The tendency has been, since the brief honeymoon period of cooperation between the two major parties immediately following adoption of the *colegiado,* for them to regard jealously any attempt by other parties to share their politico-constitutional eminence but at the same time to look at each other askance and critically. It is not entirely an accurate figure to assume that they could be symbolized by a dog and a cat tied together on a low mound from which they kept other small animals at bay but on which they meanwhile snarled and spat at each other. And yet, in crude simile, this is somewhat the position they have occupied in the political life of recent Uruguay.

Let us now take a somewhat more detailed look at certain of the items of evidence as to the state of affairs in the past few years, after which it will be in order to attempt to make any pertinent interpretations.

Recent Economic Developments

It is no secret that Uruguay's economy has been unfavorably and seriously affected in recent years. Inflation has had its nagging impact on the country (the first eight months of 1957 saw the cost of living rise 13 per cent, compared with a rise of 6 per cent in the whole of 1956) and this has caused a chain reaction of consequences of other kinds. Perhaps the most obvious and spectacular of these has been the rash of strikes with which the Uruguayan economy has been plagued in the past few years. In the first ten or eleven months of 1957, for example, according to the Montevideo paper *El Bien Público,* a total of 1,154 working days was lost by strikes by some forty-four organized groups in Uruguay; the more serious instances included 172 days lost by longshoremen outside of Montevideo, 133 days by veterinary students, ninety-eight by employees of FUNSA (the Uruguayan Tire Company), eighty-seven by meat workers, etc. Railway and *frigorífico* workers conducted serious strikes in mid-1956. The catalog of others, big and little, important and unimportant, would be too long to try to enumerate, and of course redundant.

Strikes, like narcotics, can be habit-forming. In June, 1956, for example, students at the University of Montevideo went out on a twenty-four-hour sympathy strike (it was by no means the first) to express their accord with Paraguayan students who had been victims of police violence two months before. And, as with narcotics, the relief coming from a strike can often be merely illusory.

Strikes were allegedly a factor in the closing of all Uruguayan operations late in 1957 by two of the country's largest *frigoríficos* (the largest two under private operation). They were Swift and Company of Montevideo, a subsidiary of International Packers of Chicago, and Artigas, a dependent unit of Armour and Company. The two firms alleged that for the past seventeen of the forty years they had carried on operations in Uruguay their activity had been at a loss because of government policies and regulations. The facts in this involved situation are probably not all yet available but it is undisputed that the cessation of operations by these two large packing plants resulted in a loss of work by at least 6,500 employees.

Foreign trade has suffered. This is the more important in view of the great dependence which the nature of the Uruguayan economy necessarily puts on this portion of commerce. In the first half of 1957, for example, the unfavorable trade balance reached $52,000,000 as contrasted with a favorable balance of $13,000,000 in the corresponding period of 1956. The trade deficit by mid-October, 1957, was reported to be about $90,000,000. Additional detail would be superfluous.

Closely related to the unfortunate state of Uruguay's foreign trade is the series of attempts by the government to regulate—perhaps manipulate would not be too harsh a word—the use of foreign exchange. A complex set of foreign exchange regulations was adopted by the National Council of Government in August, 1956, but was subsequently modified in one respect or another. A decree of November 11, 1957, providing for withdrawal by the government of preferred exchange rates on certain exports and imports was rescinded the following month in the face of threatened lockouts by industrial employers and the forced resignation of the Minister of Labor and Industry under pressure from importers. Gold and foreign exchange holdings at the beginning of 1957 totaled $147,000,000 but by November had shrunk to about $55,000,000. The exchange value of the peso dropped in the single month of March, 1958, from 5.10 to the dollar to 5.68.

Production has fallen in certain categories. *Frigoríficos* have an annual slaughtering capacity of about one and three quarters million head of cattle but the largest recent annual slaughter has been about 700,000 head. The Montevideo cattle slaughter declined from 64,000 head in July, 1957, to 32,000 in August, to 12,000 in November. On the other hand, the estimated wool production in the 1957–58 season was 209,000,000 pounds, a 20 per cent increase over that of the preceding year, but this was the first such increase since the 1953–54 season. The wheat harvest, begun in November, 1957, would result, it was estimated, in an 80 per cent increase over that of the preceding year. This rapid increase in wheat production after the inauguration of wheat-growing subsidies by the government in 1947 was a factor, it was contended by meat-producing interests, in the decline of available meat supplies, inasmuch as large amounts of land previously available for pasture had been converted to wheat production.

Physical properties have in some instances deteriorated. A report in the early fall of 1957 indicated that a sum of $140,000,000 would be necessary to restore the railways of the country over a ten-year period to the condition prevailing in 1948–49 when the government converted the remaining privately owned lines to public ownership. The debt structure, especially as it involves public units, has reached complex proportions and alarming heights. Cattle producers in the hinterland have at times refused to sell to the Frigorífico Nacional because of failure to be paid for previous deliveries and "Frigonal" on its part responds by pleading the failure of the municipality of Montevideo to pay it. It was reported within the past year that debts between autonomous entities and other governmental units approached a quarter of a billion dollars.

All of this, and a great variety of additional evidence that could be adduced, adds up to an alarming state of economic affairs. *The New York Times* on Christmas Day, 1957, commented editorially, in sorrow rather than anger, that Uruguay was "on the brink" and the economy "close to bankruptcy." The editorial, appearing as it did in this country's most prestigeful newspaper, naturally drew critical responses from Uruguay, but in previous months various Montevideo papers of different political coloration, such as *El Día, Acción, El Debate,* and others, as well as a variety of public figures, had on their part been critical of the direction in which the Uruguayan economy was tending and of government policies which propelled it in such a direction.

Recent Political Trends

It is elementary to point out—and the conclusion certainly need not be labored—that a basic and inevitable relationship exists between economics and politics. Each reacts upon the other. If a country is economically prosperous the government and the governmental system will be the more secure; if the reverse is true the instability of the political regime will almost inevitably correspond to the adverse economic conditions. Conversely, the government can do many things, both positive and negative, which will affect the country's economy. It is now in order to attempt to examine possible political responsibility in Uruguay for the sad state of the country's economy which has developed in recent years.

Nationalists have been admitted, as noted, to an official and fixed share of top-level executive positions by the constitutional changes of 1951. The initial interparty harmony which then prevailed did not last long, and indeed its collapse was a certainty. Uruguay is as "party-minded" as any country in Latin America and the adoption of the *colegiado* operated to make it even more strongly subject to party control. It was inevitable that Colorados and Nationalists on the National Council of Government, and their followers in lower levels, should blame each other for the failure of specific government policies and that each group should renew and redouble its efforts to woo possible independent political support.

A climax was reached in April, 1957, when former President Luis Batlle Berres called publicly for the removal of the Herrerista members of the National Council and their replacement by representatives of splinter Colorado groups. The feuding has not been confined to that between the two major parties, however. Within the Colorado party the internecine political rivalry has been especially evident between Lists Fourteen and Fifteen, headed respectively by César Batlle and his cousin, Luis Batlle Berres. These two lists, or wings of the party, represent in some degree substantive political differences, but the distinction is to a greater extent one between the rival followings of two members of the same family, one the nephew and the other the son of "the" Batlle, and each claiming to be his proper political heir. Cabinet reorganizations have come on several occasions in recent years, the most dramatic being that of May, 1956, when all nine members of the cabinet resigned because of disagreement over the 1956–57 budget. A year later the continued feuding led *El País*, the influential and reliable Independent Nationalist paper, to say, in effect, "a plague on both your houses."

Let me call on two or three expert witnesses—who must, for obvious reasons, remain unidentified. One of them, a thoroughgoing student and devoted friend of Uruguay, wrote me late in

1957 that "Atomization, therefore, seems [to characterize] the present situation, an unhappy reaction in the face of real economic crisis. Whether it will extend to civil disobedience on a grand scale, I can't say. The parties are proceeding toward the election as if it made no difference, however."

Another well qualified observer, one who knows Uruguay at first-hand and whose affection for it is indicated by his description of it as "a lovely, friendly, and potentially stable and prosperous country," wrote ten months earlier in a manner that deserves to be quoted at a little greater length:

... it is quite obvious that the Uruguayan government has come to a grinding halt. It has reached a stage of semiparalysis, from which it is almost impossible to extricate itself. . . . The country is paralyzed with politics and suffers a scarcity of people who are willing to put the welfare of the country above their own petty politicking or personal interests. There is almost a parliamentary stalemate in that people do not vote for the interests of the country but rather by party lines, regardless of whether they are for or against a given measure in principle.

. . .

The Herreristas, Socialists, and Communists apparently are doing everything possible to overthrow the present regime by blocking everything possible in Parliament. On the other hand, the list 15 (Batlle Berres) and the list 14 of the Colorados, the governing party, are not always in accord and frequently are unsuccessful in achieving effective measures because of party disunity. The nine-man Council . . . is proving itself quite ineffective by dividing responsibility and authority in a country which already lacks effective authority, leadership, and centralization of responsibility—a remarkably weak government with a relatively strong minority opposition. . . . The current [early 1957] theme is that everything is wonderful, the country is progressing, the economy sound, and everybody prosperous.

Finally, I may quote briefly from an Uruguayan writing early in 1958, a man of the highest degree of perceptiveness as well as patriotism, and possessed of a wide international reputation (the italics are mine):

Up to recent years there was a good control against inflation, but that evil has been moving with great impetus in 1957, much to the detriment of the economic situation in my country. *The difficulties arise*

*mainly from the political parties' lack of fortitude to put into effect
unpopular measures within a sound content of policy. What we need
is courageous leaders who would assume the responsibilities involved.*

An Appraisal of the Colegiado

It seems only reasonable to indict the *colegiado* for a significant share of the political responsibility for these times that trouble other souls than just the Uruguayan. It is a creation which
runs contrary to all Latin American political tradition and philosophy. That in itself is not sufficient ground for its condemnation, of course. It simply means that to the degree to which Uruguay shares a common cultural inheritance and denominator
with other Latin American states, any bold deviation from practices consonant with such tradition must be unusually well conceived and sincerely implemented.

The institutions of Latin America, especially those of Spanish
America, are basically authoritarian in character, whether those
institutions be familial, social, religious, economic, military, or
political. Democratic development makes headway in spite, not
because, of such institutional organization. Uruguay has departed probably further from this basic Spanish inheritance and
coloration than any other country in Latin America. An admir-
ing (and possibly slightly envious) Cuban friend of mine says,
when I hold Uruguay up to him as an example of the great
progress Latin American countries can make, "But Uruguay is
not really Latin American." Evidences of the departure of Uruguay from norms that are typically Latin American are to be
found in the significant role played by the middle classes (perhaps a relatively greater role than in any other Latin American
country), the reasonably important progress made by industrialization, the entirely peaceful deflation of the traditional power of
the Catholic Church, the consistent demilitarization of the country, and the absence of any false or artificial pride built upon
caste.

It is a matter of relativity and perhaps of personal judgment as
to whether the degree of this departure is sufficient to justify and
undergird so radical a political experiment as the *colegiado*. It
may be that Batlle—and no one maintains he was infallible—was
too optimistic in assuming that what worked satisfactorily in

Switzerland could be transplanted to a different political soil and be expected to flourish equally well. We must not, of course, judge the *colegiado* by the experience of 1919 to 1933; that would be an unfair test of it because, in the face of the bifurcation of executive function at that time, responsibility could not be centered squarely upon the National Council.

It may also be questioned, particularly in the light of the perspective provided by the half dozen years since 1952, whether the political milieu of the early 1950's sufficiently resembled that of a third-of-a-century earlier to make the same kind of governmental prescription as feasible and desirable at the later time as at the earlier. Batlle, who was of course the sole architect of the first *colegiado*, thought of it as an antidote to dictatorship. He knew dictatorship: he had experienced it and fought against it in the years of his young manhood. Hence, the potential menace of dictatorship was very real to him, and to others of his generation, even as late as 1916–17. The same situation did not prevail in 1951–52. Uruguay's only intervening experience with dictatorship had been at the time of Terra, more than a decade and a half before, and the Terra dictatorship was, at least by comparison with many others in Latin America, mild. There is, so far as I know, no evidence to indicate that Martínez Trueba or others active in the reinstitution of the *colegiado* were motivated by the experience of the 1930's. Dictatorship was not a real threat in the early 1950's and it is not a real threat now unless complete economic collapse should indicate an undisputed political bankruptcy of the present governmental system.

It is obvious that the experience since March, 1952, provides a fairer test of the *colegiado* than did the earlier experience inasmuch as no continuing presidency complicates the assessment of responsibility. But, again, the circumstances are not so simple as to permit an easy evaluation. The Council is not chosen on a basis of proportional representation, even were it to be limited to the two major parties. And the presidency of the Council, an office which has somewhat more than merely protocolary significance, rotates mechanically among members of the leading party —normally the Colorado. Hence, in part at least, the cards are stacked against the successful operation of the system. The dog and the cat are tied together and find it increasingly difficult to cooperate save in the face of an exceptionally strong opposition. Each, in fact, is schizoidally affected within itself, as the feuding between Lists 14 and 15 and the leaders personifying them indicates, at least for the Colorados.

The Planned Society

The whole situation is not, however, merely a product of politics *per se*. Uruguay has become the archetype of the planning state in Latin America. It would seem, though, that an insufficient distinction has been made between various types of planning. The term itself is not intrinsically bad, even if it has become a devil word of sorts. A businessman who did not plan intelligently would soon go bankrupt. A valid distinction can be made, however, between planning that is substantive and that which is merely manipulative. If Uruguay undertakes planning aimed at reducing brucellosis or at improving the breeding stock in the cattle industry (both of which illustrations would of course increase production) it can be regarded as substantive planning. If the government erects a complex system of both producer and consumer subsidies we have an example of manipulative planning. The economic system of any country which is at all advanced is an extraordinarily involved thing and efforts to control it manipulatively require both wisdom and courage. They are not to be undertaken casually or ignorantly, as Perón found out to his sorrow in Argentina.

It is not easy to draw the line between these two types of planning: one can readily shade into the other. If, for example, a country wants to undertake an initial industrialization—a desire which is in many situations entirely legitimate if soundly approached—it can do so, even in the face of competition from more developed countries, by the device of a protective tariff. This enables industry to become established and adds to the wealth of the country. But "infant industries" develop a fondness for swaddling clothes and bottle feeding and often insist on a protective tariff long after they are walking or even running in successful competition with older industries elsewhere.* In such circumstances a protective tariff ceases to be substantive and becomes manipulative.

* For a critical appraisal of the value of protective tariffs, see the article by Wendell C. Gordon in this volume. [Editor's Note]

If a Klein and Saks mission, for instance, were to undertake an objective and impartial survey of the Uruguayan pattern of planning it probably would quickly become apparent that no real or at least sufficient distinction has been made between what I have chosen to call substantive and manipulative planning, between that which obviously adds to the wealth of a community and that which merely (and probably artificially) reorganizes economic activity.

One of my correspondents earlier quoted wrote (in somewhat jaundiced terms, admittedly):

There is no national economic planning body, no national economic development plan, no agricultural development plan, and no industrial development plan, and no indication of any desire to have any planning. National economic policy, if one can call it such, is done on a piecemeal basis, with political rather than economic considerations forming policy at many times. There is no indication whatsoever of an interest in having Raúl Prebitsch and ECLA . . . make any recommendations for sound economic policy or sound planning—this would upset the political convenience of the present regime.

Governmental planning has been defined as rational calculation or the process of intelligent preparation for making wise decisions in the field of public affairs. From such a point of view, planning is the monopoly neither of a socialistic or Communistic regime nor, on the other hand, of a capitalistic or free-enterprise system. Nor is intelligent planning to be restricted necessarily to dictatorial regimes; democracies can well and effectively make use of such procedures, as was amply illustrated by the experience of the Allied Powers in World War II.

Admittedly, the problem is a more complex one for democracies. A dictatorship can, to the degree that it is a dictatorship, act irresponsibly and in disregard of public opinion or popular controls. In a democratic system the two basic problems are how to maintain rationality in planning and how to keep officials accountable to the people. Defects on both scores appear to have developed in recent Uruguayan experience.

If planning is undertaken on a piecemeal basis it is all but inevitable that it will develop a progressive imbalance as it becomes more involved and complex. It will also, in all likelihood, present perhaps glaring illustrations of duplication and extravagance. It may additionally fail to give the government valid answers to problems that cut across planned and unplanned (or differently planned) areas.

The planning operation in Uruguay needs to be undertaken not merely in terms of its over-all integration and coordination but also in terms of its targets. The latter should be primarily concerned with a great increase in production, both national and per capita. ". . . the difficulties from which Uruguay is suffering at this time," a well informed and perceptive correspondent writes me, "arise from the fact that it is necessary for it to increase its productivity in order to meet the great demands imposed upon it by the development of its social programs. Uruguay's political trends have brought it to the point where it has developed a broad program of state socialism and a very expensive bureaucratic machinery created by the establishment of so many government enterprises."

A major aim of socialism is the redistribution of wealth, and, quite apart from the political implications of one ideology or another, few persons who are acquainted with the age-old social imbalance and maldistribution of wealth in most parts of Latin America would argue that such an objective is not desirable, at least within reasonable limits. But if a large and expensive bureaucracy simply undertakes the *redistribution* of the available wealth, that wealth will be progressively diminished. A more imperative aim should be to increase the total wealth; this is the more necessary in the light of (a) growing populations, (b) an expanded program of public services, and (c) higher costs due to inflation. West Germany has made its remarkable postwar recovery largely because of the emphasis put on increased production. Its results have been a greatly improved economic stability, political independence, and psychological contentment.

Although Uruguay would remain, as long as its economy continues primarily colonial, considerably at the mercy of foreign economic policies, attitudes, and circumstances, a significantly increased national productivity would place it in a correspondingly improved bargaining position vis-a-vis other countries. Economic planning should be directed toward such ends.

Uruguay's recent planning unfortunately appears jerry-built and in some instances the product of emergency and erratic response to exigencies as they developed one by one. What is probably needed is another Batlle, not necessarily a son or nephew of Uruguay's outstanding figure, but a figurative Batlle, a man of great moral stature, influence, and wisdom who could lead the country out of the political and economic difficulties into which it has fallen.

The new Batlle would have to be a consummate politician to be able to sell a democratic country a program and policy which would of necessity be initially unpopular in greater or lesser degree. But more than that, he would have to be a statesman of outstanding character, integrity, and vision who would provide constructive rather than simply machinative leadership. There seems little doubt that the economic policies and actions of Uruguay have in various instances been unwise. The remedy for this may have to be an unwonted austerity. A perceptive young Argentine professional man told me several years ago in analyzing the current difficulties of his own country: "Churchill could preach 'blood, sweat, and tears' and persuade the English people to accept that program. Perón can't. We can't bring ourselves to accept a policy of austerity." Perhaps their neighbors across the Plata will face a similarly difficult choice.* As one person who knows Uruguay well writes of it, "You can't keep taking things out of the economy without putting something back in!" The phrasing is homely but profound. And "a veteran diplomatic observer" was recently quoted in *The New York Times* as saying: "Everybody knows the country is living beyond its means."

Prospects for the Future

Where is Uruguay headed? In facing a question of this sort we see only as through a glass, darkly. It seems obvious that the country cannot go on indefinitely in the direction and at the pace it recently has. Overpadded personnel rolls are an item: three-fourths or more of the budget is normally allocated for payment of personnel and 20 per cent or more of the whole Uruguayan

---

* The startling victory of the Blancos or Nationalists in the late 1958 elections, occurring several months after Professor Fitzgibbon had completed his article, has been interpreted by some as a manifestation of impatience, especially on the part of the rural population, with heedless government spending. If this appraisal is valid, there may be an indication that Uruguayans are willing to accept a greater degree of austerity here and now, in the interest of long-range national welfare. Whether an Uruguayan de Gaulle will be needed to complete the process remains, of course, to be seen. [Editor's Note]

population (including family members) depend for their livelihood on wages, salaries, or other income from the government. The proportion of Uruguayans in government employ is significantly higher than is the case in the United States despite the fact that this country has a federal and hence more elaborate form of governmental organization.

Another item is the nature of the retirement system. Uruguay is justly famous for the conscientious care it gives to the superannuated and for the advanced social security legislation it has adopted with regard to them. There is grave question, however, as to whether the pattern is actuarially sound. A by-line correspondent in *The New York Times* points out that some employees can retire at age fifty if they have by that time worked for thirty years, and adds: "One of the attractive features of retirement is that the pensions are higher than the take-home pay received before retirement. This increase, which may amount to 15 per cent, results from the ending of deductions for social security." Even if such a situation could be actuarially defended it would still be subject to question on psychological grounds.

A further item is the apparently increasing practice of borrowing from Peter to pay Paul. Within recent months, for example, unemployment insurance payments to wool industry workers were as much as two months in arrears. The railway management in August, 1956, had to request additional government funds to pay overdue and current obligations. In the last nineteen years of government fiscal operations at least sixteen annual budgetary deficits have occurred.

Several years ago I wrote:

Democracy presupposes a tough-minded and tenacious acceptance of the nation as deserving a continuing loyalty which transcends loyalty to class [or, it might be added, party]. Democracy assumes that the proper adjustments and accommodations among classes, probably accompanied by vigorous debate and pulling and hauling, will be made peacefully within the framework provided. If loyalty to a class, whether a proletariat in the professional sense or an elite group, supersedes the common loyalty then democracy suffers correspondingly.

Not all parties—or groups or classes—in Uruguay have suffered this atomization in recent years. The party as an entity deserves mention first because Uruguay has become so party-conscious and because political parties have so significant an impact on the course of public affairs.

It seems likely that the considerable elements of political strength represented by Luis Batlle Berres and Luis Alberto de Herrera and their followings (respectively a wing of the Colorado party and the dominant fraction of the Nationalist party) are open to grave criticism on the score of allowing party loyalties to transcend devotion to the *patria*. (Not all "intransigents" are to be found across the Plata under Frondizi's banner!) The same charge certainly can be made against the Communists; it possibly can be levied against the Socialists. Unión Cívica, the Catholic-oriented party, and the Independent Nationalists appear to have reflected a considerably higher degree of statesmanship in recent years. Such assessment of party attitudes represents generalization, of course, which is always unsafe, and which, at a distance of several thousand miles, must naturally be advanced hesitantly and humbly. The influential press generally reflects attitudes of the parties or fractions to which individual papers belong. *El País* and *El Bien Público,* respectively Independent Nationalist and Unión Cívica papers, have probably taken the most detached and "above-the-battle" attitudes toward politico-economic problems of late years.

Three therapeutic prescriptions might be proposed for the ills with which Uruguay is currently beset:

1. A selflessness which will willingly subordinate individual, party, and class interests and ambitions to the general good of the nation as a whole.

2. A politico-administrative system which will permit and demand the centralization of responsibility.

3. A well conceived program of austerity which will ultimately relieve Uruguay of any hint of its present after-us-the-deluge psychology.

None of these is a placebo. Each would in some instances be an astringent or bitter remedy, but the present condition of Uruguay is not a healthy one and stern curative measures are called for. One can only hope that the innate and profound common sense of the Uruguayan people will be equal to self-administered remedies of the kind. The alternatives are not pleasant to contemplate.

CONCLUSIONS

Can we still regard Uruguay as an example which the other Latin American states might emulate with profit? I regard the answer as definitely yes. The Uruguayan bodies economic and politic have, it is true, been subject to abnormal conditions recently but that does not mean that the nation is near death or even permanently injured. Uruguayan integration is so considerable, her basic situation so sound, her sense of balance and sense of humor so reassuring, that the current pathological condition, while not to be passed off as superficial, is at the same time probably not to be interpreted as permanent.

Uruguay has experienced an accretion of successive gains which temporary injury to the economy and polity of the country cannot efface. Many other Latin American states are still far behind Uruguay when criteria of any practical or useful variety are applied. Virtually all Latin American states have experienced times of stress and strain, some of them much worse than the troubles of recent Uruguayan history. The Perón period brought to Argentina a travail, both political and economic, that was far in excess of what Uruguay has suffered. That austerity, though bitter, could also be helpful has been proved in part by Chile in recent years. Peru has discovered that a freeing of the economy from artificial and manipulative regulation resulted in beneficial changes, although that country has also found that the cure for a plagued economy comes from no simple or single remedy.

Other countries in Latin America would do well to avoid certain political excesses which Uruguay has demonstrated recently. It is a natural and deep-rooted tendency for Latin American governments to assume far more of a managerial role than is characteristic for Anglo-American governments. If carefully controlled and kept within due bounds this is probably a useful course to follow in many parts of Latin America, given the underdeveloped conditions and the lack of integration which often prevail. The danger lies in taking the easy path toward an exaggerated and misdirected planning function, an expanded and expensive bureaucracy, and ill-considered and selfish economic policies and political programs. A siren lure can lead to an ever steeper declivity which may or may not end in Avernus, but at least will involve a particular government in geometrically compounded difficulties before it changes its course.

Various other Latin American governments would also do well to avoid Uruguay's somewhat prodigal fiscal operations. Fortunately, very fortunately, Uruguay fails to be possessed of at least two characteristics which would make its financial plight still worse: (a) it has no psychosis of "keeping up with the Joneses" which would lead it into extravagant expenditures simply to maintain governmental fashions or appearances; and (b) it has no pathological urge to develop a large military establishment, that voracious devourer of pesos, dollars, pounds, or whatnot with which so many contemporary countries are saddled. And yet, Uruguay's fiscal management has not, especially in recent years, been sound. No government can operate on a basis of deficit financing as frequently as has Uruguay's and not find itself in increasing fiscal difficulties.

In the third place, other countries of Latin America would do well to learn a lesson, at least tangentially, from Uruguay's experience of recent years that national integration is hard won but easily lost. Half a dozen years go I could write that "very large numbers of the people, . . . irrespective of whether they individually are Colorados or Blancos, Montevideanos or *campesinos,* loyally Catholic or religiously indifferent, feel they are all Uruguayans. . . . Allegiance is more to the nation than to the part or fraction. . . . Country has taken precedence over party." Some people now allege that class and caste, *agrupación* and *fracción* have come to occupy a higher place than does *patria* in the loyalties of many influential people. To the extent that this might be true—and I am not at all sure that it is seriously so—it would be evidence of a sorry deterioration in national psychological integration. It would be a dry rot to be diligently avoided by other Latin American countries. But be that as it may, it is evident that most Latin American countries are still far short of the degree of integration which Uruguay had long since attained, whether that cohesiveness may now be affected unfavorably or not.

On the other hand, there has been no diminution—nor could there well be—in the political consciousness and articulateness of the average, humble Uruguayan citizen. In this fact is to be found a basic factor which virtually every other country in Latin America could emulate with profit. It may be true that some Uruguayans have become disillusioned with the particular manner in which the political process contemporarily operates and that on the part of some the emotion may have crystallized in a positive form varying from irritation to downright anger. It means much, however, that political consciousness remains basically unimpaired regardless of the manifestation which that consciousness may take in becoming articulate. Disillusionment or even cynicism can be temporary reactions but to remove the political perceptiveness of more than two million Uruguayans would necessitate removing or denying not only the high degree of literacy prevailing in the country but also a half-century tradition of political awareness and participation on the part of the mass of the population—and that is obviously impossible.

Other Latin American countries could also well seek to develop, for its political implications and importance, the finely matured Uruguayan balance between personal dignity and that false pride which makes many other Latins see political phenomena through distorted lenses. *Dignidad* can easily become overinflated in Latin America and when and where this happens the political process works less easily and naturally. Even though they still occasionally fight duels, Uruguayans of almost all classes temper their *dignidad* with the saving graces of humility and a sense of humor. This means that as political participation becomes more diffused in this twentieth-century world it is hedged about—at least in Uruguay—with less of the mores and behaviorism which might befit an Athenian type of democracy or a nineteenth-century Latin American variety but do not comport well with the contemporary, broadly popular sort. Uruguayans, in other words, have a basic attitude as political beings in which democracy can flourish, given proper economic and political circumstances, whereas in many Latin American countries the individual approach to politics is such as almost implicitly to deny democracy much chance of success.

There are still other essential factors in the contemporary picture which, without conveying the impression of being simply rationalization, give comfort to those foreign friends of Uruguay who remain convinced that the country, despite her lapses of the moment, continues as one of the fundamentally great democracies of the world and certainly of Latin America. Let us not pretend that all is currently well in Uruguay. The conscientious, patriotic, and perceptive Uruguayan cannot at this moment hold his head quite as high or his back quite as straight as would be desirable. Certain conditions and certain political habits badly need modifying. But, broadly and generally, Uruguay is sound. Freedom and reform still hold as much promise on those rolling oriental plains as they do anywhere in Latin America.

CHAPTER XI

[ARTHUR KARASZ *]

Experiment in Development:

Bolivia Since 1952

About Technical Assistance in General

The purpose of this study is to examine a special case of technical assistance which a United Nations team has been giving to Bolivia. The case was not what we currently call technical assistance; it was more than that. While technical assistance usually consists in advice given by foreign experts who work as outsiders, the experiment in Bolivia consisted in technical assistance given by foreigners who became part of the country's Civil Service, that is, who worked almost as nationals of the country itself, one may say, "from the inside." Opinion about the experiment in international circles is divided. It will be for future generations to decide whether, in effect, it was a success or a failure.

* Born in Kolozsvar, Hungary, Arthur Karasz received his LL.D. from the University of Budapest. Beginning in 1932 he served as a staff member of the Bank of Hungary, and from 1945 to 1946 was President of that Bank. The following year saw him commence his academic career, serving as Professor of Central Banking at the Economic University, Budapest. From 1949 to 1950 he was a Lecturer at the New School for Social Research, and from 1950 to 1952, Professor of Finance at De Paul University, Chicago. During the 1952–1956 period, he was a member of the United Nations Mission to the Bolivian government, in the capacity of economic advisor. He has also been a visiting lecturer at the Universities of Chicago, Montevideo, La Paz, Cochabamba, and at the Center of Latin American Monetary Studies (CEMLA), Mexico City. Since 1956 he has been an Economist with the International Bank for Reconstruction and Development, Washington, D.C. The views expressed in this paper do not necessarily correspond to those of the Bank.

Let us first agree on some definitions. The word "underdeveloped" is much discussed nowadays. It is undoubtedly somewhat undiplomatic, for it implies, as Gunnar Myrdal says, that the "economic upper class of nations" [1] is on a higher level of values than are the poor, the "backward" nations; however, the word also has some dynamic qualities; it is—to quote Myrdal again—"value-loaded . . . it implies the value judgment that it is an accepted goal of public policy that the countries so designated should experience economic development." [2]

What is an underdeveloped country? "To designate a country as underdeveloped . . . implies that its present economic performance . . . could be improved by means which are known and understood." [3] Jacob Viner expressed the same idea in the following way: "An underdeveloped country has good potential prospects for using more capital or more labor or more available natural resources, or all of these, to support its present population on a higher level of living." [4] What is common to both definitions is, among other things, that the underdeveloped areas would probably be better off were there more capital at their disposal.

However, capital is really not all that is needed to develop a country. The best and most modern plants will easily be ruined if there are no experts to run them. Therefore, expertise is needed too; or, if we prefer the word "capital," we can say that in addition to financial capital, human capital is required. An essential function of technical assistance, therefore, will consist in helping to "transfer skills from people to people and from area to area." [5]

This is the generally accepted form of technical assistance practised by the United Nations as well as by national organizations like the International Cooperation Administration (ICA) of the United States. Missions are sent to give technical advice to a country which has applied for such advice. The technical assist-

[1] Gunnar Myrdal, *Rich Lands and Poor* (New York, 1957), p. 3.
[2] *Ibid.*, p. 8.
[3] Norman S. Buchanan and Howard S. Ellis, *Approaches to Economic Development* (New York, 1955), p. 4.
[4] Jacob Viner, *International Trade and Economic Development* (Glencoe, 1952), p. 125.
[5] David Owen, *Technical Assistance for Economic Development,* quoted in L. W. Shannon, *Underdeveloped Areas* (New York, 1957), p. 320.

ance expert works in an advisory capacity and is responsible to his own national or international agency. It remains the sovereign right of the receiving country to decide whether, and how much, it will accept of such advice.

Technical assistance in Bolivia departed from this generally accepted formula in certain important respects. In Bolivia several members of the United Nations Mission had not only advisory but also important executive powers. Although they were nominated to their position by the United Nations and received most of their salary from that organization, they were appointed by the Bolivian government; in theory, at least, they were considered as part of Bolivia's Civil Service and worked as part of that country's administration.

The Setting

Knowledge of the extremely difficult geographical problems of the country and its population will help the reader to understand why the United Nations had to invent this special form of assistance for Bolivia and also why the Bolivian government accepted it.

As far as geography is concerned, all of us know that Bolivia is in the middle of South America and that it is at the top of the world. La Paz, the actual capital of the country (the legal capital is the city of Sucre), is situated at an altitude of about 11,000 feet, a "two-mile high city," in a canyon that resembles in many respects the Grand Canyon. The canyon of La Paz is situated between a plateau, one of the highest in the world, called the Altiplano, and the eastern range of the Andes mountains, the so-called Royal Cordillera, one of the highest and most beautiful mountain ranges of South America.

If one goes east from La Paz it is necessary to cross at an altitude of about 15,000 feet a pass that leads over the Royal Cordillera. East of that point begins the way down and within a distance of 100 miles one is at the edge of the tremendous jungle of the Amazon Basin, only a few hundred feet above sea level. Thus, only a few miles east from the high snowy pass begins an endless tropical jungle with parrots, snakes, wild orchids, malaria, yellow fever, and all the other attributes of tropical life. The Bolivians like to use colorful expressions. They call their country the synthesis of the world. In a sense this is true. Bolivia is probably one of the few countries of the world where one may find every kind of climate concentrated within short distances of a few miles.

It is the synthesis of the world, but at the same time this great variety of altitudes and the location of the mountains means a great disadvantage for Bolivia as compared to its neighbors, Argentina or Brazil. While the South American countries on the Atlantic Coast consist of vast plains mostly facing the ocean, with mountainous regions behind complementing the economy of the plains, in the Andean republics the mountains go right to the Pacific and the big plains are inside; moreover, the plains are separated from the seaports by one of the highest and most rugged mountain ranges in the world. This is particularly true of Bolivia, and this may be one of the reasons why the majority of the population is concentrated on the Altiplano, isolated from the rest of the world by snow-covered peaks, while about two-thirds of the country—approximately twice the size of pre-War Germany, or the state of Texas—is practically empty. Transportation from the plains is too difficult and people prefer to withdraw into the isolation of the rugged Altiplano; thus, the Altiplano has become overpopulated and hungry, while the remaining two-thirds of the country, which could produce enough food for several Bolivias, is deserted.

In short, Bolivia is a vertical country. It is built on several floors; the first floor is almost at sea level, a hot tropical region, with all the problems the Amazon Basin can create. The second floor, way up at about 8,000 feet, is a region of extremely narrow valleys so steep that there is practically no place to turn around with a plow. And finally, there is the Altiplano, the third floor, at altitudes varying between 11,000 and 13,000 feet and surrounded by the towering summits of the Royal Cordillera. These are the three floors of the country, each with a different climate, ranging from extreme cold to tropical heat. The three floors are not always tied together by normal valleys; often the mountain just falls down from one floor to the other, and the valleys are often so narrow and steep that the railroad (if there is a railroad) has to zig-zag up by means of reversing stations. In consequence, rail or highway transportation between the different regions is costly and sometimes impossible. For instance, between La Paz and the Amazon territory practically everything is transported by plane. Meat is flown into La Paz as are lumber and even empty beer bottles.

Bolivians also like to say, with a slight exaggeration of course, that from the political point of view their country is again a synthesis of the world. In any case, with scarcely three million inhabitants (no one knows the exact number because, for understandable reasons, the census is not yet complete in the jungle or among the glaciers), Bolivia has staged up to 1952, that is, in 125 years of national independence, 179 revolutions or one revolution for every eight or nine months. As in other Latin American countries, revolution in Bolivia has not always meant a step forward; more often it served to strengthen the hands of those in power and enable them to keep the majority in a sad state of misery.

This majority is Indian—another special feature of the Andean republics. While in Argentina or Chile, for example, the population is white and homogeneous, for the simple reason that there are no Indians left, Bolivia has always had a native, sedentary population which was used as forced labor by the Incas as well as by the Spanish conquerors. The conquerors at first were colonial aristocrats; later they were replaced by an aristocracy of land, and of mines, first of silver and later of tin.

The Bolivian revolutions have mostly consisted in fights between these aristocrats, ending merely in the substitution of one "baron" for the other. The fall of silver and the rise of tin at the end of the nineteenth century did not mean too much for the Indian population; it simply meant a change in the mineral laboriously extracted from the ground, and sometimes in the person of the boss.

Thus, in the course of the last three or four centuries, Bolivian history has been characterized by the existence of two distinct blocs in the nation: a stubborn, silent majority of Indians on the one hand, a busy, clever minority of managers or owners on the other. The two blocs still speak two different languages, materially as well as spiritually, and it will probably take a long time and great effort to get them one day to meet.

The Andean problem is very much in vogue these days. There

is practically no agency interested in technical assistance which does not have at least a small mission in the Andean republics. Each of them is endeavoring to find a solution to the "Indian Problem" as it is generally called, although this name does not cover the problem of the area. A diplomat from one of the Andean republics was probably right when he said: "Please do not fight against the 'Indian problem' in my country; the problem my country really has is a white one." What he meant was that about 80 per cent of the population is Indian in his country and only a small minority is white, but the power in the hands of that small minority is disproportionately big. The diplomat, incidentally, was a white man himself.

In Bolivia, until 1952, only the literate had the right to vote. The Bolivian Indian, Quechua or Aymará, does not yet read or write; therefore he could not vote or be elected to office, and all the powers of the state were in the hands of the approximately 125,000 people who were entitled to vote.

Bolivians live on the production of mines and agriculture. Most of Bolivia's problems are related to these two branches of production. Among the Bolivian minerals, tin is the best known today. Tin is used mainly in the canning industry and so its price depends very much on the state of business in the industrialized countries and on the competition of synthetic products.

A modern Bolivian writer, until recently Ambassador of his country in Rome, published a book after the Second World War under the title of *Metal del Diablo*.[6] The book is about tin. Why is tin the "metal of the devil"? Mortality is extremely high in the tin mines of Bolivia. The average life expectancy of the tin miner is said to be forty-five years. One is tempted to say that a young man, when making the decision to go to the tin mines, is committing suicide because he knows in advance how long, or rather, how short a time he will live. If he spends some years in the mines he will die either of tuberculosis or of silicosis. The entrance of most of the mines is on the Altiplano at altitudes between 11,000 and 15,000 feet. The mine itself is generally a few thousand feet below the entrance. Among the worst Bolivian mines is Pulacayo in southern Bolivia where the galleries of the mine are at such a depth that the naked body of the working

[6] Augusto Céspedes, *Metal del Diablo* (Buenos Aires, 1946).

miner has to be sprinkled continuously with cold water to enable him to resist the heat. The entrance to the mine is high up on the Altiplano where the temperature can easily fall below zero during a South American winter. One can imagine the dangers the miner is exposed to when living and working in such tremendous differences of temperature.

Tuberculosis is not the only enemy of the lungs in the mines; silicosis is the second. While in countries like the United States or Canada there is one case of silicosis for every four industrial accidents, in Bolivia, at least until some years ago, there used to occur seven cases of silicosis for each industrial accident. This meant that the Bolivian ratio was twenty-eight times the normal. The miner, moreover, has become addicted to chewing coca leaves because coca helps when one is hungry and it also helps one to resist the rigors of the altitude. In modern times he also got accustomed to alcohol which had been strictly prohibited in times of the Inca.

Curiously enough, it was an Indian or half-Indian, Simón Patiño, who toward the end of the nineteenth century discovered a mine that was to become one of the great tin mines of the world. Patiño was an excellent organizer and became a very rich man. Unfortunately his wealth was built up in foreign nations, and his own country and fellow Indian countrymen continued to be poor.

Bolivia has other important mines, mostly tin. Until 1952 they were owned by the companies of Aramayo and Hochschild. Patiño, Aramayo and Hochschild are called the Big Three in Bolivia. It would be an understatement to say that the present Bolivian regime is not too friendly toward the Big Three. One of the many accusations made against them is that they were a superstate within a state. In this respect Bolivians generally quote two incidents in Bolivian history. Even if only coincidences, they are interesting. There were two Bolivian Presidents who tried to regulate the financial activities of the mines. One was called Busch, a young and energetic man who is said to have committed suicide, quite curiously just when he had to sign a decree on state regulation of mineral exports. A successor to Busch, Colonel Villarroel, had the same ambitions as Busch. He wanted to bring mineral exports under more control but he was lynched under circumstances that have repeatedly been described in the American Press. The job of a Bolivian president is sometimes risky.

Agriculture is the second basis of Bolivian wealth, or maybe it would be better to say, of Bolivian subsistence. Until 1952 most of the cleared land was in the hands of a few landowners. Some of the farms were well managed, but most of them were in the state of neglect which generally characterizes absentee ownership. As a consequence of the system of land ownership, as well as because of some social and economic reasons, agriculture was stagnating and the country spent almost 30 per cent of its foreign exchange income on foods like wheat, sugar or rice, which could have been produced in the country itself. It was an easy task for the political agitators to blame the big landowners for all these shortcomings.

Absentee ownership, lack of reinvestment, sickness, corruption and wars have made Bolivia one of the poorest countries in the hemisphere. Income per capita is estimated at $58 per head as compared to $2,000 in the United States. Electric consumption is 139 kwh. per capita as compared to 4,000 in the United States.[7]

Such was the situation when on September 14, 1949, the government of Bolivia transmitted an urgent request to the Secretary-General of the United Nations to send a Mission to the country. The task of the Mission was to present definite views on how the government could be aided to draw up a concrete program of economic and social development and how the recommendations of the Mission could be implemented. The Mission was headed by H. L. Keenleyside, a Canadian, who submitted his report in 1951.[8]

The Keenleyside Report

The report is an excellent survey of Bolivia and it is all the more useful because statistical data are rather scarce in the country and traveling is not always easy. The Mission found that there were ample natural resources in the country and the reason for the failure of the Bolivians to "translate that wealth into the agreed evidences of a prosperous national economy was to be found . . .

[7] U.S. Department of Commerce, *World Trade Information Service*, Part III, No. 58, p. 3.

[8] *Report of the U.N. Mission of Technical Assistance to Bolivia* (United Nations, New York, 1951).

in the governmental instability that has consistently marked the history of that nation." [9]

The report continued: "No legally elected Bolivian president has served out his term in the last quarter century; there have been 7 presidents and 8 revolutions in the last 10 years; there have been 18 ministers of labor in 4 years . . . there have been 8 ministers of finance within 18 months."

Governmental and administrative instability could be greatly reduced, it was affirmed, if foreigners could be hired to work permanently in the country. Therefore Keenleyside proposed "that the United Nations assist the Bolivian government in obtaining the services of a number of experts and competent administrative officials of unquestioned integrity drawn from a variety of countries, and that the Bolivian government appoint these officials on a temporary basis to positions of influence and authority as integral members of the Bolivian Civil Service." [10] In other words, Keenleyside was of the opinion that Bolivia would probably have the potential of producing enough for her population if she had able, and even more important, stable administrators to help direct the destinies of the country.

The presence of foreign administrators in a country is not new. When, following World War I, the League of Nations granted stabilization loans to some Central European countries like Hungary and Austria, a trustee of the League of Nations was despatched to the debtor country to control its finances. A similar experiment was made in Greece after World War II when United Kingdom and United States aid to that country was made contingent upon the membership and executive powers in the Currency Council of Greece of a British and an American representative.

However, there is an important difference between these formulas and the Keenleyside experiment. The League of Nations trustees as well as the members of the Greek Currency Council were sent to the debtor countries to control the use of funds received from abroad; they were parties in a *quid pro quo* and the debtor country was forced, in a very diplomatic and gentle way, of course, to accept them. Not so the "Keenleyside expert." He did not have any loan or grant-in-aid to offer (incidentally, that

[9] *Ibid.*, p. 2.
[10] *Ibid.*, p. 3.

was also his greatest handicap); he was accepted as a result of an agreement between an international organization and a sovereign country, just for his knowledge and nothing more.

When the Bolivian government agreed to the idea, the United Nations initiated a broad and entirely new program of technical assistance. The principal and most unusual feature of the system was that the receiving government took so-called "administrative assistants" into its own service, its being understood that they would serve both in an advisory and in an executive capacity in the reorganization of various ministries and agencies and assist in the development of a new economic and social program for the country. Not only La Paz but even the great world centers followed with keen interest the development of the project because of the special combination of advisory and executive functions and because of the emphasis laid on improvement of administrative organization and methods.

The project was started in 1952 and administrative assistants from the United States and several European countries were engaged to work in the Ministries of Finance, Agriculture, Labor, the Central Bank, and with the General Accounting Office.[11] Regular United Nations experts assisted them in the fields of education, mining, taxation, etc. According to Bolivian Decree No. 2752 of October 1, 1951, the functions of the administrative assistants were the following:

(1) To have direct access at all times to the Minister or Chief of the unit in which they serve.

(2) To participate in all recommendations and determinations concerning appointment, transfer, promotion, demotion and retirement of all senior personnel within the unit in which they serve.

(3) To direct the administrative and technical training of the personnel of the unit to which assigned.

(4) To advise the Minister or Chief of the unit in which they serve regarding organizational and operational changes and to participate in the carrying out of these changes.

(5) To cooperate with and to advise the Minister or Chief of the unit in which they serve in supervising the activities of the unit.

[11] The writer of this article became administrative assistant at the Central Bank of Bolivia, and, according to his contract, he was expected to "formulate and put into practice a currency and exchange plan with a view to achieving monetary stabilization and the establishment of a sound exchange system."

(6) To participate and to collaborate in the preparation of the budgetary estimates of the Ministry or unit in which they serve for submission to the Director-General of the Budget.

(7) To examine items of contemplated expenditures before they were made and, when necessary, to inform the Minister or Chief of the unit in which they serve of the undesirability of any expenditures.

(8) To have access to the Coordinator General of the Technical Assistance Program and to the representative of the United Nations.

It was a courageous project, full of unknowns which could be worked out only in the country itself and with the active cooperation of the government. However, there were good possibilities for at least a limited success because the country really needed assistance and, at the date of the conclusion of the agreement, wanted to obtain it even at the price of exceptional procedures.

The Revolution of 1952

On the 9th of April, 1952, a revolution broke out in La Paz. It was not the customary Latin American revolution in which the Army takes care of everything and a General takes over from his predecessor, another General. It was an uprising staged by civilians, by the miners and peasants against the military junta, against the Army itself. It was a bloody movement which lasted several days and took thousands of victims in La Paz alone.

On Good Friday, the revolution came to an end. Its leader, Siles Zuazo, who is now President of Bolivia, halted the bloodshed with the help of the Archbishop of La Paz. On the request of Siles, the Archbishop led a procession around the city, and wherever the procession appeared the fighting subsided and peace was restored. As a result of the revolution, Víctor Paz Estenssoro (who had been elected President in 1951 but had been forced to stay in exile because the military junta would not allow him to return) became President, and his Party, the MNR, took over the political leadership of the country.

MNR stands for National Revolutionary Movement. (The political parties of Bolivia like to be called "revolutionary"; even one of the conservative parties uses this adjective.) The MNR is a coalition of the discontended, impoverished middle class, leftist miners, and Indian peasants. Organization of the party began during the Chaco war; in its principles it was not far from those of the already mentioned President Busch who committed suicide in 1939; according to some observers, during World War II, it was not far from Hitler or Mussolini. The Party's first President of the republic was Colonel Villarroel who was hanged from a lamp-post near the Presidential Palace in 1946. Thus the Party was ousted in 1946 but returned to power in 1952 backed by a great majority of the population.

At the beginning the new regime was not very favorable to us, the United Nations Mission. There were several reasons for this disfavor. First, Paz Estenssoro had been in exile when the agreement of technical assistance was signed by the military junta and the United Nations. It was easy for him to write an angry article against the idea of foreigners in the Civil Service, an article [12] in which he used all the arguments about foreign imperialism. The only thing he did not know, however, when writing the article was that three months later he would be President himself and would be in need of the expert advice of some of the foreigners.

There were other reasons, too, which explained the government's hesitancy about openly cooperating with the Mission. One of them was the attitude of the Communist parties (there are all sorts of Communists in Bolivia: Stalinists, Titoists, as well as Trotzkyites). Although they were fighting each other bitterly, they seemed to be in agreement that the United Nations Mission was full of "imperialist agents." This was the main theme of Communist propaganda against several members of the Mission. Thus, the nationalist right as well as the so-called "extreme left" turned against "foreign intervention" and waited anxiously to see whether the President would decide for or against the Mission.

In the first year of his term, the President preferred to wait and watch. Although uneventful, this was a valuable year for the Mission whose members were given enough time to study the country and prepare for the work to be done later. It was a valuable year because it takes a long time for a foreigner (and this is true for technical assistance in every country, not only Bolivia) to learn and understand a new environment. This was particularly true for Bolivia in 1952, where most of the area outside the cities had

[12] Published in the form of a leaflet, in Buenos Aires, in November 1951.

still to be discovered and where the revolution of 1952 left a complete administrative vacuum.

The work to be done was indeed formidable: the country and its developmental possibilities had to be discovered, a diagnosis of the situation worked out, and new remedies found. It was a difficult and exceptionally exciting task.

The New Bolivia

Most of the aides of Paz Estenssoro were more expert in making revolutions than in administering a country. However, thanks perhaps to their very lack of experience, they were not afraid of cost nor of consequences, and transformed the entire economy within a few months.

One of the first acts of the new regime was a retroactive increase in wages by about 50 per cent and the introduction of important social benefits in favor of the entire working population. Labor disputes had to be brought before the Minister of Labor who had the habit of deciding always for the worker and always against management. Of course, this "revolutionary"—as it had to be called—policy of the Minister did not contribute to increasing labor discipline; on the contrary, as the worker knew that he could not be fired, he had less and less incentive to do productive work. It was, in fact, a characteristic policy of a new revolutionary regime which has to back those who have helped it come to power.

The second step was the nationalization of the big mines. The Big Three were taken over and the question of compensation to the former owners was left open. The MNR created a huge state-owned Mining Corporation which is today among the biggest mining companies in the world.

Finally came the agrarian reform. According to the new law, no one is entitled to own land beyond a certain maximum, and everybody, including the Indian, was to own the land on which he worked.

These were tremendous innovations for a country as backward as Bolivia. And what was really astonishing was the speed at which the machine was working.

It is important to make an observation at this point. The reform activities of the new Bolivian regime were taking place between 1952 and 1955, a period when the United Nations Mission was also very active in Bolivia. However, this does not mean that the Mission should receive credit or be held responsible for any of the new basic laws passed by the Bolivian government. The members of the Mission did not take the initiative, and especially in the first year of the Mission's activity they were not even asked to participate in the preparation of these basic laws. The expropriation of the tin mines, for instance, was the exclusive responsibility of the Party and it was evident that the Party had acted for political and not for economic reasons. The government did not want to be dependent on the activities of a few private companies, so it nationalized the big mines. The government also disapproved of the system of latifundia (according to Bolivian sources, one family owned ten or twelve million acres—the owners themselves did not know how much they actually owned—in the tropical region of Bolivia), and so decided to make a radical land reform.

Thus the members of the Mission did not participate in the formulation of political decisions. However, they could not fail to see that this first period of the new regime was a sort of honeymoon, the first meeting of new politicians with power, and that the honeymoon—as is usual with this agreeable period—could not last for ever. As a result of the tremendous increase in wages and the decline of productivity, it was evident that domestic costs would increase, that Bolivia would soon be on the verge of inflation, and that the political success of the revolution might be destroyed by its economic consequences.

It was mentioned earlier that the new state-owned Bolivian Mining Corporation became one of the largest mining companies in the world. Unfortunately, its deficit became very large too. State ownership always contributes to the increase of bureaucracy and state ownership does not necessarily help to reduce corruption. In short, the nationalization of the big tin mines might have been a political necessity but it certainly did not contribute to balancing the economy of the country.

The land reform, on the other hand, was not only a political but also an economic necessity. But a land reform is generally a long-term proposition: the distribution of the land has to be carried out and legalized; the new owners must feel secure; they have to be educated and convinced that the new farm methods are good. None of this has yet taken place in Bolivia and it will probably be long years or decades before the beneficial effects of the land reform become real.

It was in the last month of 1952 that the end of the "honeymoon" began to be felt in La Paz. President Paz Estenssoro, himself an economist, could not ignore this; yet, for political reasons he hesitated to take unpopular deflationary measures. Not until the beginning of 1953, when the loss in purchasing power of the Bolivian currency began to take on such alarming proportions [13] did he request the writer of these lines to prepare a plan for a new monetary system.

The Reorganization of the Economy on May 14, 1953

The plan was accepted and on May 14, 1953 Bolivia had a new monetary system. The reform consisted of the following:

1) The currency was devalued and the multiple exchange rate system considerably simplified.

2) A foreign exchange budget was prepared, for the first time in Bolivian history, which determined in advance the allocation of foreign exchange both as to expenditures and receipts.

3) A special tax of 50 and 100 per cent was placed on the c.i.f. value of certain less essential imports. Simultaneously, a tax of 35 Bolivianos per dollar was made applicable to mineral exports of the nationalized mines.

4) Quantitative and qualitative credit restrictions were imposed to stop consumption from rising.

5) Prices were allowed to grow, with the exception of rent and certain basic food items whose prices were controlled. Wages were only increased by a flat amount of 4,000 Bolivianos for everybody (about US $10 at the rate prevailing at that time). The wage increase covered only part of the increase in the cost of living; it was a novelty for Bolivia because it meant that the well paid were going to receive relatively less than those in the lower categories.

6) The plan laid the greatest emphasis upon a wage freeze to

[13] For a detailed description of the Bolivian inflation, see ECLA, *El Desarrollo Económico de Bolivia*, Document No. E/CN.12/430/Add.1 (April 30, 1957), pp. 156–221.

keep costs down and make Bolivian exports competitive. A "Stabilization Office" was created whose director was to be responsible for the fight against inflationary wage increases.

In short, the main purpose of the reform was to stop the increase of consumption by creating monetary contraction. These measures did not contain any new ideas of economic policy—anyone interested in economics can find them in any basic textbook. What *was* new in the Bolivian experiment was the fact that the devaluation was not carried out as an isolated measure (as had happened so many times in previous devaluations) but that it formed part of a whole integrated net of legislation covering the entire field of monetary, fiscal, economic and social policy.[14] From the point of view of technical assistance, the new system was particularly interesting because it was carried out by the government on the recommendations of a foreign expert or, to use the terminology of the Keenleyside report—on the recommendations of an administrative assistant.[15]

While, for reasons which will be explained later, the legislation did not result in a definitive stabilization of the currency, the measures of May, 1953, did have important short-run effects. Inflation was checked for some time and, as a result, in May, 1953, business returned to normal. Some months later, following a visit to La Paz by Dr. Milton Eisenhower, the United States decided to grant aid to Bolivia—to a country which had just nationalized an at least partially United States controlled industry! The main reason the State Department used to explain this sensational decision was that the Bolivian government had made a courageous effort to stabilize its currency. In the ensuing years, 1954–56, United States aid totalled about $60 million in the form of surplus goods, machinery and technical advice. United States aid became, and still is, the most important factor in Bolivian finances.

The Development Plan

Of course, it could not be the ambition of the government and its advisers to let the country depend on foreign aid indefinitely. Foreign aid was needed first to save the country from starvation,

---

[14] Arthur Karasz, "Algunos Aspectos de la Política Monetaria," *Revista de Derecho* (University San Andrés, La Paz, March 1954).

[15] Carter Goodrich, "Bolivia, Test of Technical Assistance," *Foreign Affairs* (April, 1954).

but second, and this was more important, to help develop domestic resources which later would make foreign aid unnesessary. Therefore it became very important that the government prepare a development plan. This plan was worked out in 1954 with the cooperation of Bolivian experts and members of the United Nations Mission.[16]

One of the most important purposes of the development plan was to establish a system of priorities. What should be produced and when, in order to maintain or, better, to increase income?

The basic assumption on which the plan was based was that the mines could not be expected to continue much longer to be virtually the country's sole producers of foreign exchange. Numerous mines are near to exhaustion as, for instance, the famous Cerro de Potosí which used to be the greatest silver mine in the days of Philip II, but having been worked for around 400 years, is practically exhausted today. In addition, for reasons explained earlier in this paper, it would probably be better for the Bolivians to close down as many mines as possible and find healthier and more satisfactory jobs elsewhere. Of course, such problems cannot be solved in a short time. Thus it is likely that for the next five or ten years or even more, the Bolivians will be forced to continue working their mines, even those which are high-cost producers, and other healthier and more profitable occupations will only open up after considerable effort and a long period of time.

Agriculture may very probably be one of these new occupations. It was well known, particularly since the publication of the Bohan Plan [17] that the eastern area of Bolivia had great agricultural possibilities. However, the area had only a very sparse population and there was no road connecting the eastern area of Santa Cruz with the inhabited provinces of Cochabamba and La Paz. Bohan proposed the construction of a first-class highway of about 500 kms., cutting across the extremely difficult mountainous region from Cochabamba to Santa Cruz. The highway would make it possible for Santa Cruz to sell its corn, rice and sugar cane to the urban population of the valleys of the Altiplano. An equally

---

[16] Walter Guevara Arze, *Plan de Política Económica de la Revolución Nacional* (La Paz, 1955).

[17] Merwin Bohan, former U.S. Ambassador, prepared an economic diversification plan for Bolivia in 1942.

interesting possibility lies in the agriculture of the Amazon province of El Beni. It lies east of La Paz, but again the lack of highways makes road transportation impossible.

In short, the first part of the development plan consisted in a plan of transportation. It might be illustrated by the following somewhat oversimplified diagram.

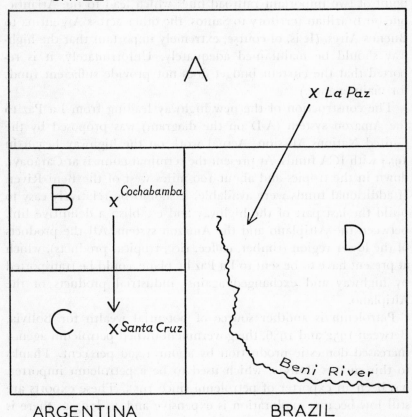

CHILE (PACIFIC OCEAN)

X La Paz

A

B   X Cochabamba

D

C   X Santa Cruz

Beni River

ARGENTINA   BRAZIL

The two arrows on the diagram represent the two main highways to be built. B-C is the Cochabamba-Santa Cruz highway; A-D is the highway from La Paz to the navigable Beni River. That river ends, after some 600 miles on Bolivian territory, in the Amazon system.

The government of Paz Estensorro agreed with the plan and

made great efforts to carry it out. Thus the highway to Santa Cruz (B-C) which had been under construction with long interruptions since 1945 (at a total cost of about $45 million, most of which was procured in loans granted by the Export-Import Bank) was finally inaugurated in 1956. As a result Santa Cruz, which some years ago was a completely isolated area in the middle of South America, is today the terminal of a first class highway leading west toward the Pacific. In addition, Santa Cruz became the meeting point of two important railroad lines which lead to the Atlantic, one on Brazilian territory to Santos, the other across Argentina to Buenos Aires. (It is, of course, extremely important that the highway should be maintained adequately. Unfortunately, it is reported that the current budget does not provide sufficient funds for maintenance.)

The construction of the new highway leading from La Paz to the Amazon system (A-D on the diagram) was proposed by the United Nations Mission. Actual work on the highway began in 1954 with ICA funds. At present the terminal point is at Caranavi, down in the tropics and about 100 miles west of the Beni River. If additional funds were available, it should be relatively easy to build the last part of the highway and establish a definitive link between the Altiplano and the Amazon system. All the products of the lower region (timber, coffee, rice, tropical products), which at present have to be sent to La Paz by plane, could be transported by highway and exchanged against industrial products of the Altiplano.

Petroleum is another source of potential wealth for Bolivia. Between 1952 and 1956, the government-owned petroleum agency increased domestic production by about 1,500 per cent. Thanks to this success Bolivia, which used to be a petroleum importer, has been an exporter of petroleum since 1955. These exports are still low because exploration is expensive and, as long as there is no pipeline leading from Bolivia to the ocean, transportation has to be by rail or highway.

Bolivia does not have the resources to meet the high costs of oil exploration; therefore it would seem extremely important to attract foreign capital into the Bolivian oil industry. However, as foreign oil interests had been expropriated in the 1930's and there was no legislation to insure new investors against a repetition of nationalization, foreign capital refused to come to La Paz. The nationalist and radical factions of the MNR were not unhappy about this situation because their attitude toward foreign petroleum capital was as negative as has been the case in Brazil and Argentina. However, by 1955, the lack of foreign exchange became so acute that financing with Bolivian capital, even of a reduced exploration program, became an economic impossibility. The President of the Republic extended to the writer the unusual invitation of participating in a meeting of the Political Committee of the MNR and asked him to review the monetary situation and the problems of future production. The meeting ended with the acceptance of the suggestion that a new petroleum law be prepared which would contain sufficient guarantees and incentives to attract foreign capital to come to the country and explore possibilities.

The law was prepared by an American expert, Wortham Davenport. Today foreign-owned companies are reported to have invested several million dollars in new petroleum exploration. In addition, a pipeline leading to Arica, Chile, is nearing completion, which means that for the first time in history, Bolivian petroleum will have a direct outlet to the Pacific Coast.

Such, in brief, are the main features of the Bolivian development plan.[18] The idea essentially was to make the country self-sufficient not by means of reducing consumption still further (although this may be theoretically right, it is not always appropriate to reduce the consumption of under-developed countries whose people are already rather impoverished and sometimes hungry), but by trying to increase production until it reaches the level of a minimum consumption, a situation which is politically less explosive.

New Difficulties and Appraisal of Past Performance

As mentioned earlier, the success of the monetary measures of 1953 was not long lasting. Difficulties arose in two fields:

(1) First, in the field of *foreign exchange*. The government was well aware that real stabilization should rest upon two pillars, one domestic, the other foreign. Thus, the ideal solution would have

[18] For more details: Arthur Karasz, *La Solución Económica de Una Inflación* (Cochabamba, 1954).

been to postpone stabilization until the moment when foreign exchange reserves could be rebuilt either from foreign aid or from growing exports. However, the inflationary psychosis became so strong that in the month of May, 1953, the reform could not be postponed any longer although the second pillar was practically non-existent, the reserves of the Central Bank being almost completely depleted and its being impossible to obtain foreign loans.

Difficulties became even greater when the price of tin fell from $1.21 per pound in May, 1953, to 78¢ by July of the same year. (At that time each cent of decline per pound in the price of tin meant a loss of $700,000 in the foreign exchange income of Bolivia, or roughly about 1 per cent of normal income.) As there was no aid forthcoming from abroad,[19] and export proceeds fell catastrophically, foreign exchange became scarce and imports had to be curtailed. As a result of low imports there were not enough machinery and spare parts for the mines, and production declined. It was, in fact, the typical vicious circle of the scarcity of dollars creating additional scarcities of dollars; or, as in the words of Nurkse, the country became poor just because it was poor.[20]

(2) The second difficulty arose in the field of *domestic finance*. As a consequence of low productivity, the mines began losing on the exchange rate. Very soon the government was forced to subsidize mineral exports and later to subsidize the imports of essential goods. The amount of subsidies increased practically in geometrical progression, and by 1956 their total was higher than the entire amount of the normal budget expenditures.

In short, the excessive creation of money to finance both the public and private sectors of the economy, coupled with acute commodity shortages, constantly fed inflation. At the end of 1956 the free exchange rate for the dollar was around 14,000 as compared to the official rate of 190, and inflation was near to the galloping stage, so well-known from the German and Hungarian postwar periods.[21]

---

[19] And even when aid began to be granted it consisted mainly of "surplus goods" (PL 480) instead of cash, and therefore did not always help to solve the country's temporary balance of payments difficulties.

[20] Ragnar Nurkse, *Problems of Capital Formation in Under-developed Countries* (Oxford, 1953), p. 4.

[21] For more details, see ECLA, *op. cit.*, pp. 156–221.

The question can rightly be asked: What did the administrative assistant do under these circumstances? Did he not have the right to veto; therefore, should he not have disagreed with unhealthy wage increases and highly inflationary practices in general?

The answer is that he should have done so if by that time he still had been an administrative assistant. However, by 1954 his position was basically changed: in 1954 he received a new title and was called technical consultant. The new title meant a considerable reduction of powers and responsibilities. The technical consultant was only expected to give advice and help to execute the policies decided by the government.

Politically, the new formula was more palatable to nationalistic public opinion than the old one had been. However, there are situations which call for real power as well as advice giving. The development of the recent inflation in Bolivia is proof of that. Technical assistance, especially in economic matters, can only be effective if the expert is not only giving advice but also is responsible for the execution of what he has been advising. In other words, the original Keenleyside formula is probably the only good approach. Perhaps it should be tried again with new people and in another country.[22]

Technical assistance is only justified by its usefulness to the receiving country. In the case of the Bolivian experiment, observers generally agree that without the Mission's cooperation (not only in obtaining foreign aid but also in merely technical matters) Bolivia would probably not have had the relative stability that it has been enjoying since 1952. The following may help prove this point. Certain governmental activities could only be carried on thanks to the cooperation of the foreign civil servants. For instance, the preparation of the national as well as the foreign exchange budgets, the reorganization of budget auditing and the simplification of the extremely complicated wage system were all the work of the administrative assistants in the Ministries of Finance and Labor, in the General Accounting Office and in the

[22] There is hope that the experiment will not only be repeated but even considerably enlarged. The Economic and Social Council of the United Nations, at its twenty-sixth Session held in Geneva in July 1958, adopted "on a limited and experimental basis" the Secretary-General's proposal for an International Civil Service. This proposal envisages the United Nations recruiting and paying part of the salary of men who would be absorbed in the regular government service of various under-developed countries. (ECOSOC E/3159 of July 15, 1958.)

Central Bank. Moreover, such technical assistance was not always confined to administration and legislation, as in the cases referred to above. To give only one example: when a United Nations expert found new water for the Santa Cruz area, this was a very tangible contribution to the physical well-being of its population.

The fact that the number of such practical improvements is not greater and that not enough could be done until now to "transfer skills from people to people" is mainly due to the almost continuous emergency in which the Bolivian economy finds itself. Very little technical assistance, in the classical sense of the word, can be accomplished in a country where the expert has to be continuously on the alert and has to find solutions for emergency problems instead of being free to look for the underlying causes of the emergency. In such a country, technical assistance can only achieve its basic purpose if it is given enough time to wait until the emergency is over so that the real work of the expert can then begin. (However, if the expert had not contributed to solve this series of emergencies, the need for technical assistance itself might not exist any more because the regime would probably have disintegrated.)

The most important "emergency contribution" of the Mission was its cooperation in what we may call the "discovery of a new Bolivia." After the revolution of 1952, Bolivia became a *terra incognita* politically as well as economically. Within a short peroid of time everything has completely changed in the country: there is a new managerial class, new and powerful labor forces, and Indians who suddenly have become owners of land; in short, a new population with new needs and new political objectives. New economic resources had first to be discovered in order to see how these new needs and objectives could be satisfied.

It was in this unknown environment that the Mission prepared its diagnosis and evaluated the short and long-term possibilities of the country. According to the diagnosis, the lack of foreign exchange was threatening to become the most acute and difficult problem of the country. Unfortunately the diagnosis was (and still is) right. Without important United States grants-in-aid, which were being given to Bolivia every year since 1954 and in the obtaining of which the Mission was quite active until 1956, a profound crisis would have developed probably by 1954 and nobody can tell what would have happened later.

One may ask, of course, why was political stability so important in Bolivia? The answer is that it is important everywhere, but it is particularly important in Bolivia in view of the country's geographical position. As one can easily see on any map, the Altiplano is a great potential airfield, a meeting place of rails and highways, an obstacle to, but also a potential center of transportation. And social unrest or revolution could lead to the triumph of Communism. If they once came to prevail in Bolivia, it is possible that Communists could not be stopped behind the towering mountains, behind that "Tin Curtain," but would spread their influence into all the neighboring countries of the South American continent.

In most of the young developing countries, public opinion is very ready to think that inflation is the only way to growth. Bolivia is no exception to this rule. The Mission did not succeed in suppressing inflation; however, it helped at least to slow it down. The main idea behind the monetary measures of 1953 was that they would help to retard inflation until the economy of the country could be diversified and petroleum and agriculture could begin to replace the marginal mines—in short, until stabilization in real terms could take place. If the government had been able to hold out more energetically against exaggerated wage demands, if labor discipline had been maintained, and, last but not least, if the foreign exchange income of the country had developed in a somewhat more advantageous way, the Bolivian currency would not have depreciated so greatly as it did in 1956.[23]

[23] At present (May, 1958), Bolivia is in the midst of a new monetary experiment. The basic principles of this new experiment follow those established by the reform of 1953. In addition, as an innovation, there was created in August, 1956, a Stabilization Council whose Executive Director is a citizen of the United States. He has great executive powers in all problems which relate to economic, monetary, fiscal and social matters. Another foreign expert at present in Bolivia working on these same problems is a representative of the International Monetary Fund. For details see Ernest Moore, "The Stabilization of the Bolivian Peso," *Public Finance Quarterly* (Haarlem, Netherlands, 1958), pp. 43–64. In practice the new system means that multilateral technical assistance (in which the pooled effort of many countries cannot be identified with any single country) has been given up and replaced by a bilateral agreement between Bolivia and the United States. The acceptance by the Bolivians of the new system was followed by the creation of a $25 million stabilization fund granted, in December, 1956, by the United States and the International Monetary Fund. The country's new President, Hernán Siles Zuazo, is making

CONCLUDING REMARKS

The purpose of this paper has been to try to describe the results of a new form of multilateral technical assistance. Under this new arrangement, a position of stability—one could almost say "tenure"—was given to foreign experts working in an under-developed country's administration. The results of the experiment fall into two categories:

The first is of a practical nature. Thanks to the cooperation of the foreign experts, the government of the receiving country was able both to improve its economic and social practices and also to obtain financial aid from abroad which helped to avert political and economic chaos.

The second category of results, less immediately obvious but probably more important for the longer-range future of the country, is in the field of international relations. In the first few months which followed the revolution of 1952, the international position of Bolivia was weak, for reasons which are easily understandable. The world did not know the new revolutionary regime and the young regime did not know the world. Long months of patient work were needed to explain to the Bolivians the whys and hows of international organizations, but as the leaders of the new regime were talented and intelligent people it was a relatively easy task to convince them about the necessity of international *rapprochement*. It was a great triumph for the government and a sign of the intelligence of its members that in the matter of a few years they were able to lift the Tin Curtain and that Bolivia again became a well-known and full-fledged member of the international community. Thus, the United Nations Mission served as a bridge between La Paz and those countries outside whose policies towards Bolivia and her raw materials are so vital to the development of her economy. The Mission tried to explain Bolivia to the outside world and also to explain the outside world to Bolivia. It would not be an exaggeration to say that this sort of activity should probably be one of the basic forms of international technical assistance.

courageous and honest efforts to stabilize the economy. It would be premature to pass judgement on the new experiment now when it is still relatively recent. The difficulties of the country are enormous and if President Siles does not find a way to increase the standards of living of the population, the stabilization program may easily degenerate into a dangerous depression.

CHAPTER XII

[ALCEU AMOROSO LIMA *]

Voices of Liberty and Reform

in Brazil

INTRODUCTION

It must at the outset be emphasized that the whole of Latin American civilization has been strongly molded by the spirit of the Renaissance, whereas United States civilization is rather a direct product of the eighteenth century. This means, among other features, that the spirit of authority has prevailed for centuries in the formation of the Latin American countries while the spirit of liberty has been dominant in the development of North Ameri-

* Alceu Amoroso Lima was born in Rio de Janeiro, and pursued his higher studies at the Faculty of Juridic and Social Sciences of that city. He has been Rector of the University of the Federal District (1938), and beginning in 1941 has served as Professor of Brazilian Literature both as a member of the Faculty of Philosophy at the University of Brazil and at the Pontifical Catholic University. He has been director of the review *A Época* (1912), literary critic of *O Jornal* (1919–1945), and was the founder of *Agir* in 1944. From 1951 to 1953 he was director of the Cultural Department of the Pan American Union. He was a co-founder of the Christian Democratic Movement of Latin America (Montevideo, 1947), and has been a guest lecturer at the Universities of Paris (Sorbonne), Bordeaux, Tolouse, Montpelier, the Catholic University of America, Duke, North Carolina, Louisiana State, Texas, Nashville, Fordham and Pennsylvania State College. During the 1958–1959 academic year he held the chair of Professor of Brazilian Studies at the newly established Brazilian Institute of New York University. A few of his books include: *Estudos*, 5 séries (1927–1933); *Pela União Nacional* (1942); *Pela Cristianização da Idade Nova* (1947); *O Problema do Trabalho* (1947); *Mensagem de Roma* (1950); *O Existencialismo* (1951); *A Realidade Americana* (1954); *A Vida Sobrenatural e o Mundo Moderno* (1956).

can institutions. Therefore, the voices of liberty and reform in Latin America have always come from underground, raised by vast segments of the people, by isolated personalities or by lower level political or nonpolitical groups. The fight for liberty and reform in Latin America has always been a reaction against the prefabricated frames, as we may say, imposed upon us and responsible for the general outlook of our different civilizations.

There are many Latin Americas and not just one, as is most frequently assumed. In this paper I shall attempt to outline, within the Brazilian area, the significant visible and invisible sociological forces which, during the four centuries of our historical life, have been most active in the development of a national consciousness based on responsibility and independence.

THE COLONIAL PERIOD

The Voice of the Missionaries

Juan B. Terán, an outstanding Argentine scholar, in considering the colonial period of Latin America has noted two categories of peoples who came from the Iberian peninsula: the *conquistadores* and the *anti-conquistadores*. Under the first heading he includes, as the name indicates, those who came to spread the "empire" of the Iberian crown, both Spanish and Portuguese; under the second, those who came to conquer the land for God and His Church. One of our best historians in Brazil, Capistrano de Abreu, has more or less reached the same conclusion, distinguishing between those "who came to go back" and those "who came to stay." The first were the officials and *colonos*, and the others the *missionarios*.

Those missionaries were the first to raise the voice of liberty and reform in Brazil. They belonged to four religious orders: Jesuit, Franciscan, Carmelite and Benedictine. They came to stay and to work with the people. The Benedictines founded the first monasteries. The Carmelites specialized in preaching. The Franciscans worked with the settlers and also among the aborigines. The Jesuits took upon their shoulders two of the heaviest burdens: the protection of the natives and the establishment of an educational system, from instruction in the popular crafts to the seminaries which were the harbinger of our first universities.

In their work the members of these four orders clashed frequently with the colonists and officials. The pulpit was, we can say, the first voice of liberty in Brazil. The greed of the colonists, the sins of the planters, "whose wives display more luxury in the colony than in Lisbon," according to the Jesuit Fernão Cardim in his *Narrativa Epistolar* (one of the earliest chronicles on sixteenth century Brazilian colonial life), the exploitation of the Indians and slaves, were exposed by the spoken word from the pulpits of Bahia, Recife and Rio de Janeiro, and by the written word in the chronicles and letters of the missionaries. In particular, the annual letters from the Jesuits, each referred to as an *Annua* and only recently revealed to the public, contain the most outright denunciations of the evils of colonization.

Into Minas Gerais, from where the Portuguese crown received the bulk of Brazilian wealth in gold and diamonds, the religious orders were not allowed to enter. One reason for this is revealed by a letter written by a Governor of this province to the authorities in Portugal: "Those friars place themselves always on the side of the people against the crown, and aid them in evading the payment of taxes." [1] The fight of the Jesuits against the colonists is one of the most striking traits of our colonial history. A particularly renowned member of the Society of Jesus, Antônio Vieira—whose life as missionary, ambassador, orator, writer, statesman, theologian and as a prisoner for years of the Inquisition is revealed in his thirty volume *Works*—was one of the leading and most colorful *anti-conquistadores*. He did not hesitate publicly to denounce not only the greed of the colonists but that of the crown itself, "which used to pump the wealth of Brazil to irrigate Portugal!"

The Voice of the Municipal Chambers

To study the role of the municipal chambers in the story of my country two historians must be consulted: João Francisco Lisboa (1812–1863) who wrote during the mid-nineteenth century, and Afonso de Escragnole Taunay (1875–1957) who died only very recently.

[1] The original document is quoted at length in my own book, *Voz de Minas*, which is not available here. The lack of specific references throughout this paper must be attributed to the fact that I have written it when far removed from my library and usual sources.

Both have emphasized the important part played by municipal groups in northern and southern Brazil. The local chambers were the first seeds of our self-government. In them the *homens bons* and the *vereadores,* the important citizens of the most important towns—as São Luiz, Recife, Salvador, Ouro Preto, Rio de Janeiro and São Paulo—met to organize local administration. These men represented sometimes opposite classes and policies, those from Recife, for example, being merchants and those from Olinda landed aristocrats; but by their activities they took the first step toward the formation of a national consciousness. They were always more or less at variance with the official representatives of the Portuguese government.

Particular stress must be accorded the mood of the *Paulistas* and especially the *Câmara Municipal de São Paulo,* the archives of which were disclosed and analyzed by Afonso Taunay. The renowned navigator Coreal, in his work relating his seventeenth-century voyages which took him to Santos, the port of São Paulo, tells about the *Paulistas.* He notes, for example, that they were renowned for their sense of pride and independence. They considered their territory a republic and would not allow the Portuguese tax collectors who came to receive the *dizimos* to enter São Paulo. The collectors climbed the high mountains between Santos and São Paulo and stopped at the edge of the plain. There, at the beginning of the colonial period, the first settlers had built the town of *Santo Andre da Borda do Campo* (St. Andrew on the limit of the field). To this settlement the *Paulistas* came, bringing the amount of taxes that was due. The tax collectors were not allowed to go beyond the top of the mountains, midway between São Paulo and Santos, in order that the *Paulistas* might demonstrate that they paid their imposts willingly, spontaneously and without coercion.

This reveals the mind of those *vereadores* who represented the *comunes* of colonial Brazil and who constituted the first political voices of liberty and reform.

The Voice of the Intellectuals

The third group of voices was that of the early writers, especially the poets. Poetry is, by its very nature, anticonformist. The greatest Brazilian colonial poet, Gregório de Matos (1633–1696), was the prince of the anticonformists. Born and raised in Salvador, where the Jesuits administered the sort of higher studies compatible in some ways with those of University training at Coimbra, Gregório de Matos at eighteen went to Portugal where he attained the highest posts in the Law Courts. He had already been appointed to the Supreme Court in Lisbon when he refused to preside over an investigation committee sent to Brazil to arrange one of those false trials with which the totalitarian states of our century have made a mockery of liberty and justice.

Gregório de Matos refused to participate in a farcial judicial procedure against a Governor of Rio de Janeiro who had offended Portuguese officials. He was promptly exiled to Salvador, first capital of Brazil and his own birth place. There he earned his livelihood as a lawyer but lived largely as a vagabond, a kind of Brazilian Villon, transfusing his spirit of resistance into the most fiercely satirical poetry ever written in colonial Latin America. He was once more exiled, this time to Africa, and toward the end of his life was allowed to return not to Salvador, but to Recife, provided that he write no more verse!

Notwithstanding all that can be said against his character and the questions that can be raised concerning his tendency as a poet to borrow from Quevedo, Gregório de Matos without question was a typical voice of liberty and sarcasm, attacking the evils and abuses of colonial society and administration.

Another voice, far quieter and more mediocre but projected on a higher moral level, must also be included among the intellectuals who fought for liberty and reform during the colonial period of our history: that of Nuno Marques Pereira, the author of a kind of novel called *O Peregrino da América* (*The Pilgrim of America*), written in 1628, which denounces the rotten customs of the society and urges a moral regeneration. The same can be said of another novel whose authorship is not as yet completely established. It was written either by Alexandre de Gusmão, an outstanding Brazilian statesman and counselor to King João V of Portugal, or by Teresa Margarida, sister of Matias Aires who was the first philosopher born in Brazil. If it could be clearly demonstrated that she wrote the book, she would emerge, undisputed, as the first Brazilian authoress. The name of the novel in question is *As Aventuras de Teofanes* (*The Adventures of Teofane*), published in 1752. It concerns a mythical personage belonging to the literary cycle which arose in Europe as a result of the famous novel of Fenelon, *Les Aventures de Télémaque*.

During the first half of the eighteenth century the initial literary academies, imitating the powerful academic movement that started in Italy with the Renaissance spirit and spread throughout Europe, were founded in Brazil. Organized by the established authorities, they were rather in the conformist mood. But in the second half of the century other academies, which took the name of societies and were more inclined toward the scientific spirit, arose. Organized on more anticonformist premises, these societies were soon closed by the public authorities and most of their members were imprisoned. One of these victims must be remembered: Silva Alvarenga (1749–1814), a forefather of the revolutionary ideas persecuted at that time as "French ideas."

A whole literary movement began to develop at the end of the eighteenth century. Known as the *Escola Mineira* (The School of Minas Gerais), it included in its ranks the best poets of the Portuguese language at that time, not only of Brazil but of Portugal. The movement was closely connected with the tentative political upheaval known as the *Inconfidência Mineira* (the rebellion of Minas Gerais) which was bloodily suppressed by the absolutist government of Portugal. Three great poets were connected with the arcadian movement or the School of Minas Gerais: Tomás Antônio Gonzaga who was exiled; Claudio Manuel da Costa who committed suicide; and Alvarenga Peixoto who died in prison. Most assuredly, theirs are three voices of liberty and reform to be included among the intellectuals of colonial Brazil.

In the fields of sociology and economics we must introduce the name of the founder of these studies in Brazil, José da Silva Lisboa, Viscount of Cairú (1756–1835). His was the contribution of introducing economic liberalism, as promoted by Adam Smith and his followers, in opposition to the prevailing economic colonialism. Cairú was also one of the patriots who will be discussed in the following section, but he cannot be excluded from those intellectuals who fought for liberty and reform during the late colonial period.

THE IMPERIAL PERIOD

The Voice of the Patriots

O Patriota (*The Patriot*) was the name chosen by Silva Alvarenga, referred to above, for the magazine he founded in 1813, one year before his death. It was the second magazine to appear in Brazil—the first one, *A Idade do Ouro* (*The Golden Age*) commenced publication in 1812—and its name clearly revealed that a new mood was gripping the country. The period between 1808, the date of the arrival in Brazil of the Regent Prince from Portugal later to rule as King João VI, and 1822, the year which saw our independence proclaimed, marks the transition between colony and empire.

The human type most characteristic of these times was surely "the patriot." He did not belong to a special class. He might have been born in Portugal, have studied there and remained many years outside of Brazil. He could have been an illiterate or a great poet, a scientist or a statesman, a rich man or a pauper. Nor could "the patriot" have been distinguished by color of skin, religious creed or philosophy of life. Essentially, what identified him was his striving for liberty and reform, not in the exact manner of the missionaries, the *vereadores* or the intellectuals of colonial times, but with a much more developed awareness of the national unity that bound together the citizens of the country. The cause was one: independence. The feeling was one: patriotism. And the patriots, scattered all over the country, fomented the spirit that led to independence in 1822.

It was the man in the street, the anonymous man, who was truly the new representative of the spirit of liberty and reform. For the first time in our history the "mob" assumed political and national influence. Up to that moment many limited popular movements had appeared here and there, but restricted in their scope only to local aspirations and protests. Now, a general spirit of patriotism, which had as its substance the popular hope for liberty and reform, began to mold the national character. This spirit can be considered under two aspects that we may term negative and positive. The negative was the rebellion against colonialism, and especially against the Portuguese. It is true that in the seventeenth century, during the temporary Dutch occupation of the coast from Recife to Bahia (1624–1654), some kind of national spirit developed among whites, Indians and Negroes, all fighting side by side against the Dutch. But we can safely say that in their struggle they were not motivated by desire for liberty or reform. They considered themselves Portuguese, although natives of Brazil, and it was basically the opposition of the Catholic conscience to Calvinism that united them against the invaders. Nevertheless, we can find in those wars the seeds of the mob-consciousness of patriotism that flowered at the beginning of the nineteenth century. It was, however, between 1808 and 1822 that "the patriot," with his sense of liberty and reform, was truly born, not only as an individual but as a people. The mob movements throughout the country that preceded the formal declaration of independence heralded a new consciousness and a new human type, drawing its inspiration primarily from the negative impulse of reaction against the former rulers and authorities.

To the popular and negative aspect—negative in the sense of anti, not in the sense of passive—of the new social tide, we may add the positive role of the elite.

The positive approach to liberty and reform, based on patriotism, was the planning of a new state. If one desires a general and at the same time analytical view of the conscious molding of the Brazilian Empire by the cultural and social elite, I would recommend as the most up-to-date and reliable study on the "Founders of the Empire" the ten volume work of the noted Brazilian historian Octavio Tarquinio de Souza.[2] For the purposes of this paper, I need mention only two names: Emperor Dom Pedro I and, the so-called "Patriarch of the Independence," José Bonifacio de Andrada e Silva.

One of the most remarkable differences between Brazil and the Hispanic American countries as pertains to our national character and the manner in which we obtained our independence can be symbolized by those two patriots: an Emperor and a scientist!

It was Pedro I, son of King João VI, who proclaimed on September 7, 1822, the independence of Brazil, thereby bringing to fruition the scattered movements of anonymous patriots which had been under way for many years. Pedro I, although his father

---

[2] Octavio Tarquinio de Souza, *Os Fundadores do Império*. 10 vols. (Rio de Janiero, 1958).

as Prince Regent had fled from Portugal before the armies of Napoleon, was profoundly influenced by the Napoleonic spirit. By making himself the leader of the movement for liberty and reform, he assured the transition from colonial status to national independence within the framework of monarchical traditions. The Napoleonic influence explains the existence of an Empire in America for half a century. The change from colony to Empire was carried out almost without bloodshed and amidst a minimum of violence, which fact constitutes one of the most striking features of Brazilian history and character.

The personality of José Bonifacio, the "patriarch" of our independence, is also symbolic. He was a scholar, born in Brazil, who for ten years traveled throughout Europe, regarded as one of the most renowned geologists of his time. Two or three minerals, newly discovered at the time, were named after him, one being *Andradita.* He contributed to the trend toward reform and liberty always as a statesman, scientist, jurist and even as a poet, but not as a soldier. While the fathers of Hispanic American emancipation were in general military men, like Bolívar, San Martín, Artigas and Sucre, those of Brazilian independence were civilians.

Among the patriots who incarnated the desire for freedom in Brazil we find priests, military men, politicians and even women, who were at that time, of course, much less politically minded than today. But the military men played an insignificant role. Therefore, the figure of the *caudilho* does not appear as a typical patriot, and even the word is not Portuguese. This, it seems to me, is characteristic of our march toward freedom. Compared to the Spanish Americans we are perhaps less heroic and dramatic, but at the same time more pacific, quiet, balanced and patient. We have never had dictators or leaders like Rosas, López, Gómez or Perón. Vargas was something of an exception, but even his regime has been referred to as a dictatorship without a dictator, for he was always eager to be more a leader behind the curtains than a real *duce.* When overthrown, he returned to power through ballots rather than bullets.

The Voice of the Provinces

Unlike the Spanish-American world, Brazil preserved its unity in its new found independence. Many forces, analysis of which would be beyond the scope of the present paper, contributed to this result. On the other hand, powerful movements aiming at the separation of our country into different parts were present throughout our historical past. There was, for example, talk of a northern *República do Ecuador* in 1824, and of a southern *República de Piratinin* in 1835. Separatist tendencies were, however, always strongly opposed, by the Portuguese crown during the colonial period, and by the Brazilian crown during the nineteenth century.

Even though the central or federal authorities have always had sufficient strength to avoid actual secession, various centrifugal provincial movements have a symbolical meaning in the general outline of our national movement toward liberty and reform.

Unity is not uniformity. True unity, instead of abolishing variety takes it for granted, and presupposes a certain autonomy of the parts of a whole. The unity of Brazil is based upon the existence of numerous varieties. In the majority of instances, the different local uprisings against Portugal during colonial times and against the imperial or federal government thereafter have had as their essence the desire to protect regional patterns of life. The last of these movements was the *Revolução Paulista* of 1932, which was not a separatist movement but a rebellion in the name of constitutionalism against the centralizing and dictatorial regime of Vargas.

These movements in general, it seems to me, are much less a tendency toward the disruption of Brazilian unity than a manifestation of local characteristics and ways of life and the hope to maintain intact local privileges and liberties. This trend is definitely in the tradition of the municipalism to which we have previously referred.

The provincial voices represent definitely the same spirit of freedom which is manifest throughout our history in contradiction to, even though in occasional alliance with, the strong authoritarian tradition of the Renaissance heritage. These voices have been raised to protect regional customs and ways of life against forced integration. Therefore, the provincial impulses toward autonomy that abound in the pages of our history are tangible indications of a growing local love of freedom, and not of separatist movements.

We must, however, be careful to distinguish the occasional provincial upheavals which have, in fact, aimed at separatism, from the tendency of certain regions or provinces to project into the nation as a whole, or to protect against centralistic intrusions, certain special features of local character. The first impulse, liberation from a national community, seems to me a dangerous trend. The most famous military man of our history, the Duke—the only one—of Caxias has been called the *Pacificador,* or peacemaker, because of his great missions during the Empire period undertaken to restore peace between fighting factions inside the country.

But the second kind of impulse, the one which manifests the natural and free varieties of psychology and temperament within the national unity of the whole people, is highly commendable. Within the confines of this paper it is impossible to elaborate on differences of national temperament, but we may safely allude to three sections, North, Center and South, each of which, with special traits and representing different provincial voices, has nurtured a spirit of variety and freedom and has thus contributed to the trend toward liberty and reform.

The Voice of the Democrats

The word democracy is confusing and misleading. It admits of so many interpretations and misinterpretations that it is not surprising to discover the difficulty with which it has made its way through our history—a difficulty far more extreme than in Anglo-America. The Latin and German traditions in politics have always been those of conflict and opposition, whereas the political tradition of England has been that of compromise. The word democracy in Latin America conveys both connotations, and the two currents can be seen in simultaneous motion in our nineteenth-century history.

The Empire came from a Napoleonic and Louis Philippe tradition, as we have seen, and not from one of legitimism. García Merou, an exiled Argentine writer living in Brazil, could therefore call the Empire a "crowned democracy." The most recent history of our imperial regime has chosen this terminology as the most accurate description of our monarchical institutions.[3] The

---

[3] João Camilo de Oliveira Torres, *A Democracia Coroada* (Rio de Janeiro, 1958).

liberal tradition of democracy has prevailed even in the official institutions of the country, beginning with the first Constitution of 1823.

Crowned democracy did not satisfy the more radical democrats, who from the outset enjoyed considerable strength and developed a more extreme program that was in frequent opposition to established institutions. We cannot deny that both types of democrats tried to enforce freedom and achieve reforms. The two-party system in the parliamentarian regime which was strongly influenced by English traditions, alternated both groups, in the form of the Conservative and Liberal Parties, in the administration of the country, always under the final authority of the *Poder Moderador*. The Constitution, through this moderator power, attributed to the Emperor supreme but not absolute power. We cannot speak in any way of the crowned democracy as an authoritarian democracy in contrast to a libertarian democracy, if we understand as democracy the increasing participation of people in general in public affairs. Even the so-called authoritarian democracy of Vargas in our own century pretended to "abolish the parties in order to bring more closely together the Government and the people."

The real difference between the two approaches to democracy lay in the fact that the radicals emphasized, as a first and indeed the ultimate goal, the necessity of liberty and reform, whereas the conservative political parties and the champions of the established institutions considered liberty and reform not as ends but as means.

Those who placed liberty and reform as the finality of political institutions and as the required policy of any stable government in Brazil can be divided into three categories: abolitionists, federalists and republicans.

The abolitionists, as the name indicates, were those who strove for the suppression of slavery. No social movement in the direction of liberty has had so dramatic an impact upon our history. Slavery was an institution already in decay when American colonization commenced. The Middle Ages had crossed the line between slavery and serfdom. The industrial revolution, in turn, had abolished serfdom and was projecting the economic system toward the use of free labor. But colonialism, which antedated industrialism as one of the features of the Renaissance period, returned to the use of slavery so as to exploit the new continent. Africa, where slavery still prevailed in undiminished strength as one of the results of primitive warfare, was plundered in order to secure low cost labor in America.

During the colonial period there was little protest against slavery, so firmly had the institution become established within the colonial mores. As soon, however, as a more national understanding of the natural rights of human nature developed, from the eighteenth century on, the reaction against slavery began. The forefathers of our independence, men like Cairú and Hipólito da Costa (1774–1823), one of the founders of our periodical press, and even José Bonifacio (1765–1838) proposed plans calling for the gradual replacement of slave with free labor, and for the immediate suppression of the so-called "traffic." The first law against the slave trade was passed in 1831, but not until 1888 did a law presented to the Parliament by the Conservative Party and enforced by the daughter of Emperor Pedro II, reigning during the temporary absence of her father, abolish slavery. The fight for abolition, waged against the "realists" in politics and the large estate owners of both Liberal and Conservative Parties, was led by great political orators like Joaquim Nabuco, by Negro journalists like José do Patrocinio, by poets like Castro Alves and by the whole intellectual generation born after 1850. The slaves themselves were too oppressed by the burdens of their infamous situation to be capable of efficient insurrection. But the formation throughout the country of groups called *quilombos,* consisting of escaped slaves, and the individual and even group effort of Negroes to buy their own *alforria* (liberation) must be included as part of the anonymous and mob contribution to the work of the intellectuals and political elites against the prejudices and financial interests of the majority. The fight for abolition was the most epic episode in the attainment of freedom in our history.

Next to this, but on a much lower level of importance, we can place the federalist ideal. It too was an ideal of liberty and reform, based upon the same aspirations as those discussed above under the heading, "The Voice of the Provinces." Reform was precisely the word used by a group of writers and politicians who in 1870 founded the *Club da Reforma* and a newspaper called

A Reforma. This movement sought to shield the aspirations of local autonomy against the centralized institutions provided by the monarchical constitution, and only slightly moderated by the *Ato Adicional* of 1834.

Among the politicians and writers participating in the federalist campaigns we may mention three of the most influential publicists of our country, whose influence was to become decisive in the historical trends of Brazil at the end of the last century: Rui Barbosa (1849–1923), Joaquim Nabuco (1849–1910) and Tavares Bastos (1839–1875).

Rui Barbosa was to be the principal author of the first republican Constitution of 1891, which to a considerable extent was modeled after the United States Constitution. Joaquim Nabuco, an aristocrat, was one of the most efficient and eloquent campaigners for abolition, both in Parliament and the press. Tavares Bastos, who died very young, was the author of the most outstanding work in defense of federalism, *A Provincia*, published in 1861. The federalist movement was the predecessor of the republican movement which started in 1870.

Republican ideas and ideals had scarcely appeared during the colonial period. Only in the nineteenth century did they produce any notable effects, when the revolutionary movements of 1817 and 1824 in Pernambuco and the *Guerra dos Farrapos* (The War of the Rags) between 1835 and 1845 in the extreme South announced republican goals.

During the same century, and especially after 1856, the ideas of the French philosopher Auguste Comte began to wield strong influence in Brazil. In particular, three persons were prominently involved in disseminating the message of positivism: Miguel Lemos, Teixeira Mendes and Benjamin Constant. The first two were civilians, the third a military man who attained great prestige among the army officers and is considered one of the individuals most responsible for initiating the victorious military uprising of November 1889, which brought the Empire to a long expected end.

The positivist philosophical ideas, as we know, favored republican authoritarianism. Another trend of the republican movement, influenced more by the purely political thought of France and America, was in the direction of liberal republicanism. Still a third group inclined toward Jacobinism. The three groups gathered together for the common purpose of rejecting the only existing monarchy in America, but strongly opposed one another in regard to the type of new political structure that should be fashioned. What prevailed, after the foundation of the republic in 1889, and especially with the Constitution of 1891, was liberal republicanism, with federalist relations being established between the states and the union.

The Voice of the Church

The Church is based on authority, but on spiritual authority. And the strength of its position depends on independence from the state. Christ Himself, once and for all times, distinguished between, but did not totally separate, the two powers—temporal and spiritual—in urging all men to give to Caesar what is Caesar's and to God what belongs properly to Him. But the rule for all historical times has tended to be tension between the two swords. Brazil was unable to avoid the dissensions which had previously erupted in Spain, Portugal and elsewhere in Europe. The ancient laws of medieval kings, establishing certain rights of the crown over the Church as compensation for the protection of Church by state, were never fully accepted by ecclesiastical authorities; nor were they rejected outright. Because of this ambiguous situation which had never been resolved during colonial times in Brazil, and owing also to the rise of Freemasonry during the independence period at precisely the time when imperial policies were being devised, relations between the Church and the Empire always lacked true cordiality. Although Church and state were united according to law, that union was transformed little by little into the submission of the Church to the state.

In this paper I cannot even summarize the conflict between the two powers that erupted in Rio and Pernambuco, between 1872 and 1875. Suffice it to say that a law of 1855, under the pretense of reforming the decadent seminaries, declared that henceforth no religious orders could open seminaries in Brazil. The real intention was to weaken the importance of the religious orders which are everywhere the stronghold of spirituality and the bulwark of the Church's independence in its apostolic duties.

A young Brazilian from Paraiba, Vital Maria de Oliveira, who had been ordained a Capuchin in France, was named Bishop of Recife and Olinda when only twenty-seven years of age, thus becoming the youngest Catholic bishop in the world at the time. Animated by zeal and reform aspirations, he opposed the intervention of Masonry in the affairs of the Church. This initiated a lengthy legal struggle, as the outcome of which the Bishop was condemned to four years of imprisonment at hard labor. A like sentence was meted out to the Bishop of Pará, D. Antonio Macedo Costa. Both went to prison, but were granted amnesty after two years.

The clash between Church and state strongly divided public opinion and evoked heated discussions which often centered upon considerations of liberty. The struggle of the Church in behalf of its freedom, not against the state *per se* but against intervention in spiritual matters, became such an important aspect of the development of freedom in Brazil that many historians assigned the crumbling of the Empire in 1889 to the so-called religious question.

The religious question in Brazil was, in reality, a fight for spiritual freedom. To a large extent this objective was realized at the inception of the Republic, through the separation of Church and state. Since then, relations between the two powers have been friendlier than at any previous time in our country's history. Freedom pays.

THE REPUBLICAN PERIOD

The Voice of the Liberals

Four divisions of politicians, of political doctrines and of public opinion can be detected if we consider the fall of the Empire and the emergence of the Republic: the liberals, the authoritarians, the realists and the Jacobins. I will mention only one outstanding representative in our political life of each of these groups: Rui Barbosa among the liberals; Teixeira Mendes among the authoritarians; Pinheiro Machado among the realists; and Aristides Lobo among the Jacobins.

Each of these four, and his own group of politicians and adherents, played an important role in the beginning of our republican life. But undoubtedly, those who tried to balance the ideal of freedom in political life with the necessity of preserving national unity, the claims of the federal government with those of the provinces, were the liberals. The federalist movement, favoring virile autonomy for the provinces, had been the harbinger of the Republic. The new Constitution granted the provinces, or states as they were now called, substantially greater autonomy than previously enjoyed. To avoid secession and at the same time to introduce a suitably enhanced degree of liberty and flexibility into the centralistic traditions of the Empire, while still avoiding too drastic a break with the patterns of the past, constituted the major trials of the liberals. In meeting their challenge, the liberals' outstanding personality was Rui Barbosa, always the champion of liberty and reform as a federalist during the Empire period and as a liberal during the first Republic—referred to also as the Old Republic to distinguish it from the so called New Republic which developed out of the 1930 Vargas revolution.

The chief author of the draft for a Constitution approved by the Constituent Assembly in 1891, Rui Barbosa had been a prominent figure in the pre-Constitutional, provisional government. He continued now to serve his country as a statesman, internationalist, jurist, orator and author, whose works in 160 volumes are now in process of publication.

His great opponent was Pinheiro Machado, the "realist," a Senator for many years and the most influential politician of the First Republic. A man of great intelligence and political ability, Pinheiro Machado inclined toward authority rather than liberty, and his cultural attainments were limited in comparison to those of Rui Barbosa. The duel between the two, lasting almost twenty years, is more than a rivalry of two men or parties. It is a symbol of the painful struggle for liberty and establishment of democracy in Latin America. Neither man became president. But the presidents were mere shadows in contrast to the two great combatants.

The two other figures representing forces in the movement of institutional reform and the transition from Empire to Republic were Teixeira Mendes, head of the positivist "Church" in Brazil, and Aristides Lobo, a minor politician but a symbol of a fighting group of radicals enjoying only limited influence. Teixeira Mendes was a very respected philosopher who observed strict obedience to the ideas of Auguste Comte and played a distinguished role in the launching of the Republic. He and Aristides Lobo, and their respective groups, were strongly inclined toward authority rather than liberty.

Parties were exceedingly loose in their discipline and in their principles, and distinctions between them during the period of the first Republic were based more on regional influences and interests than on ideological divergences. The dominant tendency from 1889 to 1930 was the strengthening of central power. The revolution of 1930 was a reaction against that tendency, a blow struck in favor of greater liberty. Rui Barbosa had died in 1923 and Pinheiro Machado was stabbed to death in 1916 by a madman, but their rivalry still endured and the 1930 revolution was promoted under the ideals preached by Rui Barbosa. A revolution, nevertheless, often takes unexpected turns. The consequence of this revolution, originating in the name of additional freedom in government, was the *coup d'état* of 1937 and the dictatorship of Getulio Vargas, lasting until 1945. Proclaiming the New State, promulgating a new Constitution, dissolving Parliament and political parties so as to remove all intermediary groups between government and the people, Vargas stressed authority and restricted freedom. The ideals of the liberals of 1891 had vanished.

The Voice of the People

Politics is a mysterious game. In the name of liberty, many liberties have vanished. The tides of authority have helped, not infrequently, the cause of freedom. The revolution of 1930 and the suspension, for some years, of democracy, with the suppression of political parties and rigorous limitations upon liberty of the press, have been the opportunity for the manifestation of a new voice in the quest for freedom and the implementation of social reform.

Nominally, most of the great historical movements have been initiated in the name of the people, but it is not difficult to distinguish those which have the consent or real participation of the people from those which are only using the name. Sometimes a political movement, in which the real people, the mass of the population, have no part in the beginning, receives during its development the spontaneous approval of the citizenry. This happened with the political upheaval of 1930. Undertaken by military men as a means of forcing the government to make certain compromises, and without a program of institutional reform, it became the point of division between the First and the Second Republics. The *coup d'état* of 1937, even if not approved in its political implications, received the loyal support of the man in the street, of the workers, of the unions (which we call syndicates), of the people in the sense of a *popular elite*—the masses are always indifferent, whether the "mass" of the elite or the mass of the people.

After 1930 the voice of the people began to be a strong and serious reality. What this voice demanded was not liberty but reform. The two ideals were separated. So often had the people heard the invocation of liberty to justify factionalism and the continuation of harsh social conditions that the word had lost its traditional prestige. Vargas, the smooth dictator from 1937 to 1945 and the most popular statesman in our recent history, voiced at the beginning of his dictatorship this significant sentence: "The vote does not fill the stomach. . . ." And the discouraging fact was that the people were insensible to the disastrous implications of those words, which constituted not simply a sentence but a policy. What the people wanted was security, better wages, low costs of living, various protective laws, strong unions, in short, tangible values, not votes. Therefore, the two ideals with which this paper is concerned were disassociated; instead of liberty first, the slogan has been reform first—reform in the sense of new social legislation and a new status for workers. This disassociation was false in itself. Freedom and reform are complementaries. Every social reform that does not bring as a result an increase in freedom will not be long enduring.*

It is said that when Lenin subscribed the decree of expropriation of the aristocratic landowners' property, he broke his pen and said: "I defy anybody to restore what today has been abolished." The Brazilian revolution of 1930 brought the *coup d'etat* of 1937, and the momentary eclipse of political freedom. The people—the man in the street, the industrial worker and the

* The author expresses a more optimistic opinion regarding the compatibility of freedom and reform than that found in the introduction. For the sake of preserving the free way of life in today's world it is hoped that his appraisal, although debatable, will prove correct. [Editor's note]

country farmer—never regretted the loss of liberty. They felt that reform—the accent on the social as the most important problem in the new political ambient—would never permit a return to the bygone era in which the social problem had been considered, in the famous sentence of a President of the Republic, as just a "police problem." Conditions, they felt, which had made possible this utterance, had forever changed. The new social laws, the new importance of labor in politics, the industrialization of the country, the new ideals in sociology, were factors that once and for all had become a central element of the new era.

When, in 1945, Vargas was overthrown by the army, the new revolution was unpopular. Five years later the old dictator, who had feared democratic elections, returned as President, elected by an overwhelming majority of votes. The landslide was proof of his popularity, and opportunism; it was evidence that the people, more than the army or the parties, had an effective voice in the framing of political and social reform. The liberals had favored liberty without reform. The people wanted reform, even without liberty. Balance had not yet been attained. Other new voices, taking advantage of the rupture between liberty and reform and the new indifference of the people to freedom, began to preach the political gospel of authoritarianism.

The Voice of the Extremists

The tendency to extremes has always been a characteristic feature of Latin American life. But it has been, at the same time, a point where Brazilian civilization is at odds with the Spanish American tradition. The Brazilian pattern, in history or psychological attitudes, is one of balance rather than violence or extremism. Therefore, I consider any political movement in Brazil based on the intent of violent minorities to impose their will on the nation in the name of the people, or a higher good, or the party, as substantially contrary to one of the most fundamental and natural tendencies of our people. A people can never in peace and justice find its way to the satisfaction of its ideals of security and happiness through the use of methods contrary to its own character or to its own *lignes de force,* as Gonzague de Reynold has called these irresistible historical determinants.

As repercussions of extremism, both revolutionary and reactionary, two contradictory political movements emerged after 1922, the centennial of Brazilian independence. The Communist Party of Brazil was founded in 1922, and ten years later "Integralist Action" was launched. The two sides of political history in the world during the post-World-War-I period were thus reflected in our national development. In both movements the split between freedom and reform was central. Both preached reform, a structural reform of political institutions. But both revolutionary reforms were to be reached and managed through authority and not through freedom. Both preached authoritarianism, not only as an end but as the means to obtain the goal. Both not only proclaimed violence but used it in fact, the Communists in 1935, the neo-Fascist *Integralistas* in 1937. Both attempts at seizure of power failed, for Brazil was allergic to the medicines of despair. Both of these minority and extremist movements were outlawed, and subsequently turned to the use of other methods, more dangerous because Machiavellian, but more in apparent and at least temporary agreement with the temperament of the folk and the traditions of our history.

Neither freedom nor reform can ever be obtained in a country through the use of expedients contrary to its history and character. If Vargas, in spite of his fatal errors, has impressed upon our history his strong mark and attached his name to a new era of social reform in our country, it is because he retreated from his false position of semidictatorship, and returned to the natural connection between freedom and reform.

CONCLUSIONS

The conclusion of this rapid excursion over the trends of freedom and reform in our country must be that freedom without reform is an empty ideal that has lost its appeal to the people of our century. A country or a civilization is the voice of the people or else it is just a voice of the void, a *flatus vocis,* and is in contradiction with the intrinsic and proper relation of freedom and reform. The goal of reform without freedom is a chimera, the most tragic of all now pursued by modern absolutism, basically contrary to the nature of things, and therefore to the true happiness and real interest of any country, people or civilization.

Freedom *and* reform, the simultaneous respect for the rights of man and the exigencies of justice, must be the twin objectives of the major policies of any government or any party concerned not with the egocentric interests of individuals or groups, but the common good of the whole nation. This is true of Brazil and of the whole of humanity, yesterday, today and forever.

Index of Names